LIES IN HIGH PLACES

DANA KILLION

Obscura Press

1

Which version of the truth was this?

Making no effort to be subtle, I glanced at the clock on the wall and let out a breath. I was sitting at a conference table with fellow journalist Art Borkowski and Erik Martin, my boss and soon-to-be ex-husband. A desperately needed long weekend beckoned me, and I was anxious to get out of the office. Unfortunately, the conversation had drifted into male bravado. The men were spouting off journalistic fish tales experienced while scouring the streets of Chicago for a recalcitrant snitch or shadowing morally flexible cops. I knew that with each telling, these stories grew more Herculean than the last. The boys were now playing a game of professional one-upmanship that stretched the imagination. And my patience. Of course, the exchange excluded me, the lone female in the room. It also made me want to retch. Just whip them out already and see who wins the prize for size. I sure didn't care.

"Guys, this is great fun, but could we get back on track?" I said, struggling to sound less annoyed than I felt. "I have a date with a beach chair in Michigan and wanted to be on the road half an hour ago."

"Of course, Andrea," Erik said, flashing one of his *you know you love me* smiles. "Sorry we got off course. You know, war stories..."

He'd somehow found a way to make me feel excluded and insecure, all in one sentence. Not that insecurity wasn't something I'd felt every day of the last six months anyway, but I sure didn't need it aired in front of Borkowski, the pro recently hired away from the *Chicago Tribune*. I was just the boss's wife who had arm-twisted her way into a career change with her husband's digital news organization, Link-Media.

"I've got two *actual* stories in the works right now," I said, moving the conversation back to the agenda items. "The proposed privatization of Midway Airport and an investigation into some funky financial transactions by Mayor Rendell—not sure if there's anything there, but I'm digging." I flipped back a few pages in my notebook. "We talked about running the Midway story next week. I'll have it pulled together by end of day Monday."

Erik double-checked his production calendar, running his hands quickly through his sandy-blond hair as he contemplated the schedule. "Perfect. We'll post Tuesday, but run it by me first."

I nodded, struggling to ignore the huskiness of his voice.

"Andrea, privatization will funnel a lot of dough into the local economy. I hope you're not going to piss on that. Non-government workers gotta eat too," Borkowski said, pushing his tortoiseshell reading glasses up to the spot on his head where five forlorn strands of hair were fighting their last, losing battle.

I gripped the arms of my leather chair and pushed myself upright.

"Are you telling me to slant a story, Art?"

"I was suggesting you think about the financial implications of this deal for the city before this story is published." A vein in his right temple pounded visibly and condescension dripped from his voice. "You're not in a courtroom anymore. Doesn't hurt to remember that this is more complex than the work you've done in the past. You've been here, what? All of four months?"

"Well, Art, it's been six months, and this isn't an op-ed piece," I fired back, not giving him time to respond. "It sounds to me like you've got a personal opinion that you'd like shared with the world. Our job is to present the facts, not my singular viewpoint. There are winners and losers in this. At all levels. Those facts, that truth, that *complexity*, is what I will write."

Borkowski's words were still ringing in my mind twenty minutes later as I drove south out of Chicago on the Dan Ryan Expressway. As was the pain of the divorce that had yanked my emotional compass straight out of my chest, placing hard jabs direct to my heart in the process. Emotionally, professionally, everything in my life was buried under a mantle of pain. I pulled some deep breaths into my lungs as I drove and pushed them out slowly, willing myself to leave the irritation behind and relax into the much-needed weekend of solitude.

A call rang through the speaker of my Audi. Erik. Damn. I thumped my hand against the wheel, then reluctantly pushed the Bluetooth connection.

"Hi, Erik. What is it?"

"I need you to come back to the office."

"Seriously, Erik? I'm almost at the Skyway." The nearer we got to finalizing our divorce, the more often Erik seemed to fabricate reasons to keep me close. "I need this time alone," I said, my voice a near whisper as I attempted to control emotions that were raw and bloody.

Please, not this weekend. My body craved the release, the isolation, the time to focus on nothing but reading a good book and taking long, mind-clearing walks on the beach.

"How far along are you on the piece about the mayor's campaign contribution?"

I sighed. "I have proof that Rendell has been depositing a number of large checks into a personal account. Campaign dollars? It's not so clear. The source of the funds is the eyebrow raiser, but right now I don't have adequate proof."

I could hear his other line ring in the background and the clicking of keys as he checked something on his computer.

"Why the rush?" I asked. "Reelection mode won't kick in for another thirty days, at least."

"Wrong. I just got word he's about to announce a run for governor."

Damn! The 63rd Street exit was fifteen feet in front of me. I pulled off, turning left on the overpass, and swung back around, entering the northbound expressway. My mood had changed from irritation to excitement by the time I'd merged into traffic. It was only 2:30; traffic was light for a Friday and moving at a decent clip. If everything went smoothly, I could still be in Saugatuck in time for sunset.

As Erik continued to fill me in on the developments, I ran through the details in my head, debating how I wanted to present the story. Circumstances were forcing my hand. I just didn't have this tied up yet, but I'd have to proceed with what I had and backfill later. If all went well, Erik could make his edits, and I'd still have my weekend.

"So you need to get on this. I'm sure I don't need to tell you how important this is. We'll work with what you've got, but, Andrea, we're going to need that source." A pause. "Or, if your vacation is more important, send your research over to Art."

"I'm already on my way back. Should be there in fifteen..."

The Chicago skyline was fully in view when a deafening boom rattled the windows of my Audi.

"What was that? Andrea, you there? Andrea?"

The call forgotten, I scanned the landscape for the source of the sound but saw only the black SUV four cars ahead of me flung into the concrete barrier. Stunned, I watched it ricochet off the embankment and veer right. Vehicles scattered like bumper cars in its wake and my world moved into helpless slow motion as I was broadsided. I gripped the wheel and struggled against the impact. Battling frantically for control, my hands were no match for the thrust, and my car was pulled into a tailspin.

Hurled into the barricade, I was punched instantly in the chest and face with the airbag. Left, right, north, south, all sense of direction and place left me. As the car came to a stop, I gasped for breath. It was as if my lungs couldn't fill completely with air. My body trembled as adrenaline and fear coursed through my veins. Lifting my head up from the dash, it felt heavy, throbbing from the jolt. Light smoke hung in the air, giving off an odd acrid smell. Afraid to move, I slowly flexed my limbs, wincing with the effort. Nothing seemed broken, at least at first impression. I fumbled for the seat belt release, then pushed into the door with my arms, terrified of staying in the crushed metal a second longer as hissing steam rose from the front end.

Stumbling out of the car, I took deep, slow breaths, trying to coax my lungs back to full expansion. Leaning against the rear door, I struggled to control the shaking that had overtaken my body. A warm wetness dripped down my forehead onto my cheek. Lifting my hand to my head, I winced at my own touch and pulled back blood. While I fought for control of my breathing and my limbs, I looked around, watching people exit their cars and fill the expressway on foot, some to escape, others to offer assistance. Debris and crumpled vehicles lined the pavement around me in the northbound lanes as drivers in the southbound slowed to gape.

The wail of sirens bounced through the fray as police and medical personnel began to arrive. Damaged vehicles hissed and smoked as EMTs scurried to assist the victims. The stink of gasoline wafted past me as I watched, fixed in place, my body quaking. I could do nothing but will my legs to support me as I watched the chaos around me. The Toyota that had hit me sat disabled about ten feet away, its hood folded like a fortune cookie. The driver, a man in his early thirties, had pushed himself out through the missing front door and lay on the ground writhing, grabbing at his twisted right leg. Bone poked through the skin of his calf, blood trailing down from the wound as the medic stabilized his limb.

In the next lane I could see a young girl who I guessed to be about eight, lying unconscious, sprawled across the pavement. Instinct and shock moved me toward her and the burgundy Dodge Caravan lying on its side. The girl's hysterical parents hovered screaming for the paramedics' attention, oblivious to their own wounds, pleading for her to wake up. She wasn't responding. I stepped aside as two techs with a stretcher swooped in to assess her injuries. Checking her pulse, her pupils, her vital signs, the men worked to stabilize the girl while I stood immobilized by the parents' panic and my own fog. Unsure what to do. Unsure where to go. My mind unable to function, unable to pull myself out of the vortex, I simply stood until the stretcher was moved to the ambulance and there was nothing more to watch.

Reluctantly, I walked away, fearful for the girl's outcome. Would she survive? What pain lay in front of her if she did?

The black Escalade that had caused the accident rested on the shoulder. Terrified by my imagination, but unable to resist, I inched toward the car. The driver lay splayed on the pavement twenty feet in front of the vehicle, apparently thrown through the windshield.

Shards of glass glistened around him like glitter, reflecting bursts of light and color against the black asphalt.

Slowly, through the haze, my basic reporter instincts kicked in. Male. Dark, matted hair. Blood pooling in large swathes.

Police and ambulance sirens continued to scream as additional support teams arrived, drilling their urgent demands into my head. Officials with dark uniforms and medical gear rushed past me, calling out codes, their voices insistent, but controlled. Blocking the chaotic activity around me, I continued toward the SUV. Unable to stop myself, I stepped closer, past the EMTs too occupied with their work to notice me. My chest tightened again as I got within five feet. Something was terribly wrong. His face was missing.

Blood ran in streams toward my shoes. I stood frozen, staring at him, unable to help. Unable to do anything. It was far too late.

I felt a hand on my arm pulling me away, but I couldn't divert my eyes or control the choking horror in my throat.

"Ma'am, are you okay?"

I looked up into soft brown eyes. A man. Familiar. Someone I knew. But I couldn't bring a name or place to the surface.

"Are you injured?" The eyes scanned my face, did a once-over on my body, then returned to my forehead. "Andrea?"

"He's dead," I said, fixated on the body in front of me.

"Were you in the vehicle? Do you know this man?"

"No." My eyes were again locked on the expanding pool of blood. So much blood. I began to crumple, my legs no longer able to support me.

Brown Eyes put an arm around my shoulder, steadying me, pulling my attention away from the body.

"Andrea, are you hurt?" he asked again. Only then did I become aware of the police badge clipped to his belt.

He seemed to know my name, but I couldn't think, couldn't place him, couldn't get my head focused on anything but the pool of red in front of me.

"My car is over there," I choked out, nodding in the direction of my pile of twisted metal.

"Let's get that gash on your forehead looked at." Gently, he steered me over to an ambulance. We stepped over scraps of plastic and chunks of metal. Past first responders. Past the injured. And the dead.

He left me with an EMT, promising to check back. Police vehicles had barricaded the area now, shutting down the Dan Ryan Expressway, a major artery into Chicago. Numbly, I watched the police officers work the scene as the female technician dabbed at my head. She asked questions about what hurt and where, but it was as if someone had turned down the sound.

As my head was bandaged, I was given instructions for dealing with the bruising of my chest that was sure to come from the airbag impact, and a cautionary note about being mindful of signs of concussion. Then the EMT rushed off to assist others.

Slowly, the throbbing in my head pushed through the blur. I could now more lucidly observe the whole of the turmoil around me from my slumped, cross-legged spot on the blacktop. Time was hazy and I couldn't tell how long I'd been sitting here. Long enough for the press to arrive. TV news helicopters hovered overhead, and reporters schemed to try to get the shot or the quote that would set them apart from the guy next to them. On the Garfield Street overpass above, I spotted Art Borkowski trying in vain to get a few comments from one of the officers pushing back the crowd.

Oh, right, this is news. I should be doing something other than sitting here on my ass. I shifted my weight and tried to pull myself up, but the world around me spun and I landed on my elbow. Leaning back against the concrete, I took deep yoga breaths, releasing them slowly, and tried to regain control of my body. Just a few more minutes, I told myself. I watched as Borkowski struck out with the cop and was forced back behind a barricade with every other journalist who'd been angling for an exclusive comment. Just then, he spotted me down below on the highway.

Borkowski glared at me across the expanse, as if somehow I had arranged to put my life on the line just to scoop him on a story. I could almost hear the thoughts running through his head: *What's she doing here? Who tipped her off?* I doubted he had even noticed I was sitting with a wad of cotton taped to my head and a bloodstained shirt. Would he have the balls to try to use me as a source? Would his ego get past the fact that he wasn't the only Link-Media reporter on the scene?

He *was* the only reporter if I was going to sit here, I realized. I kicked myself into gear and managed to get to my feet. Like it or not, I had a ringside seat to this mess, and it gave me an edge.

I looked around to get my bearings, taking note of the position of the vehicles, the personnel on the ground, the fine points of my surroundings. A medical helicopter had arrived, and the little girl would be airlifted, probably to Children's Hospital. Her mother was still sobbing uncontrollably. On my right, a crowd of state police officers, CPD officers, and medical personnel gathered around the dead man. My focus was returning, journalistic instincts were kicking in. Techs measured, photographed, and tagged pieces of debris. I pulled out my cell phone and grabbed a few photos, careful not to draw attention to myself.

About thirty feet ahead of me, a tall man in his early fifties seemed to be directing the investigation. I watched as uniformed cops and plainclothesmen checked in with him, took his lead. I didn't recognize him. He was broad-shouldered, with close-cropped blond hair and none of the swagger of a typical Chicago detective. This guy was buttoned-up, almost an FBI type; it was clear this was the man in charge. But in charge of what? I took another look. There were an awful lot of guys in gray suits running around the scene for a traffic accident, even one with fatalities. Was something else going on?

"How's your head?"

Brown Eyes was back at my side. I tucked the phone quickly back into my pocket. With the shock of the accident subsiding, I was now lucid enough to recognize the man in front of me as Detective Michael Hewitt. We had worked together on a case a few years back, before I had resigned my position as a Cook County assistant state's attorney for the dream of a journalism career.

"Did they give you anything for the pain? You're going to have one nasty headache." He winked, but his eyes were soft and full of concern.

"Hi, Michael. I should make some pathetic joke about not meeting like this, but my head hurts too much to come up with anything clever."

"You recognize me now. I'll take that as a good sign."

"No permanent damage, luckily. I have meds to get me through the night and firm instructions to see my physician in the morning." I smiled back, grateful for the inquiry and now clearheaded enough to appreciate the rich timbre of his voice. "Not everyone had luck on their side today. What happened? Why is this place crawling with detectives?"

"No, unfortunately, not everyone was lucky," he said, ignoring my questions and flipping open a pad. "Can you tell me what you saw?"

I ran through the SUV swerving and striking the embankment, the other cars unable to avoid contact, and one bouncing me into a spin.

"Did you see anything that might explain why the SUV driver lost control? Debris in the road? Maybe an animal?"

"No. Nothing. Could have been out of my line of sight, but I didn't see anything like that."

He continued his notes, frowning as he tried to piece everything together. We ran through the typical questions of where I was and who did what when that could help diagram the accident.

When he seemed to be wrapping up his questions, I said, "You didn't ask about what I heard."

He lifted his head and looked at me. A flicker of confusion shaded his eyes.

"A loud bang. Possibly a gunshot," I replied, waiting for a reaction. "Is this another highway shooting?" I held my gaze as steady as I could, watching for a glint of confirmation.

The pieces had started to click into place. Over the past month, two shootings had occurred on this stretch of the Dan Ryan; in one an electrician from Gary had been struck on his way to a job site, and in the second, a tourist driving his family into Chicago for a weekend vacation had been hit. Both men died at the scene.

CPD had attributed the shootings to an expanding gang turf war and initiation rites required of new members. Gang problems weren't exactly news on Chicago's South Side, but this was pushing the killings into civilian territory. Was this accident a third shooting?

"Hang tight for a bit. I'll have someone take you home as soon as we can. Obviously, your car will have to be towed."

"Is that a 'no comment,' officer?"

He gave me a hint of a smile. "We're still investigating," he replied, handing me his card.

Now fully alert, my mind raced with the implications—not just for the city at large, but at the opportunity that had been forced into my lap.

"Who is that guy?" I asked, not ready to abdicate my insider status, tipping my head in the direction of Mr. Gray Suit. "The one who looks like he's a fed from central casting?"

Michael chuckled. "That's Karl Janek. He's heading up the investigation."

"What's his story? Was he formerly with the Bureau? Or maybe the IRS? He has that *don't mess with me because I have no sense of humor* look about him."

"No, he's cool. He used to head up the Gang Enforcement Task Force before Mayor Rendell disbanded it."

Michael turned to head back into the fray, giving me another wink over his shoulder.

There it was. I'd been dropped into the middle of Chicago's hottest crime story. A story that, if done right, could forever eliminate any accusation that I was nothing more than the boss's wife. A story that could solidify my career.

2

I watched the snarled traffic from the front seat of a Crown Vic as a uniformed CPD officer snaked his way toward my Gold Coast co-op. The benefit of a ride with flashing lights and permission to drive on the shoulder was immediately obvious. Too bad my escort was the strong, silent type. Pumping him for details on the cause of the accident, or Janek, or a connection to the highway shooting investigation, *or anything,* was yielding nothing more than "you'll have to speak with the public affairs officer." Obviously he'd been well prepped. After exhausting my immediate list of questions, I surrendered to the pounding in my head that rattled the contents of my brain with each pothole, wondering why the hell my tax dollars weren't being spent on highway repair. Leaning back against the headrest, I closed my eyes for the balance of the ride and prayed for smoother streets.

The EMTs had insisted that a responsible adult meet me at the other end of the trip, so I called my closest friend, Cai Farrell, and asked her to come babysit. We'd been friends since the first year of law school at the University of Chicago, where we'd forged a bond over my struggles with contract law. She was brilliant, beautiful, and tough as nails, and I had bribed her with good wine until she'd agreed to tutor me. After graduation, she was the person who'd talked me through my decision to become a Cook County assistant state's attorney in the Criminal Prosecution Division, while she went on to a much higher-paying gig with Chicago's largest corporate law firm.

Cai had been there, too, when I'd walked away from ten years of tenure with the State of Illinois. The jail cell suicide of a teen I'd prosecuted had thrown me into turmoil. It had been a terrifying decision, particularly when I'd been walking toward something so nebulous. Racked with guilt and self-doubt, I hadn't been able to live with the consequences. And now, six months in, my nose was still barely above water—but a life preserver might just have been tossed in my direction.

The officer pulled up in front of my eleven-story 1920s brick building, lights flashing as he made a U-turn and double-parked in front of the door. A concerned doorman rushed out as the officer assisted me out of the car.

"Ms. Kellner, let me help you," he said, taking my arm. "Ms. Farrell is in the lobby waiting for you. She told me about the accident. I just can't believe it."

"Thank you, Norman. Could you bring in my suitcase?"

"Of course, of course, don't you worry about anything. You just go on up and get rested," he said to me, then turned to the cop. "I'll take good care of her."

I thanked the officer and then walked the fifteen feet into the lobby. Each tiny movement of my head brought a new stab of pain. Cai sat in one of the leather wingback chairs, tapping at her phone, her face glowing in the dark wood-paneled room. She jumped to her feet as she saw me and sprinted over.

"Honey, you're a little confused about the concept of vacation," she said, holding my shoulders, her brown eyes creased with concern. "Let's get you upstairs. You're looking wobbly."

She gave me a once-over, pushed her long jet-black hair behind her ear, then pulled me across the room.

"Not exactly the afternoon I had planned," I said, letting her lead. "Am I going to be ruining a hot date for you tonight?"

"Shut up and get in the elevator already, will you? There's no date hot enough to leave you hurt and stranded." She took my suitcase from Norman and we headed up.

Stepping off into the spacious vestibule on the eleventh floor, we could hear Walter meow even before I turned the key in the lock. Just the sight of luggage threw him into a bad case of separation anxiety. As I swung open the door, the little gray fur ball shot at my legs. His mournful cries echoed into the hall until I gently scooped him up and felt his body go limp.

"While you make nice with that furry dishrag of yours, I'm going to put your bag in the bedroom."

"He's a Ragdoll cat, not a dishrag cat," I laughed.

"Whatever. All I know is that the damn thing seems to have rubber bones. Now sit your ass down. Last thing I want is for you to pass out or something on my watch." Cai wagged a finger at me as she left with the satchel.

Becoming a couch potato could wait another minute or two. I had a feeling that once I was down, I'd want to stay there. Instead, I walked through the dining room, past my tarp-covered table and around the stash of toolboxes, nail guns, and ladders that filled the corners of the space, turning my home into a remodeling war zone. The beautiful herringbone floors I'd fallen in love with at first sight were covered with paper. The marble fireplace mantel was shrouded in plastic, a gift to be rediscovered when power tools no longer accessorized the room. Provided I'd be able to keep the apartment post-divorce.

Anxiety over my uncertain financial future could wait for another day. I shut down the thoughts and opened a closet near the kitchen. I grabbed a bottle from the wine rack and returned to the living room with two glasses, a corkscrew, and a Cakebread Dancing Bear Cabernet.

"Is that a good idea?" Cai asked as she caught me wrestling with the cork. "I know it is for me, but you're an invalid. I'm fully prepared to rush you over to the emergency room at Northwestern Hospital if I need to, but I can think of better ways to spend an evening." She grabbed the opener from my hand. "Yum, I see we're opening the good stuff." Parking herself on the couch next to me, she poured a finger of the rich burgundy liquid for me and four for herself.

"It's a horrible idea, but I'm going to do it anyway. If I can't have my beach weekend, I at least deserve some good booze." I lifted the glass off the walnut coffee table, and we clinked, toasting the fact that I was only bruised and battered. Leaning back against the down cushions, I winced with the effort, feeling sore from the airbag impact. Walter rubbed against my arm, demanding to be loved.

Cai stood, walked over to open the three sets of French doors to the terrace, then returned to the sofa.

"You need some fresh air in this place. All I can smell is tile adhesive. Now that you're settled, tell me what the hell happened."

"Four cars. One guy with a broken leg, a little girl who had to be airlifted. Didn't look good. And one fatality that I know of." I spouted off the salient points first, then filled in the gaps, answering her questions as I relived the incident. "It's going to be a long time before I can think about what was left of that guy's face without hyperventilating," I said, shuddering again at the image of torn flesh. I laid my head back and let the gentle breeze of the early-summer evening wash over me, hoping it would combine with the alcohol and ease the hammer pummeling my head. If not, the pain meds were in my bag. I looked over at Cai and sighed. "I think the driver was shot."

"Shot? Does that mean this was another highway shooting?"

The insistent thump of a hand against the carved wood of the front door resounded through the room. "Andrea!" came Erik's unmistakable voice.

"Not now...," I said, closing my eyes. In the insanity of the afternoon's event, calling Erik with an update had not even been a thought, but another confrontation was more than I could stomach right now.

"Do you want me to get that? I'd be happy to tell him where to go."

"And I'd love to watch." I laughed, which only increased the throbbing in my head. "Tell him I'm okay and I'll call—"

Just then the door swung open. I hadn't latched the door. "I've been calling you for hours! You said you'd be in the office in fifteen minutes. Then the phone goes dead. What the hell happened? Oh, I see. Playtime get in the way of your job?" He glared at Cai as he crossed the room, as if she, somehow, was responsible for my failure to return.

Not having the energy for his temper tantrum, I let him rant until he was standing in front of me and finally noticed my condition, watching his face shift from anger to confusion to concern in the span of three seconds. Cai stood patiently alongside him, ready to act as bouncer if I gave the nod.

"I was in a car accident on my way back to the office," I said. "Multiple cars. One fatality. Didn't you hear about it? Shut down the Dan Ryan. Borkowski was covering the story. He saw me. Didn't he call you?"

Noting the shock in his eyes as he shook his head, I softened my tone, but only slightly.

"I'll be okay, but checking phone messages wasn't a priority. Sorry to worry you, but you really shouldn't be storming in here like this."

I watched his body deflate and his eyes stray off as he racked his brain for something to say.

"I, ah, was in off-site meetings. I'm sorry, I didn't know you were involved." He scanned my face, my body, as the magnitude of the incident slapped him sober. Fear and horror at what might have happened all washed over his face as we looked at each other. "Are you sure you're okay?"

"The car's totaled, but I'll heal," I said, reaching for my wineglass, forcing any remaining feelings I had for him into the pit of my stomach, where I couldn't reach them. At least that's what I told myself. I had to stay strong. I couldn't allow this moment to make me vulnerable again, regardless of the pain in his eyes. I'd been there already. I had that T-shirt, and it was three sizes too small.

Cai remained at attention, her eyes on me, alert for any sign that it was time to give Erik the heave-ho and escort him out. I could read the mix of amusement and contempt in her eyes despite her practiced lawyer mask. She knew my pain and what a manipulative son of a bitch I had married.

"I'll be in on Monday," I said, signaling that it was time for him to leave.

Ignoring my cue, he moved around the coffee table to sit next to me. Walter hissed his disapproval of the intrusion. Smart cat. Looking at my bandaged head, Erik said, "That looks painful. What can I do? Do you want me to stay?" His eyes were soft and expectant, his lush voice concerned, having sensed an opportunity to nurse me back to health. And back into his bed.

Cai coughed, fake and hollow. A reminder to me of Erik's games.

"I need a few days of rest, that's all. I'll see you on Monday. At work," I added, shutting him down.

This time he got the point. After asking me to call anytime, day or night, if I needed him, he left.

Cai was already heading over to flip the deadbolt. "You have to stop leaving that door unlatched. I know it's a private foyer, but women who live alone shouldn't be so cavalier about their safety."

"I know, it's a bad habit. The doormen look out for me."

Cai gave me a long, hard stare. "Then why did they let lover boy come up without a call? Never mind, I'll save the lecture for another day. But I am wondering what had Erik so tied up that he didn't know about this." She settled on the couch and poured another glass of wine.

"Knowing him as I do, it was most likely his latest conquest. A twenty-two-year-old model, ready, willing, and able, could keep him occupied for a long time."

"Please, half an hour, tops. Wham, bam. There's always another twenty-two-year-old model."

I shrugged, trying to hold back the painful memories.

"Thankfully, it's none of my business any longer."

"Maybe," she said, her tone skeptical. "But it sure gives you leverage in your divorce. What is it about middle-aged men and young party-girl types, all cleavage and too dumb to ask questions? Sure ain't the conversation..."

I closed my eyes again as she spoke, forcing down the thorny knot in my throat and holding back the tears that threatened to spill from behind my lids. Cai's words were true, but a sad, painful testament to my discovery of Erik's betrayals three months after I'd started working at Link-Media. I was still raw, the wound only starting to crust over. No longer able to tolerate being the collateral damage in his midlife crisis, I had filed for divorce. But could I keep that damage out of my professional life? I looked around at the wonderful apartment we had purchased together—the home I might need to give up—and was filled with sadness.

"I'm sorry. I'm upsetting you," Cai said, seeing me start to curl into a ball. "Ignore me. I should know better than to rip off the Band-Aid, especially after the day you've had."

"Just bad timing." I shifted a pillow into the small of my back, searching for a position that would ease the ache, and took another sip of wine, trying to shake off the dark cloud. "Do you remember Michael Hewitt?" I asked, anxious for the conversation to move toward more constructive ground. "I worked with him about two years ago on that case with the vigilante deli owner."

"Of course I remember the case. Damn near devastated you. Hewitt, I can't place."

"Well, he worked this afternoon's accident. He tells me that his partner, the lead detective assigned to this incident, is also the former head of the Gang Enforcement Task Force."

I pulled myself upright and leaned my elbows into my knees. If a former gang officer was leading the charge, that could mean this incident was related to the prior shootings. The throbbing in my head might have become a barrage, but speculation about a connection between incidents pushed through the pain.

"Janek is in charge?"

"Yeah, you know him?" I'd heard his name in the past but had no context beyond his title.

"Well, I know that he and Police Superintendent Wachowski had a huge blow-up over the disbanding of the unit."

"I thought it was consolidated into the Organized Crime Division due to budget cuts. Was there something else going on?"

At the time, it had seemed a nonevent. Nothing more than a little housekeeping by a city with big budget problems.

"You know that our firm handles the personal affairs of a few of the guys in the mayor's inner circle, and, ah, we hear things."

I could see the conflicting emotions pass over her face. Which meant she knew more than she could say.

"Obviously I can't name clients, but what I hear is that Mayor Rendell appointed Wachowski after some dirt bubbled to the surface that could have pulled CPD into the shit hole again. Pulled a quick management switcheroo to handle the cleanup."

"The abrupt leadership change surprised everyone."

"Rendell started tossing anyone that added to the baggage. Public pressure will push buttons when a mayor wants to get an agenda passed."

"You mean when he wants to get reelected." Rendell's gubernatorial plans flowed back into my mind. Scandal and failure to police the police didn't have good optics for a run as the state's top administrator. "So what were they hiding?"

"An Internal Affairs investigation into cops taking payoff money from the Gangster Disciples. A little money flowed into cops' pockets, and in return, they looked the other way on the gang's smaller drug deals. There was major turmoil in the force, but it never went public. The hubbub over Rendell ignoring the police board's recommendations when he appointed Wachowski was enough of a distraction to keep things quiet long enough for the problem to be solved."

"Solved?"

"More like illusion is reality until proven otherwise. CPD kept up the appearance of heavy-handed discipline but in reality, they only threw a smokescreen on the problem."

"And Janek was one of the supposedly dirty cops?"

"He was investigated and cleared of any wrongdoing, but as head of the unit, it knocked off the glow. No one was prosecuted. There wasn't enough to indict, and since CPD didn't want the public scandal, the situation went into the vault. But a couple of his guys did go off quietly. I don't know if they were muscled out or just couldn't handle the taint."

So why was a guy with funky gang history heading up the highway shooting investigation?

3

"Why didn't you call me last night?"

I'd fumbled and answered the cell phone vibrating on my nightstand, only to hear my sister Lane barking instructions. Her nasal voice was demanding and urgent. Nothing new, but my head was too foggy to push back.

"What time is it?" I glanced around the bedroom. Dappled sunlight shimmied through the linen drapes, which fluttered in the soft breeze of the open window. Walter lay sprawled at the end of the bed, keeping watch, oblivious to my annoying sister.

"I had to hear from Erik that you were in a car accident," she continued. "Really? You couldn't have picked up the phone to let me know?"

She'd talked to Erik? Who had called whom? My mind churned in confusion as I shifted my body back into the deep pile of pillows and blinked, trying to get my eyes to focus and the room to stop spinning. My body groaned at me with each tiny movement, and the details of yesterday's accident flooded back into my mind.

"Sorry, Lane, I had a few other things going on," I said, closing my eyes, trying to shut off my annoyance.

I didn't have the energy to jab at her self-absorption with my typical gusto, but the fact that I had a comeback at all after a rough night was a good sign. Sensitive, self-aware, responsible—not part of Lane's personality profile; those qualities were left to me, the younger sister. Growing up, I'd needed enough for the two of us. Was it screwed-up birth order? The death of our mother when we were teens? The debate over nature versus nurture could keep a shrink employed for a long time, not that it would ultimately affect anything. The pattern of our relationship was well established.

Hard to believe we were products of the same parents. Lane was five feet ten, with a sturdy Midwestern body and wild hair the color of Tupelo honey—although that was enhanced by magic liquid in a squeeze bottle these days. I was delicately built and closer to five five, but only if I stretched every vertebra, with dark shoulder-length hair that obeyed when I brushed it. Lane got Mom, I got Dad, and the only physical thing we shared was our mother's clear turquoise eyes.

"Well, I'm coming over. You shouldn't be alone, and I don't want to hear any of your stubbornness. Erik offered to stay with you last night, and you had to be your normal independent self and turn him away. All he wanted was to help you."

I tuned out as she blathered on. Lane's insecurities, Erik's hurt feelings, their conspiracy against me—I wasn't in the mood for any of it. Not today.

"Cai was here. I'm fine. You don't need to come over. I'm running out to see the doctor later this morning. Rest and pain meds are all I need. I'll call you if there's anything you can do." With that I hung up, shutting down the opportunity for rebuttal.

Walter's low purr reassured me from the end of the bed as I reassessed my aches and pains. My body leaden and bruised, I rolled on my side and gingerly pushed myself upright, swinging my feet to the floor. The slightest movement of my head brought sharp stabs and dimmed my vision. There was one last dose of pain meds from the EMT, and I greedily washed it down with water I'd left on the nightstand, then shuffled to the bathroom.

Wild, matted hair greeted me in the mirror I'd avoided last night. My skin was sallow, my eyes hollow, and the wad of gauze on my forehead was tinged brown around the edges. I lifted the corners of the tape and pulled back the cotton. Raw flesh, dried blood, skin swollen and mottled. Not pretty, but I was alive.

After a quick visit with my doc, who thankfully kept Saturday morning office hours, and a stop at the pharmacy, I was home parked on the couch, flipping through the local news channels, stopping as a shot of the Garfield L station filled the screen. A young male reporter stood about thirty yards from yellow police tape strung from chain-link fence, retelling the highlights of the incident. His emphasis was correctly placed on the one fatality, now identified as Jackson Gunderson, fifty-two. After they cut to a clip obtained at the scene yesterday, Karl Janek's face appeared as a reporter probed for additional details. I listened as Janek deflected questions about any connection between this and previous shooting incidents with "We're still investigating. It's too early to make that assessment."

Too early, my ass. I knew full well from my legal days how the PR machine worked: avoid, divert, give half answers until you knew things for certain, so you didn't look stupid when some bozo with a Facebook page posted a video recording from his cell phone. Controlling the flow and timing of information was standard operating procedure for any investigation. I watched Janek's body language. Listened to the tone of his voice. His word choices. The man was practiced, I had to give him that.

He handled the weak-ass questioning from the reporter like a pro. Revealed nothing that he didn't want broadcast.

Having been on Janek's side of the media when I was a prosecutor, I'd had occasion to observe the laziness of what sufficed for journalism these days. It was easy to control the message when the average fifth grader could ask better questions than today's reporters. Now that I was in the job, I found myself wanting to shout questions at this twit with the microphone, questions he should be asking instead of letting his subject get away with crappy non-answers.

My cell phone pinged on the coffee table, jarring me out of the media coverage. I flicked my eyes over to the phone out of habit, then forced myself to ignore the ringing. Voice mail could take it. Shifting deeper into the pillows heaped on the sofa, I pulled a cashmere throw around my shoulders and settled back. Not twenty seconds later, there came another ring. I pulled my arm out of the wrap and reached for the phone. Missed call from the condo's front desk, and now Lane was calling. Shit. I picked up.

"I know you're home, so tell this charming man here at the desk that it's okay for me to come up."

"I'm resting. Can we do this another time?"

I heard her mumble something to the doorman, then a male voice came on the line.

"Ms. Kellner, is it all right if I send up Miss Lane?"

"Fine." It wasn't, but the path of least resistance was all I had the energy for. Hopefully I could get away with a quick pop-in, just enough for Lane to feel that she had done something.

I was barely untangled from my makeshift bedding when Lane breezed in, her honey hair artfully tousled, her leopard-print blouse casually undone, and her Versace Woman fragrance ten paces ahead. She stopped next to the sofa and put her hands on her hips.

"Honey, you look like shit." She shook her head as she looked me up and down. "They give you anything good?" She picked up the prescription bottle from the table, read the label, and nodded her approval before taking a seat next to me.

I re-wrapped the throw closer to my neck to ward off the shivers that lingered despite the warm air, and grabbed a drink of water just to show her I was taking care of myself.

"See, I'll be fine. No concussion. Nothing that won't heal. I'm hydrating."

The words felt odd as I said them. Although Lane was three years older, caregiver was my role—the one I'd adopted after our mother's death when I was fourteen. Our father had disappeared into depression and work, overwhelmed by his grief and unprepared to raise two teenage girls. Lane had immersed herself in party life, taking full advantage of the loose supervision to play with boys and pot on countless late nights. Meanwhile, I'd fretted over everything she did like a tiger mom, feeling responsible for every adolescent show of rebellion. It wasn't a tradeoff I'd appreciated at the time, but most days I felt I'd gotten the better end of the deal. My life was a bit messy at the moment but didn't mirror the constant crises that Lane seemed to fall into.

I didn't know how to handle her attempt at concern. As feeble as it was, I had to give her credit for the effort, even if it was just an illusion.

"Not the weekend you planned, is it?" She inspected the edges of her gel manicure as she spoke.

"Another reminder that we don't always get what we want."

She looked up from her hands, her brows drawn. "Why did you send Erik away? What if you have a concussion and you black out or something? This isn't the time to tough it out. Sometimes even you need to be cared for."

Cared for? Yes. Controlled and manipulated back into a relationship because of poor timing? No. I didn't want that security blanket. Whatever I had to face, I'd face alone. The price of that relationship was soul-killing.

"He's really worried about you and still loves you, you know. Can't you forgive him?"

I clenched the cashmere into a ball and closed my eyes, counting a few breaths before I responded. "When did you start teaming up with Erik on the win-back-Andrea campaign? You know he devastated me. I can't believe you're even questioning my decision, let alone operating as his advocate."

I could hear my voice grow shrill and felt the tightness in my chest that clamped down and overpowered me every time I was forced to confront my pain. It had taken nearly three months just to get to a place where I was no longer crying myself to sleep. Or explaining away my bloodshot eyes as newly developed allergies. Yet here Lane was suggesting that I forgive and forget, oblivious to the ravages of his betrayal.

Erik was an icon to her, a symbol of the success and charisma she longed for but hadn't achieved. She seemed unable to comprehend that I could give up living in his glow when she wanted it so badly for herself.

"He made a mistake, and he's sorry. Can't you accept that everyone makes mistakes, does something stupid now and then?" She looked at me through eyes gone flat. "Except for you. You're always perfect."

"That's enough. I can't have this conversation now. You need to leave," I said, keeping my voice low and controlled. But my body trembled with anger.

"What are you afraid of? Turning out like Dad? That Erik will cheat again if you take him back, just like Mom did?"

"Yes!" I shouted, losing my patience. My head throbbed. "Our father is broken because he trusted a woman who didn't deserve to be trusted. She's dead and all he has is empty, hollow memories."

"Haven't you let go of that old childhood trauma yet? Dad chose his life. He could've said 'screw her' and moved on. I did. Why do you make her mistakes your problem? This is ancient history. Besides, Mom died in a car accident."

"A car accident with her lover, as you well know," I hissed. I stopped myself from letting loose all the hurtful things that were running through my mind, years of hurtful things that haunted us both. Instead, I let out a breath and tried to regain composure. "Lane, that's enough. I don't want to hear anymore." I pulled the blanket close, curling inward. "Not now. Please."

"All right, but don't forget that you're benefiting from Erik's vulnerability. Do you really think anyone else would have hired you as a journalist?"

"I need you to leave." I couldn't handle one more word. Lane grabbed her bag, flipped back her hair, and left in a huff as tears stung my eyes.

4

I stepped off the elevator in front of the entrance to Link-Media late Monday morning, hot tea in hand, my pace still glacial. My morning had begun hours earlier with the necessary work of insurance claims, copies of the police report, car replacement, and other practicalities.

Although the visit to my physician on Saturday had given me post-accident peace of mind, my body still protested the trauma. The weekend had been one big haze of sluglike recuperation, once I had pushed Lane out of my thoughts and out of my apartment. Moving from my bed to the shower to the couch, and once or twice to the door to accept delivery of tuna rolls and miso soup, had augmented my body's healing.

Luckily, sleep had come easier last night as the pain had finally subsided. My bruises had peaked and I looked like shit naked, but that was the least of my problems. Shaking the image of the dead man was proving difficult.

Obsessed with the media coverage, I had spent the weekend glued to the TV and the news feed on my phone. CPD had confirmed the shooting death of one individual. Questions about the shootings had replayed on a loop in my mind as I followed the media focus on blood and body counts. CPD hadn't confirmed the connection between Friday's shooting and the two previous, but with three shootings along the same one-mile stretch of roadway, conclusions were easy to draw. Too bad the reason these deaths were occurring didn't seem to be a relevant question.

Even before the highway shootings had started, Chicago's gang violence issues had become common enough to warrant national attention, with some even labeling Chicago the country's newest murder capital. Gang tensions were woven into the fabric of many Chicago neighborhoods, particularly on the south and near west sides. Conflict ebbed and flowed between the Gangster Disciples, the Vice Lords, the Black P Stones, or any of the nearly six hundred factions in the city. Some controlled an area as small as one city block; others had thousands of members spread across many neighborhoods.

And as gang numbers swelled, there was only so much territory to go around. Rivalries increased in the shift, as did shootings. Tension between the increasingly demanding public, tired of hearing weekend victim counts, and the police, seemingly unable to quell the violence, was running high.

But unlike most shootings in the city, the first two victims appeared to be random, with no reported gang affiliations. With the shootings staged midday on a major highway between Indiana and Chicago, the pattern had changed, and the city was feeling vulnerable. And dead bodies splashed across the evening news were hardly a stellar ad campaign for the city's significant tourism industry. If confirmed, shooting number three would move the public, and the Mayor's Office, into outright panic.

The idea that gang rivalry or initiation rites had been the impetus for these shootings hadn't even been questioned. But having been on the scene, literally in the middle of the action, seeing the distance and the angles, the logistics of the shooting had nagged at me over the last twenty-four hours. This wasn't a stray bullet or drive-by shooting—the types of killings that typically found their way into the news. I wondered if this was a territorial feud related to changes in drug trafficking. Perhaps a new gang had moved into the area. The sad reality was that the public had simply come to accept surface-level explanations for violence in the Englewood neighborhood.

"Whoa, wasn't one accident enough?"

Art Borkowski had passed the elevator, engrossed in a document, just as I stepped through into the hallway. His stack of manila folders and paper tumbled to the floor, skittering across the tile as he stopped short.

"Sorry, Art." I stooped to assist, annoyed with myself for apologizing.

"I don't need your help."

He bent down and yanked the documents out of my hand, as if I'd just gotten a glimpse of his porn stash.

"You know, Art, IT can get you an iPad." I nodded at his stack.

He glowered at me, did a once-over of my battered face, and said nothing. He began scooping up pages even faster.

Buddy, you work for a digital media company. Erik had brought him into the organization because of his stellar reputation as an investigative journalist. The all-digital news concept was still in transition—hell, the entire industry was struggling with print versus digital, free versus subscription, particularly at the local level. Link-Media's board of directors had needed some assurances that historic operational methods weren't being totally abandoned, by way of classic newspaper talent on staff. Snagging Borkowski away from the *Tribune* had been a major coup for Erik, and he refused to hear anything other than how Art Borkowski was a journalistic god who'd won five Lisagor Awards for excellence in reporting. My caution that his transition and ego might get in the way had been dismissed as quickly as it had been offered.

Borkowski lumbered down the hall, muttering, probably something unkind. His disdain for the way I'd secured this job was a constant presence. I followed him through the frosted glass doors toward my office in the timber-beamed loft space, nodding hello as I wound my way past the handful of coworkers buzzing around their desks, my heels clicking on the polished concrete. Heads turned and confused looks were shot my way as the staff noticed my bruises. The sound was barely noticeable over the white noise of CNN and Al Jazeera streaming from the five televisions hanging from the ceiling. I dropped my bag on my desk, set down my tea, and winced as I twisted into the chair. Some of my body parts were still relearning how to bend, and it would easily be another week before my skin was no longer blotched with eggplant patches. I lifted my cup to my mouth and wondered how often I'd need to explain my battered face.

The glass box office I was housed in suddenly felt like a terrarium, rather than the hip workspace Erik intended, and I was the chameleon on display. What color is she today? I grabbed my phone and returned a couple follow-up calls from my insurance company and the Audi dealership, then opened my email, hoping to head off any emergencies before the questions about my banged-up face slowed me down.

"How's your head?"

No such luck. I looked up from my screen. Erik stood there, leaning against the door frame, his body effortlessly filling the space. I still had serious reservations about our ability to work together as exes, but I was locked in. Hell, we'd barely established a professional rhythm in the office as husband and wife before I'd filed for divorce. But I'd known the risks when I'd pushed Erik to give me a chance. Like it or not, Lane had called it. No one else was going to hire a journalist without credentials.

I had taken advantage of an opportunity and needed to live with the consequences. My professional existence as a journalist was tied to Erik, and to Link-Media, until a major story could help me stand on my own.

"Still have a goose egg on my forehead, and the bruises will take a few days, but it's manageable," I replied, then focused back on my computer. "I'll have the Midway privatization story wrapped this morning and send it over for your comments."

He walked over to my side and tenderly pushed the hair off my face to inspect the damage. I pulled away, knowing the staff could see us.

"And what a beautiful goose egg it is. I've been so worried about you, Andrea. To think what could have happened..." He seemed adrift in the possible outcomes. "Were you asleep yesterday when I called? Babe, I've been frantic thinking about you being alone."

For a split second, I felt the old tug of affection, then forced myself to summon the image of finding Erik in the break room with his hands up the skirt of our former copy editor three months ago. Nothing like reality to kill warm memories.

Sadness and regret for what we had lost washed over me as I looked up at him, as did renewed resolve for the mission at hand. One big story would allow me to cut the final ties I had with Erik, get a new job, and uncomplicate my life. It might even allow me to keep my apartment.

"Please stop calling me 'babe.' It wasn't appropriate at the office when we were married, and it sure as hell isn't appropriate, *ever*, now that we're divorced." I held his gaze, not wanting there to be any question of my thoughts on the subject.

Erik just flashed a crooked smile, leaned in, and placed his hand on my shoulder. "The divorce isn't final yet."

"Knock it off, Erik." I shrugged off his hand. "Batting those baby blues at me doesn't work anymore," I said, knowing it wasn't entirely true. Damn, just being in the same room was ratcheting up the pounding in my head. I stole a glance at the bottle of Advil on my desk.

"Old habits." He shrugged, not letting up on the sly smile.

"Yeah, I know all about your old habits."

That got him. The I'm-too-gorgeous-for-words look was gone, only to be replaced by wounded-puppy.

"You can always call it off," he said, his voice now low and hopeful.

I held my tongue. We'd been through this too many times. He couldn't change, and I couldn't live with it.

My silence got him to switch gears. "Did you see the doctor on Saturday? What did she say? And what are you doing in the office? You shouldn't have come in." He grabbed my bag and swung my chair around to help me up, deciding I was too much of an invalid to be at work.

"Hold on." I put my palm up. "I'm moving like a sloth and turning a little purple here and there, but nothing is broken. All I need is a comfortable chair and a computer. Besides, I'd be doing the same thing back at my apartment, but with the screech of a tile saw in the background."

He shook his head. "All right, but I don't like it. You get your cute little ass out of here if you feel at all wobbly."

"Erik! Enough with the language."

"Sorry." He smiled that ridiculous little-boy grin again. "Did Art speak to you? We've got a short follow-up piece on the shooting planned for today. I'd love a quote."

I shot him my best *are you fucking kidding me?* look. "Maybe he didn't think 'babe' could add anything newsworthy."

"Andrea, give him a break. He's a damn good journalist. He's not adapting to digital as fast as we'd like, but you two need to figure out how to work together. There's a lot you can learn from him."

"And I'm sure he's dying to play teacher. Don't be naive, Erik. Collaboration is not in that man's DNA. He treats me like I don't know how to spell 'journalist.' He treats everyone—other than you, that is—like we're his personal file clerks."

"Well, the two of you need to stop being children and figure it out."

His words stung, but even to my own ears, I sounded whiny and petty. I'd never have spoken to my boss in that tone as an assistant state's attorney. I wanted to blame it on my injuries, but that was only partially true. Whether I wanted to face it or not, my self-created career vulnerability occasionally oozed out of its shell and bitch-slapped me in the face.

I nodded in agreement as Erik stepped toward the door, but would have felt better if I had any confidence that Borkowski would be receiving the same reprimand. Once again it was up to "the girl" to make nice.

"Before you go, I thought we should talk about the highway shootings. I know Borkowski's been covering the story, but I think I can add a new angle. A firsthand account is compelling."

"He's got this," he said, shaking his head. "Same story we've been hearing for years. It's rampant South Side gang violence escalating. The only new angle is that CPD has allowed it to get out of hand. They've turned over control of the prison to the inmates."

I cringed at the insensitive comment but didn't trust myself to keep my attitude contained, so I said nothing as he left. Flipping back to my laptop, I sent Borkowski a short summary of my experience, then shifted my thoughts off the highway shootings and pulled up my draft on Mayor Rendell's mysterious bank account bump. The announcement of a gubernatorial run was only a rumor at this point. I assumed the bad optics of releasing that information hours after a third shooting was holding them back.

If I could connect those funds to the campaign, my piece would add an interesting wrinkle to the election coverage. I placed another call to a possible lead on the money trail, leaving a third message, then dialed the Mayor's Office for a comment.

The press liaison I was transferred to dutifully gave me a non-answer, so I asked to be patched through to Owen Platt, the deputy mayor. Platt's long-standing political career had involved over a decade in the Office of Policy and Strategic Planning, where he had risen to deputy director before being tapped by Rendell to fill the number two position three years ago. Shrewd, calculating, and connected so deeply into the fiber of city government that he was the grease that made Rendell's administration hum. No one was more intimately acquainted with the inner workings of Chicago government than Platt.

After a brief hold, while I listened to pre-recorded community announcements, a gatekeeper-type came on the line. I identified myself and the purpose of my call. Instead of the polite brushoff I expected, she asked me to wait while she checked his availability.

"This is Owen Platt." A voice thick and smooth like crème brûlée came on the line. "Do you mind if I call you Andrea? We have so many mutual acquaintances I feel as if we've already met."

"Not at all. I understand you and Erik cross paths occasionally."

The men had known each other casually, intersecting at political functions and business gatherings over the years. In the early days of EMco—a data-encryption company Erik had founded, run for eight years, and then sold for a healthy seven-figure number—Platt had introduced Erik to a hedge fund manager who had later become a key board member.

"Yes, Erik and I do find ourselves at the same functions occasionally. It's a shame those paths have not yet included you. We'll have to change that. What can I help you with, Andrea?"

Platt's polished, politically savvy approach was legendary. He was the say-the-right-thing, get-the-job-done guy behind the mayor. But in Chicago, that slick veneer came with well-filed incisors. Whisper sweet nothings in one ear, while holding a key project for ransom in the other. That's how it was done. And Platt was a master.

"I'm calling to ask about your boss. We hear that Mayor Rendell intends to make a gubernatorial bid."

A throaty laugh bounced back at me.

"An interesting idea, isn't it? After eight years of disastrous conservative fiscal policies down in Springfield that have left this state begging, we could have a candidate who has actually balanced a budget without decimating social programs."

"Is that a confirmation?" I asked, ignoring the artificially rosy campaign rhetoric.

"Andrea, you are delightful." Again the laugh. "At the present time, I can neither confirm nor deny. But given our connections, I'd love to explore this further. Come see me tomorrow. Perhaps I'll have something juicier for you then."

5

Thirty minutes later I could still feel the oiliness of Platt's innuendo like a coating on my skin. I stared blankly at my notepad, ostensibly having set out to brainstorm additional leads to the mayor's money trail. Nothing. Ideas and time had vanished as the storm surge in my head threatened to crest two hours before another dose of meds was advisable. Closing my eyes and resting my elbows on the desk, I applied pressure to both temples, and willed the pain away.

The conversation with Erik floated back. Damn! My moods around him still swung from disgust to tolerance to nostalgic, and I didn't know how to stabilize them. Even if he was legitimately concerned, his honey, baby, sweetheart shit was doing nothing to help my professional credibility. I knew Lane was right; I had to make this job work. The only thing that was going to get me out from under the shadow of being the boss's wife was a kick-ass story. Shadowing Borkowski like I was some college intern nibbling on his crumbs might be Erik's idea of fast-tracking my career, but it also involved a couple of decades of humiliation and groveling. I had neither the time nor the patience. I needed to make it happen on my own, and soon.

"What truck ran you over? I thought you were spending a quiet weekend at the beach?"

Brynn Campbell, my part-time summer intern, stared at me from the doorway, a venti cup of something highly caffeinated permanently welded to her hand. Somehow the girl seemed to exist on coffee and Cheez-Its. Her tawny skin glowed despite the junk food diet. Still I wanted to slip a bottle of One-A-Days onto her desk for good measure.

Brynn was a recent graduate of Northwestern University, where she double-majored in journalism and computer science. Inside her compact twenty-three-year-old body lived the soul of a forty-five-year-old librarian. Outstanding at research, she'd come to her job interview having prepared an entire dossier on Link-Media. The summary also included Erik's history at EMco, as well as information on my previous career as an assistant state's attorney. She'd even analyzed my major cases. I'd hired her on the spot. I'd seen enough of the usual bubbly young things without a brain in their adorable little heads that typically gravitated toward journalism, expecting to be paid for looking cute and posting selfies on Instagram. Perky annoyed me.

"I had a quiet weekend all right, just never made it to Michigan." I motioned for her to take a seat. "Car accident. I was in that mess on the Dan Ryan on Friday afternoon."

"Seriously?"

"Just bumps and bruises."

"Damn! It's been all over the news. Another sniper hit, and you were there. Wow. You're doing the story, right?" she asked, pushing up the sleeves of her oxford shirt and taking a long swig of coffee.

"Nope. Borkowski's still on it. I shot him a couple lines on my experience, which he probably ignored. I've been shut out."

Brynn looked up from her cup, eyebrows raised. I shook my

head. No need to rehash our mutual opinion of the man. She had already developed evasive maneuvers to avoid Borkowski's constant requests for help with filing and coffee fetching.

"Give me a second," I said to Brynn, tapping a couple of keys on my computer. "His piece should have just posted. Let's see what the 'Master' had to say."

Short, fact-based, utilitarian. He'd gotten the job done in about four paragraphs of text, but having been in the middle of it all, none of the horror, fear, or the agony, had been captured. It had the emotional engagement of a textbook. Wasn't he curious about the shooter? Was it the same guy or a group? What was the motive? Why these victims? Who were their families?

"Dull and lifeless?" Brynn asked, interpreting my expression.

"He sure hasn't posed any of the questions running through my mind."

"He seems to be struggling with how to tell a story in a screenshot versus an old-fashioned two-page spread. Or maybe he doesn't think the subject matter is big enough for him—at least not big enough for the reporter he is in his own mind," Brynn said.

"We have national press hovering on the sidelines, painting this town as a crime capital, despite CPD's attempt to show control of the situation. It's sounding more and more like the official PR machine is cranking at full speed and soft-pedaling reality. How can that story not be big enough to push more aggressively? There's more life in an obituary column." I closed the page in disgust. "I put in my pitch to Erik for an insider segment, but he shot me down. So, like it or not, you and I are going to stay focused on the Midway story and Rendell's money trail."

After discussing the to-do list with Brynn, I shifted gears. My Midway story had taken an interesting turn this morning with the report of an officer-involved shooting. Apparently a confrontation between some protestors and a police officer had become physical. Guns he'd been drawn, and a protestor had taken a bullet to the leg. There had to be more sludge to that one. An administrative contact from my years with the State's Attorney's Office could give me what the press liaison wouldn't.

Before reaching for the phone, I reviewed my notes, but my mind was still wrapped around the highway shooting. Maybe it was the flashbacks to the dead man's face; maybe it was my bruised chest that roared with every move; maybe it was Erik telling me no. Whatever it was, I couldn't seem to shake the tragedy loose from my thoughts. Succumbing to curiosity, I pulled up the news coverage.

The reporting was as I'd thought it would be: a territory feud between the Black Disciples and the Gangster Disciples. And the subtle suggestion that young men were being forced to kill as part of their initiation or as proof of loyalty. CPD had used that explanation after a GD had taken credit for the first shooting on Facebook. Civilians had just been just in the wrong place at the wrong time.

Gang violence had been part of the South Side's history for decades. More recently, the economic collapse of 2008 had initiated a storm of hardship. Hospitals had closed. Schools had closed. A full-service grocery store was miles away by bus. With jobs and basic services eliminated from these neighborhoods, gang life was often the only option for far too many young men.

Whether the bleeding of neighborhood resources and basic amenities were a contributing factor to gang proliferation didn't seem to matter as long as economic hardship and its consequences were confined. Put those complex problems in a box where the average white middle-class Chicago resident could read the headlines and think about it as someone else's problem.

Young black men were dying every day just because they had walked down the wrong street, with barely an acknowledgment from the rest of the city. The death toll made the news, but where was the outrage over a generation being born with a gun in hand? What about the outrage over the destruction of those young lives?

But kill a couple of tourists on their way to Navy Pier? Well, *that* got noticed.

Enough. It wasn't my story. I closed the browser and reached for the phone.

"Jacqui, it's Andrea Kellner. How's life at CPD these days? You ready to give up the glamour and riches of government life?"

Jacqui Torres had been an administrative assistant, whipping police detectives into shape, for thirty-five years. No one got a pass from her. Sloppy, incomplete reports were met with a scolding that took grown men back to their Catholic school days. Like a good cop, she was both feared and respected. She also knew everything that was going on behind the scenes.

"Are you kidding? And give up the in-office mani-pedis and daily massage breaks? Hell no!"

"I see you haven't lost your gift of sarcasm. How's that worthless husband of yours?"

"Mean and lazy. I should have divorced him twenty years ago. Too late now. I guess I'll keep him around. The roof needs replacing," she said. "And how's that sweet piece of ass you're married to?"

"Full of bullshit as always." It was our typical banter. I didn't bother to let on that my playful spouse bashing actually had teeth behind it these days.

"Well, he *is* a man. So, is this a social call, or have you come to your senses and returned to the State's Attorney's Office? 'Cause I got a problem with the last twit they sent over."

"I'm afraid not," I laughed. "I'm still pushing a pen in the private sector."

Jacqui and I were still dancing around the boundaries of our new relationship, and I probed a bit for dirt on the Midway situation, pushing as far as I felt I could. Jacqui would slap me down if I stepped over the line. She filled me in on the details. As she described the physical aggression of one of the protestors, it sounded to me like the victim was lucky he'd only gotten it in the leg. Not that even a justified shooting was going to play well for the officer, given Chicago's hypersensitive political climate, and the national media's hunt for these stories, as well.

"What are you hearing about Friday's shooting on the Dan Ryan?" The question tumbled out before I could debate myself.

"Oh, my Lord, everyone over here is in one pissy mood. The Mayor's Office is knocking heads. The vise is tightening on our favorite superintendent, and you know what that means for the rest of us. CNN is planning some big story on how gangs are controlling the city, the AMA is threatening to pull its September convention at McCormick Place, and your people are camped outside of police headquarters with cameras and microphones like we're giving away money. This is not a happy place."

"So they're certain this is another gang situation?" All the news coverage had pointed in that direction, but I had to ask.

"That's the word. Shooter was on the overpass at Garfield Boulevard, near the Red Line L stop. It's a regular open-air drug market. Guys on the force call it 'the Pharmacy.'"

Drugs would be the obvious motivator underlying a gang territory conflict, but these shootings had been described as initiation rites. This was the first I was hearing anything about the Pharmacy or a territory dispute. Was it a new situation, or was CPD keeping quiet for some reason? I scribbled a few notes to myself.

"What's Janek's story? I understand he's heading up the investigation."

"Smart, tough, all-around good cop." Jacqui was fiercely loyal to the police force, and I wasn't surprised by her praise. She would never disparage an officer, but she would call it like she saw it if loyalties were compromised.

"I hear there were some bribery allegations a while back. You think there's anything to that?"

"Janek? No way! I know they had to investigate him, but this guy plays it straight. He didn't deserve getting raked over like that. That damage is hard to erase."

I could hear the sorrow in her voice. In a world where reputation was everything, cops weren't known for their skills at forgive-and-forget. If Janek was the lone holdout in a group happy to take the money, I imagined he had a tally sheet of his own.

"Janek did have a lieutenant who I'm convinced was dirty, Matt Dubicki," she added, pausing for a moment, deciding how much to say. "The way he was spending money, something had to be coming in on the side, if you know what I mean. A cop's salary doesn't get you a two-million-dollar restored greystone in Hyde Park, or thirty K a year to send your kids to Chicago Lab School. They could never pin anything on him. He had some story about an investment that paid big, but in my mind, that just means he was a little slicker than the investigators. Or he had help hiding it."

"Is Dubicki still with the force?"

"No. He bolted as soon as soon as Internal Affairs stopped overturning rocks. Wachowski would have booted him anyway. He came in as superintendent about a month later and started tossing the deadwood. Dubicki was probably afraid that one day his backup wouldn't show. Now he's heading up security for some commercial real estate developer, making a couple hundred grand a year. Talk about making lemonade."

I ended the call wondering how much money it took to buy a cop these days.

6

"That was a waste of an afternoon," I grumbled to myself, slumping into my desk chair and kicking off my shoes. I'd spent the past few hours pounding the pavement and working the phones, trying to overturn the rocks hiding Rendell's private bank account. My efforts had yielded nothing but sore feet, closed doors, hang-ups, and dead ends. Even the disgruntled former staffer, who had presented me with evidence of the secret account and her suspicions just three weeks ago, seemed to be avoiding me. I wasn't even close to proving anything untoward. Instead, I was starting to feel like the chump in someone else's revenge story.

I pinched the bridge of my nose to ease the pounding behind my eyes. It was nearly six and the office had cleared out for the day, aside from the usual stragglers. Borkowski was still hunched over his desk, his head buried in a stack of files. I didn't know if it was dedication or he simply had no personal life, but the man never seemed to leave the office before 8:00 p.m. The office scuttlebutt had it that Borkowski had lost a son tragically, but I'd heard no mention of a wife or partner. Maybe that explained his charming disposition.

I glanced briefly at a few notes Brynn had left for me while listening to the local evening news replay footage from Friday's shooting. I lifted my head toward the TV hanging in the corner of my office, drawn to the image of the overpass, my conversation with Jacqui fresh in my mind. A second later, Karl Janek's angular face filled the frame as a clip from this afternoon played. Gang dispute. CPD is devoting every resource. Blah, blah, blah. Then why wasn't anyone in custody? And why wasn't Borkowski down in Englewood needling Janek for answers?

Grabbing the files Brynn had pulled together on Mayor Rendell's early political career, I shoved them into my tote for a little bedtime reading. My body complained about the length of the day, but unless I wanted Erik pounding on my door at midnight, I needed to stop in his office and find out what the four phone messages he'd left this afternoon were all about before I went to meet Cai for a drink. As I headed down the hall, Borkowski lifted his head from his computer and scowled as I passed.

Erik was on the phone when I paused in the doorway. He motioned me in and pointed to the chair. I ignored his offer, hoping to make this a quick visit. Leaning back in his chair, his loafered feet rested casually on the edge of his Herman Miller desk, the sleeves of his linen shirt were rolled up and his wavy blond hair looked tousled as if he'd been running his fingers through it. Images of a happier past looked down at me from the photos dotting the bookcase wall behind him. A trip to Florence three years ago. An afternoon on the boat. Christmas with my father. I turned away, needing to tamp down any and all warm and fuzzies. When the hell was this roller coaster going to end?

"John, let's talk next week." He wrapped up the call and came around the desk, stopping close enough that I could smell the lemongrass soap he had used this morning.

"Baby, are you okay? I called several times."

The term of endearment annoyed me, but I let it pass, needing to modulate my emotions. Another tiff with Erik would only complicate my dinner plans and my mood.

"I'm fine. I was pressing my leads on the mayor story, not that it got me anywhere. What's up?"

"I was worried. You've been out all afternoon. When I didn't hear back, I had visions of you passed out somewhere. I cautioned you this morning about pushing yourself so hard. A head injury isn't something to mess with. Let me take you home."

He placed a hand on my shoulder and I stiffened at the touch. Too much had happened over the last few days for me to have any emotional stability. I didn't trust myself not to collapse against him in defeat.

I also wanted to slap myself for giving a toehold to self-doubt. Suck it up. This was just his macho male protector role coming out. *Sorry, Erik, you've been fired from that job.*

"Look, I appreciate your concern, I really do, but I'm okay. Don't magnify this injury into something more serious than it is. I'm perfectly capable of doing my job and knowing when I've pushed too hard. Was there another reason you called?"

"You should be resting. Get your things."

The man was infuriating. Speaking to me like I was a child who needed to be told when to put on her mittens was *not* going to be part of our divorce.

"Erik, you have to stop this. This isn't the relationship we have anymore."

His face softened as he stepped closer, his fingers stroking along the curve of my cheek.

"It could be. We could still have that." He leaned in for a kiss.

Caught off guard, my breath froze in my throat and I stopped him by placing my hand on his lips. I had always loved his mouth, so sensuous and strong. The urge to run my finger along that lush curve overwhelmed me. Memories flooded in. Memories of tenderness and passion and love. Memories igniting a hunger that I hadn't felt in such a long time.

His hand moved to the back of my neck, the other around my waist. He pulled me in until no space remained between us. His lips brushed my forehead, nuzzled my hair, and I melted. In that instant, I forgot all the pain and anger and felt nothing but how well our bodies fit together.

"Baby, I miss you so much," he said, as his hand slowly ran down the curve of my backside.

"Erik?"

A voice at the door pulled me out of my lustful reverie. I jumped away from Erik like a teenager caught coping a feel.

"Sorry to interrupt your, um, meeting? I need this expense authorization signed before you leave tonight."

Shit! Borkowski. Another thirty seconds and he would have walked in on something far more embarrassing. What the hell was I doing?

"No problem. I was just leaving," I said, bewildered and frustrated, but grateful for Borkowski's interruption.

"Can you wait ten minutes?" Erik implored me, desire still in his eyes.

"I'm sorry, I, ah...no, I have dinner plans," I said, my voice shaky, thrown off by my response to Erik. I spun for the door, desperate to get some distance.

"Andrea..."

"No, Erik, I have to go."

I turned—afraid to meet Erik's gaze, afraid to let him see the weakness in my eyes—and sprinted down the four flights of stairs rather than wait for the elevator, ignoring the muscle spasms in my side. My thoughts were spiraling. Confusion, lust, anger with myself were all rolled up into a whirling ball of emotions I couldn't process.

"CAN I get you something to drink while you wait?" asked a young man with a lumberjack beard and a plaid flannel shirt.

He appeared seconds after I'd been seated at a table on the sidewalk patio at Nico Osteria, where Cai and I were meeting for dinner. The cab ride from the office to the restaurant had released a little of the tension, but I was still trying to process my response to Erik.

What the hell was going on? Was I so sex-deprived that I had responded to Erik out of pure animal instinct? That at least was a more palatable thought. I had been scarred so deeply that the reminder I still had feelings for him was too painful to contemplate.

"Vodka martini, rocks, olives," I said to my server, who scurried off, apparently recognizing that I needed booze now. Good man.

I was halfway through my drink when Cai slid into the seat across from me. She threw her navy silk jacket onto the back of the chair and pulled her long hair loose from the clip she always wore at work.

"Going hardcore tonight, I see. A martini? What's the occasion?"

"Just trying to forget my day. Join me."

I motioned to my new bearded friend.

"Let me have a Dewar's, neat," Cai said.

One of our many shared traits was that neither of us had ever been into "girl" drinks—nothing fruity, no chocolate 'tini's. We liked our booze unmasked.

Her drink delivered, Cai raised her glass and took a nice swig. "To forgetting. Ah, that's better. Now hurry up and tell me about your awful day so I can tell you about how wonderful mine was."

I hesitated, not because I was uncomfortable, but because I was struggling to understand my response. It would be easier to put the encounter with Erik out of my mind and pretend it hadn't happened. I took a deep inhale of the geraniums trailing over the edge of the planter next to me and reveled in the languorous rhythm of the city around me before Cai brought me back.

"Come on, spill it already. Or do we need to get another martini into you before you can talk about it?"

I laughed and took another sip, letting the warmth of the summer evening on my bare arms relax me. Cai lifted her sunglasses to the top of her head and shot me a look.

"Okay, okay! I had a... ah...a 'moment' with Erik just before I came over here that I would have been better off without."

"A 'moment'? What the hell does that mean?"

I knew I was stalling. Going into the gory details meant admitting that I was still confused about my feelings for Erik. And I didn't like being confused. Particularly about this.

"He's not being a dick over your financial settlement, is he? I know you didn't want my SOB divorce-attorney friend to represent you, but just say the word and Nelson will crush his ass. Erik will be trading that fancy sailboat of his in for a kayak after Nelson gets done with him."

The boat was Erik's obsession. A competitive sailor since college, he had treated himself to the boat of his dreams six years ago after selling EMco. I had no interest in his boat and no interest in bleeding him dry as the woman scorned, but, if I were inclined, nothing would push his buttons more than a bulldog attorney coming after his baby.

"No, no, nothing like that. We were in his office, he made a move on me, and I was right there with him in all of five seconds."

Cai's hand froze as she lifted her glass to her mouth, and she stared at me as if I'd lost my mind. "My God, put that drink down. You obviously hurt your head more than you realized in the car accident. What could you have possibly been thinking?" she said, shuddering.

Cai knew, more than anyone, how deeply Erik had hurt me. She'd held me as I sobbed. Handed me tissues when my face was red and bloated. Listened to me rail at 2:00 a.m. when sleep was elusive.

"I know. I'm too traumatized to analyze it right now. Nothing happened, really, but I don't know where that came from. One minute we were talking, and seconds later his hands were on my ass and I wasn't pushing him away. I don't have an explanation." I shook my head and reached for my martini. "To top it off, Borkowski walked in on us mid-grope," I said, disgusted with myself for giving him more ammunition.

Cai burst out with a laugh that came straight from her gut. I couldn't help but join in. The options were either to laugh or cry.

"Look, sweetie, your neglected lady parts just need some attention, nothing more. Go out and get laid. Problem solved. Erik will be neutered."

I raised my eyebrows, pretending to take her seriously.

"Metaphorically speaking," she said, smiling. "Unless you want me to pull out the Ginsu knife. I can play out that Asian chick stereotype." Cai flipped her hair over her shoulder, then fingered the butter knife next to her plate.

"I thought Asian chick stereotypes revolved around submission."

"Or the female assassin who can kill a man with her thighs."

"You got the best of both parents: delicate Vietnamese exterior strikes back with balls of steel."

"Exactly right. Based on most of the men I meet, one of us has to have a pair." She scanned the bar, dismissing the lot on sight. Two women at the neighboring table sniggered in agreement.

"For someone trying to push me out of the self-imposed celibacy nest, you're not exactly painting an inspiring picture."

"Honey, I know it's been a long time since you've been in the market, but I'm suggesting a good fuck, not a relationship. He just has to be good with his hands, if you know what I mean."

"I have a vague memory..."

We laughed, the tension of my moment with Erik gone, and ordered another round of drinks.

Cai had a talent for cutting through the clutter and distilling any situation into its most basic elements. Normally, I could hold my own in that regard. Years of legal training had drilled simplicity and order into my approach to the world, but my feelings for Erik were still too raw, more of a sliding scale than an on-off button.

"Enough about my sex life, or lack thereof. Distract me with the juicy details of your life. You had a trial start today, didn't you?"

"I did, and if I do say so myself, my opening argument was brilliant. 'Ladies and gentlemen of the jury, my client was not embezzling eight million dollars. He was investing that money in a new venture on behalf of his employer. Perhaps his supervisor was experiencing one of his many moments of alcohol-induced amnesia at the time he authorized the funds.'"

I chuckled. "Let me guess, that new venture was something that your client personally profited from, also on his employer's behalf?"

"It's not a crime to make a profit."

"Creative strategy," I said, admiring her chutzpah.

Cai was born to be an attorney. By the time a jury finished listening to her version of events, they had trouble imagining any other possible truth. She could switch on either her soft or tough side for maximum impact, based on the objective at hand.

"I thought so. Speaking of profits, do you see who I see?" Cai said, her eyes fixed across the street, an amused smile on her face.

I turned and followed her gaze.

"Who are you looking at? There are dozens of people on the street."

Nico Osteria was at the intersection of Bellevue, Rush, and State Streets, a virtual restaurant row for moneyed Gold Coast locals and tourists alike. And on a beautiful July evening, the area was teeming with people at the outdoor cafes, enjoying a gelato in Mariano Park, or walking the few short blocks to Oak Street's designer boutiques.

"Across the street at Gibsons. The three middle-aged white guys at a table on the far-right corner of the patio."

"Yeah, I see them."

"See the big guy, white hair, with the ridiculous poufy comb-over facing us? That's Nelson Ramirez. He owns Rami Concrete. They handle every large-scale construction project in the Chicago area. He was just released from prison."

Rami Concrete was known throughout the area for its graffiti-painted trucks and aggressive advertising. The trial had consumed major airtime on local news stations because Ramirez was well connected politically. Rami Concrete took in millions of dollars in revenue from city contracts every year—at least it had, prior to its owner becoming a convicted felon.

"Yeah, I remember. He's the guy who got nabbed for manipulating environmental impact studies."

"The very same. He was paying an engineer to 'rewrite' bad news so he wouldn't lose contracts. Eventually he got caught when some toxic sludge started bubbling up in a Dollar General parking lot. Spent the last eighteen months in federal prison in

Terre Haute." She turned her attention back to her Dewar's, then leaned across the table toward me.

"His legal team was cocky and arrogant from the start," she said softly. "They tried a kitchen-sink strategy, muddying the waters with a technical data dump, hoping it would become too complicated for the jury to follow. The strategy backfired, and the case unraveled." Cai's eyes lit up in delight as she leaned back in her chair. "That was a fun one to watch."

Allegations had circled that cooking the reports was common practice at Rami and highly profitable, but the prosecutor had not been able to build a firm case for additional incidents. Ramirez and his engineer had both taken plea deals, paid their fines, kept up their stories, and agreed to jail sentences, hoping to minimize the personal damage. The engineer would be lucky to get a janitorial position when his time was up, but Ramirez would probably step back to his desk, and his bank account, barely missing a beat.

Cai might have been enthralled with Ramirez's legal wranglings, but it was his dinner companions that had my curiosity piqued.

"Interesting that one of the first things he does is have dinner with Alderman Anthony Langston—from the 20th Ward. That's Englewood." I looked at Cai, wondering if she also found the timing curious. Englewood was a South Side neighborhood plagued with high unemployment and crime. "What do you think that's all about? The way they're huddled over their drinks, they seem to be having an interesting conversation."

"Maybe they got to know each other over the South Side Walmart deal? Rami must have put in bids on that project. I think they break ground in the next few months."

"Who's the third guy?" I asked.

"I don't know. I can't see his face."

Just then the unidentified man stood and left the table,

heading back inside the restaurant and giving us an opportunity for a frontal view. He was younger than the others—closer to forty—with a head of thick, slicked-back dark hair, biceps that strained at his shirt, and a jaw so square I could measure by it. He wasn't familiar. As I watched, a fourth man arrived and began working his way around the table, clapping the guys on the back and shaking hands.

"Well, look who's joined the party. Art Borkowski."

7

Borkowski, Langston, Ramirez? The image of the three men at dinner was still on my mind this morning. The ease of their body language and laughter told me the meeting had been social, and not uncommon. Langston and Ramirez having a personal connection, I got. Borkowski, on the other hand? Should a personal relationship between a business leader and a journalist concern me? Maybe it was my predisposition to caution, or just my dislike of the man, but it was tough to be journalistically objective about one's friends in high places.

Juggling my travel mug of tea in one hand and my tote bag in the other, I unlocked the glass doors to Link-Media. Flipping on the overhead lights, I cringed, regretting the out-of-character second martini the previous night. Plopping my bag on the floor, I settled into my desk. The solitude of an empty office in the early morning gave me a chance to pour myself into my work while colleagues were still sitting in traffic on the Kennedy Expressway.

As usual, the message light on the office phone blinked at me, and I lifted the handset to retrieve my voice mail, hoping that some of yesterday's prodding had yielded a call back. As I punched in my code, a loud, angry outburst reached me from somewhere in the near distance. The outer hallway? Or was someone in the office?

I clicked off and quietly stepped past my desk, peering out over the empty worktables and silent computers. No one.

The crash of metal against something hard and unyielding came from the back, shaking my body to attention. Erik's office.

I grabbed my cell and tiptoed slowly toward the sound, hugging the brick wall, my finger hovering, ready to dial 911.

The voice was sharper now. The anger restrained but coiled. Ready to rear up again and strike.

"We had an agreement!"

Erik? On an angry phone call at 7:00 a.m.? I relaxed my grip on the phone and slid it back into my pocket before edging closer to his door.

"The money supply isn't endless. I'm not the Federal Reserve."

His words glued me to the spot. Money? Who was he giving money to? Were we in financial trouble? If he was in trouble, personally or professionally, then so was I. My mind raced back over the reams of paper my attorney had forwarded. The financial disclosure documents for our divorce hadn't raised any red flags at the time, but that had been two months ago. Had something changed? Wouldn't be the first divorcing son of a bitch who tried to get away with squirreling away assets.

"I can't leverage this anymore. We need another player at the table. Someone who can buy in," he said, his tone lower now, but still icy and demanding. "We need more skin in the game."

Whatever was going on was putting a knot in my stomach. My entire life was still enmeshed with Erik's, and any financial pain of his would eventually be mine.

The call appeared to be almost over, so I crept back the way I had come and immersed myself in the balance of my unheard voice mail messages. As I listened to the stream, my mind teetered back to my own situation. If Erik was bringing in an investor, we were all about to be looking for new jobs. With Lane's reminder that my journalist resume was pathetic playing on rewind, financial vulnerability loomed in front of me, daring me to misstep. Lost in the implications, I trudged on through the messages, painfully aware of the risks as I charted my course for the day.

"You ready for me? I didn't see any love notes on my desk."

I looked up from my computer to find Brynn waiting for the day's schedule. Her close-cropped afro was still damp from her morning shower and her uniform button-down shirt perfectly pressed as always. Wash-and-go had never been my look, but she pulled it off flawlessly.

"Is it nine already?" I asked, shocked to see that nearly two hours had slipped by. "Sorry, I got pulled into something. I have a list right here." I turned over half a dozen papers that were strewn across my desk and came up with nothing. "Umm, give me a second and I'll jot down a few things to get you started. We can touch base later."

"You sleep okay last night?"

"Sure, why do you ask?" I said, fumbling for a notepad and pencil.

Brynn was silent as I scribbled. I tore off the brief list and handed it over, only to be met with a confused stare.

"What?"

She lifted the crisp, typed, prioritized list of last week's tasks up against the hastily jotted scrap I had just handed her.

"Again, are you sure everything is all right?"

I smiled and shook my head. "Guilty as charged. I'm a little off my game this morning. Give me five minutes to get myself together and we'll chat about priorities."

"Okay, I'll resist the urge to feel your forehead—for the

moment." She turned on her heel, but not before shooting me a look that was more mama bear than lowly intern.

Erik, what are you up to? My gut clenched as the possibilities rolled through my head. A new partner would want changes, would want to bring in his own people—which meant I'd be the first to get axed. Did he have an investor on the hook? Sounded like early planning. but if something was going down, a kick-ass story could be my saving grace. Even if I had to use it to find another job.

I left message number three with my source on the mayor's funky cash transaction, asking for another meeting, then glanced through the day's headlines. Tourism was projected down twenty percent. Revenue numbers would start to tank if there was another shooting. And without a suspect in custody, that possibility felt very real.

I wandered out to Brynn's cubicle and pulled up a chair. She swung around and raised her coffee to her lips, watching me over the rim.

"Humor me for a minute. I need to throw a question at the wall, brainstorm a bit." The images of Friday's accident were still not far from my mind, but were now layered with the puzzle of a messy police history and the Pharmacy. The story felt underinvestigated. Was it because I now had a personal connection? Or did I want there to be more because I needed a story? "CPD has attributed these highway shootings to gang violence. Natural conclusion based on the location, the history of violence, gang behavior, drug activity in the area..."

"Right." Brynn nodded. "Are you questioning that premise?"

"I guess I'm wondering if it's an assumption instead of a fact. Whether there is any real evidence of gang activity versus what the appearance suggests. We're not talking about stray bullets or some drive-by shooting where the wrong target was accidentally hit, so I'm wondering if we've all rushed to judgment because of preconceived ideas? What connective tissue might exist between the shootings?"

A huge smile crossed her face, and she shot her eyes over her shoulder to see who might be within hearing range. "I knew you wouldn't sit back and not make a run at this story."

"I'm not sure I'm making a run at anything, yet," I said, keeping my voice low. "Just thinking out loud. Pull up what's been released on the victims."

She tapped at her keyboard. "First victim, Angel Velasquez, thirty-six, a resident of Gary, Indiana, an electrician employed with Hoover Electrical, also in Gary, on his way to a job site in Schaumburg. He was alone in the vehicle. Second victim, Mark Walsh, forty-two, a self-employed accountant from Kalamazoo, Michigan. Mr. Walsh was traveling with his wife and two young children, who sustained minor injuries in the crash."

"And Gunderson?"

"Chicago resident. Computer programmer with a small outfit in the Loop."

"Where is this conversation going?"

I turned to find Erik at my elbow. His normal Captain America grin was dampened by the weariness in his eyes and his wrinkled dress shirt. I couldn't stop a chill of apprehension from creeping up the back of my neck. Whatever was going on with him clearly was taking a toll. Borkowski was a half-step behind him, a smug smile straining his face. I looked at him with a critical eye, wondering again about his connection with Ramirez and Langston.

"We were discussing the highway shooting victims, wondering if there were any connections between them," I said.

"Playing detective now, are you?" Borkowski said, looking at me over the top of his glasses. "Questioning CPD's police work? Or formulating the prosecution's strategy before anyone's been arrested?"

"None of the above," I shot back. "Shouldn't journalists question what has been presented?"

"I think I was clear with you yesterday, Andrea, that the highway shooting story is not yours," Erik said, his voice tight. "Focus on your own work. And, by the way, I'm still waiting on that Midway draft, which you committed to yesterday."

He stomped off as Brynn and I stared at the back of his head in confusion and Borkowski moved on to chastise someone else.

"I'll be right back," I said, following Erik to his office.

"What?" he shot at me as I entered.

"I sent you the copy yesterday afternoon. Check your email."

"Fine," he mumbled, taking refuge behind his desk. His attention focused on the foam in the cappuccino he clasped between his hands.

"Is there an issue we need to discuss? Is this about last night?" *Or the phone call I'd heard this morning?*

"No, just reinforcing the roles you've very clearly established. I repeat, you are not assigned to the highway story. Stepping on toes won't change that."

"Stepping on toes? Erik, I'm just speculating. Wondering if these specific people were targets. Shouldn't we all be playing what-if? I was there. Saw all of it with my own eyes. Felt it with my own body. Don't you think I have something to add based on that experience?"

"Drop it! It's not yours. If I want a contribution from you, I'll assign it. In the meantime, get back to your own work. Owen Platt is expecting you at eleven thirty to discuss Mayor Rendell's gubernatorial run. I made the arrangements."

And did you write my interview questions too? Thanks, Erik.

8

Phone. Notepad. Hand sanitizer. All the tools of the trade. I wasn't even in Platt's office yet, and I was already feeling dirty. As promised, I was on the fifth floor of City Hall, having passed through security, and now on my way to my 11:30 a.m. appointment with Owen Platt, Chicago's deputy mayor, to discuss Rendell's future. Despite the advantage of an early statement from the Mayor's Office, my ego was still bruised by Erik's condescension. Arranging my appointment. Ordering me over here like I was some kid sent to take dictation. What was next?

The marble-paneled hallway was eerily quiet as employees navigated from meeting to meeting. Their voices were hushed, in deference or anxiety.

There was no mistaking the entrance to the mayor's suite. The custom-made rug with the City of Chicago seal, the glass doors lettered in gold. After checking in with the attendant, I was shuttled through the maze and left standing in front of Platt's receptionist.

"I'm here to see Owen Platt," I said, identifying myself to the young woman sitting stiffly at the desk. She looked at me with blank eyes, then typed on her keyboard. Mayor Rendell's bulbous face stared down at us from the formal portrait behind her head. I noticed the artist had been generous in shaping his jowls.

"Yes, Ms. Kellner, I see that you're in Mr. Platt's calendar, but unfortunately he's been called away. Can we reschedule?"

"When do you expect him? I'm happy to wait."

"He's with the mayor at his residence. They're prepping for a press conference." She turned to the clock on the wall to her left. "They'll be down in Daley Plaza in about fifteen minutes. After that, his schedule is quite full for the balance of the day. The next availability I have is at the end of the week. I can get you on the calendar Thursday at two p.m."

A press conference? Were they making the gubernatorial announcement? If so, that blew my early lead to hell. Or perhaps it was news on the highway shootings. I told Platt's scheduler that I would phone later, then hurried downstairs. I rushed through the main corridor that connected the city government side of the building to the Cook County side and out onto Clark Street, darting into Daley Plaza, a landmark courtyard adjacent to the Richard J. Daley Center and home of Chicago's circuit courts.

I followed a handful of people past the fifty-foot Picasso sculpture into the plaza, which was famous as a location for weekly farmer's markets, summer festivals, and an untold number of movies. The usual mix of tourists and workers sat scattered at tables along the edge of the square or cross-kneed under the sculpture. Not yet noon and the day was already sweltering. I could feel a trickle of perspiration glide down the small of my back. Near the building, I saw a group milling around a temporary stage. Must be the place. Scanning the crowd, I saw the usual faces. Local network news types were primping and doing their sound checks, while camera operators juggled their bulky gear. The rest were glued to their phones, oblivious to the rush of pedestrians and the constant drum of buses and cars that bounced off the surrounding high-rise canyon. No sign of Borkowski. Oh well, his loss.

"I hear Wachowski's going to be emptying parking meters in Elgin if he doesn't get a head on a stick ASAP."

"Ought to get the damn National Guard in here."

Two reporters next to me were batting around the same issue being debated at coffee shops, bars, and Little League practices all over the city. Could Wachowski get these shootings under control? What *was* Rendell doing? Guess I knew what this press conference was about now.

In the shadow of shooting number three, the city's two top dogs were under mounting pressure to end the madness. Residents were flooding City Hall with phone calls and emails, demanding a resolution. Political pundits around the country were questioning who held control of Chicago, the mayor or the gangs? For a mayor who prided himself on building Chicago into the largest tourist destination in the Midwest, the millions of dollars being lost in the local economy—as travelers moved their plans to Minneapolis or the Wisconsin Dells—simply made him look impotent.

Rendell's relationship with Wachowski was onerous, but shatterproof. Rumor had it that they'd buried too many bodies in their symbiotic rise for either to be toppled alone. It must have burned Rendell's ass that he couldn't offer up Wachowski as the sacrificial lamb.

Why had the media been summoned? My Twitter feed was telling me word was getting out, and based on the tone, people wanted answers. Short of an arrest announcement, I was having a hard time imagining what words would placate the community in this hastily arranged press conference.

A handful of uniformed cops now hovered around the edges

of the stage—the advance team. I saw Brian Coogin, a cop I'd worked with on an auto theft ring case a few years back. His attention was focused on chatting up the young female officer next to him rather than on the crowd. *Sorry, Coogin, your love life will have to wait.*

More than forty journalists were now congregated in front of the platform, getting antsy in the heat. I moved through to my right, squeezing around an obnoxious guy who wrote for the *Chicago Truth*, a snarky right-wing political blog that delighted in finding fault with the current liberal administration. He was barking orders into his cell phone as I passed. Taking issue with my maneuver in the crowded space, he jammed an elbow square with my ribs. Damn! I sucked in some air as the pain shot up my side. For a second, I contemplated a rebuttal, but decided he wasn't worth the time.

Coogin looked in my direction as I got to the front. A broad smile deepened the creases around his full, ruddy face.

"What the heck got the likes of you out here? Whose ass you kickin' today?" He held out his hand, then introduced his colleague.

"I decided I liked representing both sides of a story," I said, handing him my card.

"Press? Well, ain't that a gear shift." He laughed and scrunched his face, baffled by my career change. "This little lady is, or I guess *was,* one tough-ass ASA. Not that you can tell by looking at her," he said to the female cop.

The look she gave me told me I was about as welcome as food poisoning.

"So, you're here for front-row seats to this performance." Coogin nodded at the throng.

"What's this all about? We going to hear anything new?" I asked.

"Beats me. Rendell calls, we gotta jump." He shrugged.

"Are they going to announce a lead on the highway shooter?"

As far as I knew, Coogin wasn't directly involved in the investigation, but word got around on prominent cases.

"I hear we're shakin' up a few of the usual bangers. A couple of those toads are always on the short list." Coogin leaned in close and lowered his voice a notch. "Got nothing, but you didn't hear it from me."

"What's Janek's story? Do you have any history with him?"

I eyed Coogin's friend as I spoke, looking for a flicker of interest. Nothing but a peeved stare.

"He's solid. If anybody can nail this, he can." Coogin's eyes swung over to his colleague to make sure her attention wasn't wandering before he turned back to me. "Shitty the way he got screwed over by that dog turd of a cop Dubicki, though. Changes a man to have his partner stick the knife in and twist. And then to kick sand in his face, Dubicki parlays that mess into a job payin' serious green. Let me tell you, I, for one, will be takin' my sweet-ass time showin' up at any calls to his job sites. No telling what kind of unfortunate accidents might happen, given the friends he's burned over the years."

With the advance team assembling, Coogin and his partner shifted over to their posts before I could ask the name of Dubicki's employer. Dubicki wasn't winning any person-of-the-year awards. If someone as mild-mannered as Coogin was fantasizing about a construction calamity, a few other officers would be itching to do worse if he'd crossed them. If I were Janek, I'd be praying for a crane to fall on my former partner's head.

I held firm in my position along the front edge of the stage and watched tourists pose for photographs with Chicago's landmark Picasso. Its Corten steel bulk also offered some of the only shade in the park. The heat bouncing off the concrete made the urban canyon feel like a sauna. I fished a water bottle out of my bag and took a swig, then dabbed a tissue at the back of my neck.

A flash of lights on the Dearborn Street side pulled my attention. Unmarked police cars and a cadre of black SUVs with dark tinted windows arrived. A swarm of cops and security types in dark suits descended. Showtime.

Mayor Rendell's burly frame strode toward the podium, smiling and raising his hands in greeting to constituents as he walked, already moving into campaign posture. Superintendent Wachowski marched behind, looking as if he had swallowed dung. As the men and their minions moved into position, so did the press, jockeying for best advantage. A low chant began to grow somewhere in the background, but the sound bounced off the glass and steel of this man-made gorge and cloaked the direction. The words were unintelligible, but the angry tone was clear.

"Ladies and gentlemen, thank you for coming," Rendell began.

Flanking him on stage were Wachowski, my former boss Cook County State's Attorney Denton Tierney, Detectives Janek and Wolman, and a handful of other cops I didn't know. The men stood lined up like sentinels, their mere presence a silent oath of support. Platt hovered two steps back and to the right, his arms crossed casually; a slight hint of satisfaction played at his eyes, as if he was pleased with himself for making this happen.

On my side of the dais, cameras, phones, and the occasional pad of paper and pen were all poised for whatever came next. The plaza was now teeming with people who had gathered to hear the press conference or who had stopped, curious about the spectacle on their way to lunch.

The hum I had noticed moments ago was now muffled as the protestors were pushed to the back, becoming part of the expectant crowd of close to two hundred. Galvanized by social media, their hastily written placards read, "Wachowski, do your job," "Who's in charge here?", "Rendell doesn't care."

The officers on the podium stood strong, their steely eyes alert, their bodies poised for anything that might occur. Detective Michael Hewitt's gaze found me as he scanned the crowd. A brief smile flicked at the corner of his eyes, followed by confusion. I nodded a greeting, smiling as I remembered the compassion he had shown me during Friday's accident. Damn, he looked good all suited up.

"As you are all aware," Rendell continued, "Chicago has experienced some recent troubling situations on the Dan Ryan Expressway."

"Yeah, dead people are troublesome!" a voice in the crowd shot back.

Rendell ignored the outburst. "I'm here to assure you that every resource the great city of Chicago has at its disposal is being utilized to find the individual responsible."

"So you're confirming there's only one shooter?" my buddy with the wayward elbow shouted.

"Superintendent Wachowski and his fine team are pursuing every lead they have. We are working night and day," Rendell continued, unwilling to yield control to the crowd. "Gang violence will not define Chicago."

"Tell that to the victims' families!" another voice called out.

Wachowski pulled his barrel chest up a little higher into his five-foot, nine-inch frame giving us a power pose. His dark eyes hammered into the back of Rendell's head, but whatever he might have wanted to say or do was irrelevant. This wasn't his show, and he knew his place in the pecking order.

Signs began to sway and low voices of discontent murmured through the plaza as the protestors grew even more annoyed. A few of the video guys had swung their attention away from the officials and onto the crowd. Shots of angry people were more interesting than this drivel. Had Rendell staged this just to issue hollow platitudes? This crowd wasn't going to sit quietly by while he doled out meaningless answers.

As Rendell droned on with empty words and promises no one was confident he could keep, I watched the men assembled on the platform, all stone-faced and probably resentful about being called away from real work for this dog-and-pony show. A dozen questions about the shootings filled my mind as we waited for something of substance to be presented.

I also watched Tierney for a hint that there would actually be some type of announcement, but as usual, he wasn't showing his hand. I'd always joked that he washed his face with Botox, but every now and then, an extra steeliness to his eyes gave him away. Although a skilled politician who used his tools to his best advantage, he resented the hell out of being part of seedy used-car sales pitches, and this stank of nothing but distraction. He was probably drinking Maalox by the gallon these days. I had been hesitant to use our relationship to get information so far, but I knew the time would come when I would need to play that hand.

Enough of this. "Superintendent Wachowski," I shouted. "Can you comment on the possibility that we are dealing with a sniper intent on killing innocent victims and not random gang violence?"

Wachowski jerked his head hard in my direction, looking for the source. "Andrea Kellner, Link-Media." I raised my phone, set to video record mode, even higher to catch his response.

As the possibility rumbled through the crowd, Janek glowered at me from the podium. Tierney looked at me as well, puzzlement in his eyes. I held my ground, ready to push back if I needed to.

With the crowd now agitated, it was going to be difficult for

Rendell to pretend the question wasn't on the table. Would he keep Wachowski on his leash?

"CPD is investigating. Any additional information will be shared as it's available," Rendell replied, lobbing back more drivel and pushing the volume of chatter around me a few notches higher.

"Can the police superintendent answer the question?" I volleyed back, hoping to engage Wachowski.

The crowd picked up the thread, and someone yelled, "Answer the question!" Another, "Who's killing our citizens?" and "Why can't you catch him?"

The simmering frustration was palpable. Working the politician's playbook, Rendell pulled out his most reassuring smile and raised his hands to shush the throng, trying to diffuse the tension. The crowd wasn't buying it. As he struggled for control, Superintendent Wachowski stepped forward and took the microphone. Rendell shot him a look that said, "Fix this!"

"As we've indicated repeatedly, CPD's investigation has determined these shootings are a result of recent gang territory disputes that have unfortunately placed new pressure on the Englewood community." Wachowski swung his eyes to me and continued. "To suggest anything else is both unproductive and foolish. My men are exploring all avenues, and we have every confidence that the perpetrator will be apprehended."

Wachowski stepped back, and Rendell delivered a pandering wave before being whisked away. End of conversation. The mob, however, wasn't willing to let it go. The volume rose, a unified voice fed up with empty rhetoric. And I didn't blame them. This "press conference" had been a waste of everyone's time. Probably something Platt had fabricated, convincing the Mayor's Office it was better than saying nothing.

As Rendell left the stage, the protestors at the back began to push forward after him, dissatisfied with the outcome. Reporters and tourists were herded right along with them, wedged between the dissenters trying to get at the mayor, with the camera crews not getting out of the way fast enough.

Protestors yelled after Rendell, their voices full of anger and distrust. Bodies jostled, pushing tighter into the wedge formed by the stage and the nearby Picasso, as the cops tried to hold back the swarm. I maneuvered another step to the right as the horde of bodies pushed all around me. A sharp elbow to my back slammed me forward and my shins into the steel frame of the stage. Screams rang out somewhere behind me, as did the crash of what I guessed was an expensive camera hitting the ground. Pinned between the platform and the crush of bodies, I clung tightly to the phone still in my hand, and tried to pull myself up to the stage as shoulders and elbows and hands pummeled my back.

As I struggled to free my foot pinned below, hands reached under my arms and pulled me up, releasing me from the tangle of bodies and metal. I fell into a solid chest. Enveloped in the warmth and security of strong arms, I inhaled the lightest whiff of sandalwood and looked up into Michael Hewitt's concerned eyes.

I smiled, overtaken by this small bit of comfort in the midst of the mess. "Rescuing damsels in distress again?"

"There are worse parts of the job." He grinned. "Let's get you out of here before this gets ugly."

His arm around my shoulders, Michael led me across the platform above the chaos and behind the police line, escorting me over to Dearborn where the officers had formed a human fence between the horde and the mayor. Janek's ramrod straight frame greeted me at the curb. His eyes were icy, filled with the desire to ream me out, I imagined. *You've got more to worry about than tough questions.*

"That's some job change you've made," Michael said, removing his arm from my shoulder. "You okay from here?"

I nodded. "Thanks. Go ahead and get back to more important things," I said, glancing at the protestors.

He grinned and eased back into the police line as Rendell's SUV drove off, leaving me with the aftereffects of the adrenaline rush. With Rendell off-site, the protestors would probably disperse or move across the street to City Hall, hoping to shake up a few aldermen. I tapped the screen of my phone and replayed the video. Hopefully it was more than just pictures of feet and muffled voices.

A hand on my arm pulled me away from the screen, and I stared into Denton Tierney's dead blue eyes.

9

"What the fuck was that question all about, Andrea? Do you know something, or are you just trying to create a story?" Tierney snapped.

Leave it to Tierney to be the one guy with a spine.

"Come on, Denton, you don't believe that this is just a bunch of gangbangers going at each other. The victims took direct hits."

"Don't play semantics with me. And don't play cop." Tierney clenched his jaw and glared at me. "If CPD says some twerp with a gun is shooting from an overpass, just to prove he has the balls for the life, then that's what's happening. Unless you have proof to the contrary, I'd keep my mouth shut about anything else."

He walked away, leaving me staring at the back of his head, before I could frame a rebuttal. I snagged a cafe table in the plaza as the crowd thinned out, and contemplated what I'd just witnessed and what to do about it.

Too bad the political side of Tierney's personality was more dominant than his bulldog side. Our days of old-fashioned heart-to-heart conversations were probably over. Total honesty didn't fit in with our new roles, and he wasn't about to admit to any doubt about CPD's current stance on the shootings. From his point of view, the press was something to use. And I knew the game. Still, I wondered where his instincts were leading him on these shootings. It was obvious that public discussion of a possible sniper had rattled him, but it had to be one of the theories, even if it didn't sit well with the mayor's agenda.

Jacqui's revelation about the drug trafficking at the Garfield L station ran through my mind as I took another swig of water. If the station was a hub of drug activity, then stray bullets weren't out of the question. But the shots were too clean and direct. A sniper trying to put notches on his belt to prove he had the cojones wasn't magical thinking, but why these people? Somehow the idea that drug activity tied the shootings together didn't feel like a slam dunk, and I didn't know why my gut was whispering caution.

And what about Janek? Even if he hadn't taken bribes, he could be blinded to other possible causes of this violence because of his past. Revisiting the accident scene might help quell my discomfort. I left a message for Platt asking to reschedule, put in a call to Brynn to update her on my plans, then walked over to catch the Red Line at Washington and Dearborn.

A fifteen-minute train ride and Chicago was an entirely different landscape. As we rolled along, I watched the familiarity of the Loop give way to Chinatown and then US Cellular Field, home of the Chicago White Sox. Its historic predecessor, Comiskey Park, site of four World Series, had been torn down in 1991 and rebuilt on the south side of 35th Street before being renamed following the obnoxious trend that turned buildings into ad space. From the elevated tracks, I watched this, the last of the tourist destinations on the train line, give way to the decidedly non-touristy South Side. Loop high-rises became shoddy low-rise industrial structures or multifamily homes that had seen better days.

I exited the train at Garfield, the open platform a stretch of concrete, pillars, and system maps. The occasional whiff of stale urine or ripe trash wafted past me as I looked around, standard fare for public transportation. This wasn't what I'd imagined after hearing it called "the Pharmacy." People were simply going about their business of trying to get to work or to the grocery store, just like any other stop on the CTA system.

The station sat in the rumble of the highway, smack-dab between the north and southbound lanes of the Dan Ryan Expressway; auto traffic whizzed past on the outer edge of the tracks. I wasn't sure what I'd expected. Dirty needles littering the platform? Small plastic baggies with white powder residue on the floor of the shelter, having been discarded after a few snorts? Maybe some strung-out guy in a dirty sweatshirt offering me a hit? I was embarrassed by my own stereotyping. But if the cops were on to this, then the drug activity was real. Maybe it was simply too early in the day for shop to be open.

I walked the length of the platform, taking note of any graffiti on the support pillars. Tagging was often a marking of territory, a "Joe was here" type of symbolism. This was a language where colors and marks had subtle, sometimes subliminal meanings. As with any successful, growing business, competition was at the core. Which gangs were claiming this terrain? I pulled out my iPhone and shot some photos of the ubiquitous six-pointed star of the Gangster Disciples.

Scanning the expanse, and the strategically placed security cameras on the roof above, it seemed an unlikely spot for a guy with a gun to go unnoticed in the middle of the day. Moving toward the southern end, I looked for evidence of police investigation. Seeing nothing else that piqued my curiosity, I took the escalator up to the small station. With the tracks below at highway level, street access was on the overpass. There was only one way in or out of this particular station, unless you jumped both the tracks and four lanes of heavily trafficked freeway. Not exactly an easy getaway.

I stepped out onto the sidewalk, took a spot next to a "Building a New Chicago" sign that hung from a tall chain-link fence, intended to make it hard for some suicidal fool to take a header, and surveyed my surroundings. I was standing on a bridge over the highway. It was easy to visualize a gunman targeting a vehicle below by putting the barrel through the mesh, but not without being on display. Garfield was one of the few cross streets that traversed the expressway, and traffic would have been steady midafternoon.

As I stood contemplating the logistics of the shooting, I was conscious of the curious looks I was getting from people on the sidewalk as they passed. I was a petite white woman in a go-see-the-mayor suit who obviously didn't belong in this neighborhood.

I walked east toward the intersection, my eyes following the fencing until I reached the corner of Wentworth and Garfield. About forty feet south, yellow police tape flapped in the wind where it had been strung from yet more fencing. Miles of the stuff lined the highway. Someone must have a lucrative city contract. I crossed the street and walked toward the remnants. Wentworth Avenue was mainly a frontage road at this stretch, although further north it was the main artery through Chinatown. Empty lots and scrub trees framed the east side, and a weed-infested strip of dirt and shrubs barricaded the expressway on the west.

I skirted the curb, avoiding broken Rolling Rock bottles and empty Romanoff pints, my eyes watching for signs of prior police activity and the occasional oncoming car. Trampled plant material and yellow tape seemed the only signs. Had the police found any shell casings? I took some pictures of the area, then looked down at the suede Chloé sandals I'd chosen this morning and shrugged. What's a little muck when there's a story at stake? I stepped over the flattened brush to the fence.

Looking through the linked couplings and around the rushing traffic on the expressway below, there was little indication of last Friday's tragedy. The shoulder was clear of auto debris, but the skid marks and paint scrapings on the concrete bulwark told me I was in the right place. Images of the dead man, flooded back and I felt my breathing quicken. Grabbing the fence, I closed my eyes, pushing back the emotion and summoning my analytical mind.

As I viewed the scene, piecing together which cars had gone where, I tried to diagram them mentally from impact to obstacle to resting place. But the haze of having been in the middle of the incident was clouding my memory. As an attorney, I'd been on the other side of this conversation many times, prodding a victim to re-create an incident. I'd heard the hesitation, the uncertainty, the it-all-happened-so-fast that was such a common part of human traumatic memory. More challenging still were the victims who were one hundred percent certain their memory was spot-on, only to be proven completely off by concrete facts. Now here I was, experiencing my own version of fluid memory.

The shooter had probably been only a few feet from where I stood. What scuffle could have inadvertently delivered that shot? None. It wasn't possible. He had *chosen* his target. I took a few more photos, then crouched down to the level of the tallest weeds to check visibility.

"Ma'am, please step away from the fence."

I turned toward the voice. Detective Michael Hewitt and Detective Karl Janek stood three steps behind me.

"You'll have to share your secret route out of the Loop," Michael said.

I got to my feet and smiled but quickly slipped the phone

back into my pocket. The set of Janek's jaw told me he wasn't thrilled to find me poking around.

Michael gave a harder look to the remnants of Friday's accident still branding my forehead before finding my eyes. "I trust we got you home safely on Friday."

"Yes, thank you. Just some nasty bruising. Nothing that won't heal." Aside from the woozy Friday afternoon and our brief encounter earlier today, we hadn't seen each other since the deli case, but my memory of those gorgeous chocolate eyes and strong shoulders certainly hadn't been faulty.

Michael's smile flickered briefly as Janek cleared his throat.

"Detective Janek, this is Andrea Kellner. She was one of the victims in Friday's incident."

Janek was tall, topping Michael by a few inches, with intense blue eyes, a chiseled face, and closely cropped blond hair. He was built more like a distance runner than a cop.

"And why are you here, Andrea Kellner?" Janek asked, ignoring my outstretched hand.

I fished a business card out of my bag and handed it to him. His brows contracted, and he pushed the card back at me.

"Keep it," I said. "You never know when we might be able to help each other out."

"Not likely. The last thing I need is somebody wordsmithing my statements. You can get what you need from the press liaison like everyone else." He turned to Michael, who swung his eyes from me back to his partner. "Did you know she was press?"

"She's also a witness," Michael reminded him, not missing a beat.

The man could stand up to Janek. Good. That scored him a point or two.

"I asked what you were doing here," Janek repeated, his gaze drilling straight into me.

As expected, he was the straight-talking type, a quality I

could respect. "I was curious about what makes gang rivals shoot across a highway. Looks more like target practice to me." I hadn't consciously formed that thought before I said it, but the idea had been gnawing at the back of my mind.

"As we've already told the press, some pressure exists between two rival gangs in this neighborhood over control of boundaries. Unfortunately, a member of the general public got caught in the crossfire." He'd pitched that line before. I guess he could dish out political rhetoric if he had to. But did he believe that was the full story?

"You mean three, don't you?" I shifted my feet, squaring off with Janek. "Three members of the general public just happened to get caught in the crossfire. And now they're dead."

Janek's jaw clenched, and a vein on his left temple throbbed as we stared each other down. Michael's expression suggested he couldn't tell whether to cheer me on or toe the company line.

"Regrettably, yes," Janek replied. "There have been three fatalities." His voice had softened, but there wasn't the slightest shift in the hardness of his face. "I know people like you think in soundbites. You've gotten yours. Gang violence. Happens every day in Englewood. Pull the official statement from the press office and just cut and paste. It's what you people do best."

"Okay, you think journalists are a step above sewer water. I get that. I even agree with you most of the time. Lazy permeates this business. Let me show you I'm not one of the pack. Work with me. Give me something I won't get on Twitter. Tell me something you haven't released. Let me dangle the bait and help you reel in someone who knows what really happened. What have you got to lose? We both want the shooter behind bars."

"I've said everything I need to say." He stepped away, dismissing me, moving south along the fence through the weeds.

"Okay. We'll play it your way," I said to his back. "Are you trying to suggest that the Gangster Disciples and the Black P Stones are fighting for control of northbound versus southbound lanes of the Dan Ryan?" I continued, shooting for incredulous.

It was a wiseass question, but I wanted to push Janek, to let him know I wasn't going to be satisfied with vague remarks about gang problems, as if who, how, where, and why didn't matter. Janek's tone also had me feeling prickly. The press was a thorn in his side, and I was just another part of the bramble. But I could use that. Would pushing his buttons loosen his self-control?

Janek stopped and turned to face me. His bitter gaze told me everything I needed to know about his fortitude. But it was progress of sorts—at least I had his attention. For a second, anyway.

"Based on your handy-dandy police tape, we seem to have a shooter who was standing at the eastern edge of the expressway fence, roughly within ten feet from where we are, aiming southwest." I gestured toward the ground between us, toward what I guessed to be the location of the shooter. "He then delivered a direct hit to a target moving about forty miles an hour in northbound lane number two. This driver careened into the right barricade, played bumper cars with everyone around him, including me, and flipped a couple times, finally coming to rest, literally and figuratively, on the far-left shoulder. Have I summed up the course of events correctly?"

"Yes." Janek said nothing more, but his glacial eyes told me he was anticipating my next question.

I paused a moment, glancing at Michael. He wisely stayed silent, scanning the west frontage and letting Janek squirm.

"If you still want me to believe this victim got caught in the crossfire, then who or what was the real target?"

10

I jumped out of a taxi at Franklin and Chestnut to meet Cai for a drink. Stepping to the curb, I checked the plunge on my Helmut Lang dress, hoping I'd achieved the proper balance between sexy and sophisticated. The smile of the guy grabbing my cab said that I had. I smiled back, getting into the mood of the evening.

It still felt odd to go to favorite restaurants without Erik, places we had shared tender moments and fonder memories. I was keenly aware of my singleness as I pulled open the glass door at MK and stepped inside. Pausing in the entrance, I gave myself a minute to adjust to the dimmer lighting. The setting sun filtered down from the large peaked skylight in the dining room, casting shadows on the tall floral arrangements and the Richard Serra prints on the walls. The double-height wooden trussed ceiling added to the elegant warehouse feel of the space. Subdued chatter and light jazz filled the air from the fully booked dining room.

"Ms. Kellner, how nice to see you." Jose, the mâitre d', had caught sight of me and hurried over to say hello. "I didn't see a reservation. If you can give me just a few moments to clear a table, I can get you seated. Is Mr. Martin joining you this evening?"

"No need to hustle anyone away from their meal. I'm meeting a friend for a drink in the bar."

"Very well. Let's get you seated." He led me over to a cafe table next to the steel-framed industrial windows. "If you decide to join us for dinner, just let me know. Chef Williams has an outstanding scallop preparation this evening."

"Thank you. It sounds lovely." No sign of Cai. A waiter appeared shortly after I settled into my seat. I ordered a Pellegrino with lemon and a glass of Nebbiolo. The heavy dose of girl time was Cai's way of keeping an eye on me. After telling her about last night's moment of weakness with Erik, she'd apparently decided I must have suffered a minor brain injury when I hit my head on the steering wheel, and insisted on another check-in tonight, despite assurances that I'd come to my senses. Bribing me with a trip to my favorite restaurant had sealed the deal.

As I listened to David Sanborn and sipped my wine, I scanned the Link-Media website, pleased to see that my Midway story had posted. I'd spent most of the afternoon tracking down the source on my mayor story, eventually cornering her as she left her new job. Unfortunately, when pressed for details, it became clear that she was nothing more than an employee with an active imagination and a pink slip. I jotted Erik a note that the story had flamed out, then opened my email. A couple of newsletters, early reader feedback on my story that suggested I'd hit a nerve, and a note from Erik that he wanted to talk about last night. *Sorry, nothing to talk about.* I was too confused and angry to respond. Angry with myself for the crack in my armor and angry at him for whatever financial maneuvering he was involved in.

Annoyed all over again, I pulled my attention back to the

mail. As usual, it was mostly junk, but on the off chance I had missed a story lead or something else of substance, I scanned the subject headings one more time.

The subject line, "Killer or Thief?" made me pause. The sender, Sgnt1764@hotmail.com, was unfamiliar. It sounded like spam for the latest health scare: *You too can be saved by sending $29.99 for our special herbal supplement.* I opened it anyway, expecting Delete to be the next key I hit. Instead, I stared at the words on the screen, reading them over and over, trying to decipher the nebulous message.

Violence and blight and injustice deceive. Discarded lives and discarded dreams. Throwaway people that nobody sees. Shielding the truth. Hiding the greed. How far will they go? How many will bleed? Will you take on the task? Uncover the deed? I know who he is.

Could the sender mean the highway shooter? Was someone trying to give me a tip? Or was this just gibberish from an individual with mental health issues? I had the feeling I was being baited. Being dared to engage with an author who chose not to reveal his name. Construing this as a message about gangs and the residents of Englewood was reaching. However, the words echoed over and over in my mind. Or was I overreacting? Hoping for a lead because I wanted one? Needed one?

"That dress suits you."

I looked up from my phone to find Michael Hewitt on the opposite side of the table. The rich indigo of his crinkled cotton shirt added depth and sparkle to his brown eyes, even in the dim light. His smile was warm and relaxed, giving me the impression he was pleasantly surprised to see me—or maybe it was just the off-duty atmosphere. If blushing were one of my tendencies, I would have gone pink at the look on his face.

"Are you coming or going?" I tipped my head toward the restaurant.

"Just finished dinner with a college buddy who's in town for a few days." He glanced at the empty chair. "Are you meeting someone?"

"A friend who seems to be running quite late. Would you like to join me?" The invitation slid out without a second's hesitation, and it felt good. Easy even. Was it Michael, or was I just getting comfortable with the idea of dating again?

"Must be a weird moon or something. I haven't seen you in over two years, now all of a sudden, three times in one day." He pulled out the chair and sat. "Your date isn't going to swoop in and play tough guy, is he? I'd hate to cause a scene that would get me kicked out of one of the best restaurants in town."

I laughed. "My 'date' is my dearest friend, Cai. And if she walked in and saw me having a drink with a man, she'd send over another round and cheer me on. I assure you, no testosterone-fueled confrontations will be required. Although given the state of my life these days, it sounds kind of appealing."

"That's a good friend to have." He chuckled, leaning back in his chair and looking at me as if he were trying to figure out if I was serious.

Our waiter reappeared and Michael ordered a small-batch scotch that I'd never heard of while I declined a refill. After overdoing it last night, one glass was plenty. We listened to the sultry horn in the background and filled the space with chitchat about work and people we knew in common until his drink arrived.

"Do you do a lot of origami?" Michael asked a moment later.

I laughed. "Where did that come from?"

"Well, the way you keep folding that cocktail napkin, I thought maybe a baby swan would be gracing the table."

I looked down at the paper mangled in my fingers, shook my head, and sighed.

"Uncomfortable?" Michael asked.

His eyes were soft, but probing, drawing me in. He twirled the ice cube in his glass, waiting for me to answer.

"No, just out of practice being alone with a man in a social situation." I answered honestly, perhaps more honestly than I should have.

"Ah, you're new to dating as a grown-up." He held up his left hand with its bare ring finger and nodded knowingly.

"Have yet to make that maiden voyage after fourteen years of marriage."

I didn't want to be reminded of Erik right now, or my failed marriage, or the uncertainty of my financial future, or even work. Tonight I needed to enjoy the moment. To feel myself flush from male attention. To feel the anticipation of a touch or a first kiss. Did I even remember how?

Michael's gaze flickered over my face as if he wanted to say something. I sat unable to meet his eyes, instead watching his fingers as they trailed over the smoothness of his glass, imagining those same fingers tracing a path on my skin. Torn between the awareness of my attraction to him and the knowledge that even the suggestion of a relationship between us was ill-advised, I let my words hang in the air. We both knew better than to make this personal. Didn't we?

"Does it get easier?" I asked after what seemed like an endless silence.

"Well, a few butterflies are a requirement of any good date, don't you think?"

We let the drinks and light conversation do their job, changing the subject, putting us both in a more relaxed mood. Our chatter drifted through families, favorites, and avoided the details of our respective failed relationships.

A server appeared, placing two small plates in front of us.

"Chef Williams sent this out with his compliments, Ms. Kellner. Enjoy," she said.

Michael and I devoured the small plates of seared sea scallops with asparagus and fava beans, simultaneously releasing an appreciative sigh.

"I don't get here often, but all I can say is 'wow.' Do your friends hit you up for your MK connection? Obviously you're a regular."

"I rarely bring anyone here. I'm afraid it will become one of those places where it takes six months to get a reservation."

I could feel my cell phone ping a new message through the leather of my clutch, resting on the seat next to me.

"I'm sorry, I have to check this," I said, pulling my phone out of my bag. "It's probably my friend officially blowing me off."

Yep, a text from Cai had landed. A deposition had run over and she wasn't going to be able to join me. The email from Sgnt1764 was still gnawing at me and I stole another look, all thoughts of Cai rushing out of my brain as I read.

"Is everything all right?" Michael asked.

My mind froze. Running through the strange poem, trying to read between the lines and understand the message he was sending me. I wanted to shake it off, turn my attention back to Michael, but there it was, taunting me from the screen.

"I'm sorry. I don't normally bow to the smartphone gods. My friend did cancel, but I also received some information on a story. A piece of the puzzle may have just come through." The urge to share the email with Michael washed over me, as did the urge to pump him for information on the highway shootings. But my timing was horrid. Nothing productive would come of that, professionally or personally. So I turned off the phone and stored it. The message could wait until I was alone and had thought through my response.

"Hey, my job isn't exactly nine-to-five either. As long as you're not scouring Amazon because you're bored. I have a bit of experience with puzzles myself. Maybe I can help?"

He laughed, but I could see a flicker of something in his face.

Annoyance? Disappointment? Curiosity? A desire to check his own email?

"Twenty-four seven jobs can be tough on relationships," I added, taking liberties with his response. We hadn't gotten to the point of sharing our romantic war stories, but something in his expression made me want to ask.

His shoulders slumped as his finger trailed the condensation on the side of his glass. "So is the possibility of coming home in a body bag."

"Your wife couldn't deal with that?"

"Theory and reality sometimes don't mesh. She had visions of me behind a desk, knocking heads with politicians, not punks."

"And you didn't?"

"I like to dig in the dirt. To solve those puzzles. Desk work isn't messy enough." He stared out the window, lost in his memories for a moment, as I watched the pain that even the cop in him couldn't hide. "It was an impasse we couldn't work around," he said.

A flush of heat ran up the back of my neck. I decided then and there that I *really* liked this guy. Despite his profession, despite his need to be a guy who couldn't be ruffled, in this brief moment and with only a few words, he had shown how deeply he could feel.

I could feel the terrain becoming unstable. Time to change the subject.

"You were hooked up with Bill Bryson, wasn't it, when we last worked together?" It seemed a good segue. Dragging deeper into the muck of our respective love lives wasn't productive.

"Good memory. Bill retired about a year and a half ago. There was some restructuring going on in the department, and Janek and I ended up together."

A year and a half? That would have been around the time of the bribery investigations.

"Restructuring?" I wondered how rooted his loyalties were. "Don't you mean an investigation into officers taking payoffs?"

Michael paused and shot me his cop eyes. I might have just ensured that this evening would be both a first and last. But he had to know that I wouldn't back down just because he smiled at me. I might get a little weak in the knees, but brain function wasn't going to shut down.

"You're direct, aren't you?" Michael said without flinching.

"I would think in your profession, as in mine, it's a refreshing change from the BS most people dish out."

His eyes softened, and a hint of a smile flicked at the corner of his mouth. "And this from a former attorney."

"I prefer to think of myself as a reformed attorney."

The tension had passed. Michael was okay with honest. *That* definitely made my knees weak.

"Since you apparently know the story, let's be clear: Janek is the straightest guy I know. He wouldn't take a ham sandwich he didn't pay for."

"Then how did his life get so complicated?"

"I apologize if this sounds like I'm going all cop on you. I'm protective, always looking for the threat. That stuff gets in your bones. Becomes who you are. I can't always turn it off. But Janek, he has good reason to keep the press at arm's length."

"I know about the allegations."

"The media did the worst thing they could do to the man—they shredded his reputation. Lumping his actions with that scuzzbag of a partner and not questioning anything. And don't think anyone reported it when Janek was cleared. He lost his wife, his daughter. He's not the same person since it happened."

"I'm sure it was quite difficult. I didn't know about his family." Journalism was never warm and fuzzy when there was blood in the water. And a corrupt cop story was always chum. Michael clenched his jaw, and I could tell bile was rising in his throat.

"Janek was set up. Framed by one of his own. A dickhead who'd been crossing those lines for years."

"Matt Dubicki," I said. Michael nodded. "But they were partners. Why would Dubicki set him up?"

"Internal Affairs was getting close to the truth. And Dubicki needed to pull out a fun house mirror to throw attention on someone else. He was also screwing Janek's wife."

11

When I poked my head into Erik's office at 8:00 a.m., he was on his cell. After last night's email from my anonymous friend, I needed to hit him up again about the highway shooting story. After rereading the communication obsessively, analyzing each word choice, each phrase, I was convinced the writer was trying to get my attention and had information about the sniper. He was telling me he knew the shooter and that CPD had it wrong. Excitement tickled my spine. This was it—this was the break I needed.

Hunched over the vintage Knoll credenza he had installed under the window, Erik spoke in a low tone as he watched something on the street below. Unaware that I was standing in the doorway, his words were clipped, his voice even deeper than normal. Was this part two of yesterday's conversation? I couldn't make out what he was saying, but he wasn't happy. I knew that edge in his voice. I rapped lightly on the door frame to let him know I was within earshot. He held up two fingers, signaling he needed time, but didn't glance in my direction.

I watched his body tense with irritation. What the hell was he up to? I hesitated for another second, then turned to go back to my desk. I wasn't two steps out when Erik shouted into the phone, gluing my feet to the floor.

"This wasn't the plan! You need to get this under control now!"

Shocked by his vehemence, I turned back toward the door, waiting for the next explosion or the words that would explain what I was witnessing. Takeover scenarios played out in my mind, and I had visions of trying to defend my position in the company to some new number cruncher intent on protecting his investment. Even I had a hard time making that argument. My work had been adequate, but far from irreplaceable. There was no doubt in my mind that I'd be the first to get booted to the curb if cuts were called for.

I needed more time.

As I stood rooted in the hallway, the wooden floor creaked with his footsteps. A drawer opened, then was slammed shut. I gave him a few more seconds, listening for dialogue, then stepped back into the doorway after deciding I had an all clear.

"Everything okay?" I asked.

Erik was sitting at his desk, feet propped up as usual, still on his phone but now texting furiously. "Just an issue with a supplier," he said, not looking up.

"Sounded pretty heated."

"Nothing you need to worry about."

Erik's face was so tight it might as well have been carved in stone. I nodded and took a seat, waiting while he wrapped up. Until he was ready, prodding wasn't going to get him to talk, certainly not to me. I'd learned the hard way the man had a PhD in secret-keeping.

"What did you need?" His voice was clipped and raw. Was this about his phone call or my rejection of him earlier in the week?

"I wanted to speak with you again about the highway

shooting story. You were clear that you feel it's under control, but I've got a new—"

The words were barely out of my mouth when Art Borkowski sauntered in, a smug smile on his face. He slid into the chair next to me. Damn!

Erik kept his eyes trained on me, flat and unyielding, the muscles in his jaw flexing as if he were grinding down a couple of back molars. My timing was shit.

"Art, it seems Andrea has some brilliant ideas on your highway shooter," he said, staring me down. "Apparently she thinks her six months as a journalist trump your twenty-five years of experience and that she can do a better job."

I felt the blood drain from my face and my body go still. He was turning my ambition into a weapon against me.

"That's not what I said," I replied slowly, trying not to appear defensive and childish.

"What do you think? Do you need help, Art? Maybe Andrea could take notes for you."

Erik's phone rang repeatedly, but he ignored it as we sat locked in our little contest of wills. Push the knife in and turn. Anger choked in my throat and I struggled to keep a poker face, resisting the urge to shoot a glance at Borkowski as he stifled a low cough.

"Well, I could use a little help with fact-checking," Borkowski said. The shit-eating grin on his face made my stomach double over.

What! Was I now his research assistant? He was speaking to me like I was some first-year journalism student who hadn't yet learned to qualify a source. One way or another, this was *my story.* Last night's email had sealed that in my mind, despite what Erik and Borkowski seemed to think. I wasn't going to hand it over without a great deal of bloodletting.

"Well, Art, I'd love to play errand girl for you, but a self-administered appendectomy sounds more appealing." I glared at the man. "I'm not your assistant," I snapped, infuriated by his arrogance.

"By the way, what were you doing at the press conference yesterday?" he replied.

I was taken aback for a moment with the question. He wouldn't have known I was there, unless he showed up long after I had.

"Were you trying to undermine me? Let me be very clear. If I need help, I'll assign it to you. Until then, back off."

"If you're so committed, where the hell was your pushback to that drivel? It wasn't a press conference, it was a distribution of talking points. I didn't hear you challenge a damn thing. Or do you intend to let Rendell and Wachowski write the story for you?"

Erik stood as it became clear I wasn't going to be subservient and shut up. He crossed his arms over his chest, face pinched, ready to referee.

"Erik and I need a word," I said, letting the rancor ooze out in my voice. The cost of divorcing my boss had just received a price adjustment. I'd been naive to think we could be business associates without things getting ugly.

Borkowski didn't move, so I swung my gaze at him and stared until he got up from his seat. He raised his eyebrows and shot a look at Erik as if to say, "Man up," but thankfully, he headed for the door without additional persuasion. I imagined he would have been happy being a fly on the wall for the conversation that was about to take place. I waited until I heard the click of the latch.

"How could you embarrass me like that? You didn't even hear me out before cutting me off at the knees. Why?" I was struggling to keep my volume low when all I wanted to do was scream, but I wasn't going to give Borkowski the satisfaction.

"You wanted in on this story. I just gave you an opportunity. Earn it."

"Did you hear him trying to relegate me to 'the research girl'? You're so blindsided by his reputation as a hardcore journalist and the fancy awards he's won, but that was fifteen years ago. The world has changed—journalism has changed. That's why you started this company, to look to the future, not the past. What's he done lately, beyond rest on his laurels and be a bully? I know you think bringing him to Link-Media was a coup for our credibility, but in reality, you just need good journalism. There are pieces to the puzzle in these shootings that are being missed. No one is challenging assumptions. I can do this, Erik. Let me have a shot."

I dug my thumb into my thigh as I struggled to control my emotions. Erik picked up his phone and glanced at the screen, more interested in the calls he had missed than in arguing with me.

"It's a shame you can't appreciate the opportunity to learn from a seasoned pro," he said, "Maybe then you'd remember who signs your paycheck. Now get back to the story you've been assigned, or I can yank that as well."

"Appreciate the opportunity?" My voice hiked up a notch. "You mean appreciate the opportunity to get fucked over by my boss?"

I'd heard enough. I picked myself up and walked out as calmly as I could, using the fifteen feet of hallway to put my game face back on. Becoming Borkowski's flunky wasn't on my agenda. One way or another, I was not going to be sidelined.

Brynn was exiting the break room as I neared the bullpen and I motioned for her to follow me. As I walked through the loft space, the eyes shooting in my direction told me everyone had been aware of the drama that just played out. Coworkers stole looks at me over their computer monitors, checking for tears or maybe waiting for me to kick a trash can or something. The snippets of argument they'd been able to hear coming from Erik's office were far more interesting than the work they were supposed to be doing.

Ever since it had become public knowledge that Erik and I were divorcing, the mood in the office had turned expectant, as if the staff were waiting for a good knock-down, drag-out fight in the middle of the afternoon. Something juicy to retell to friends over evening cocktails. After all, journalists were drama junkies. *Sorry, guys, not today*. I walked into my office and gently closed the door before releasing the silent scream that had built up in my chest. A moment later, Brynn stepped in and quietly took a seat.

"What happened? Borkowski came out of that room beaming like he'd just gotten a BJ. I was ready to smack him to Indiana just for that cocky grin," she said. "Pun intended."

I couldn't suppress a laugh as that image flooded my mind. Brynn could smell bullshit buried in a bottle of Dior J'Adore.

"I pressed Erik again to let me have a shot at the highway shooting story," I said, trying to shake off my irritation. "It didn't go well." I'd leave the gory details to her imagination.

"Borkowski only reports what he discovers in scripted phone interviews. He may have been great back in the day, but if you ask me, he's like a great actor who started his career with incredible range and now replays the same character in every movie. An easy slide into a paycheck and we're all supposed to genuflect as we pass." Brynn took a drink of her coffee, then leaned forward, resting her elbows on her knees. "You're not going to roll over on this, are you?"

"I'm not going to be sidelined, at least not without a World War III—level fight. Erik knows I'm furious, but I don't think he'll budge. Too much ego on the line. We may need to get creative." My thoughts were on the anonymous emailer, but I didn't want to get ahead of myself. There'd be time to talk about it with Brynn when I had more information.

"Okay, so what's the plan? Food poisoning? A minor accident?" she asked, her eyes sparkling with the possibility of a little cloak-and-dagger. I glared at her. "Hey, it was just a joke. You can turn off those firebombs shooting out of your eyes."

"We work in shadow, pulling out whatever we can. Victim histories, gang squabbles, drug busts—anything that might explain what's behind these shootings. If we have a breakthrough, Erik isn't going to pass on a lead story just because he doesn't like how I got there." I glanced out at the staff room. Borkowski returned the look from his office across the open space, his famous scowl turned on me. Asshole. I turned back to Brynn. "Borkowski's going to put us under the microscope, hoping I do something stupid. Expect him to make a pest of himself. He's going to try to become your new buddy just to see what I have you working on. He'll expect dumb-kid. You don't need to enlighten him, if you know what I mean."

She smiled like a six-year-old who'd just busted open a piñata. "Absolutely. I'll just use the word 'like' five times in every sentence. He'll think I'm a typical journalism girl with an IQ of ninety and a burning desire to see my pretty face on TV."

"Perfect." I chuckled. "Borkowski's the kind of guy who thinks lipstick hampers brain function, so use that to divert him." She nodded. "What this does mean is we're also under some serious time pressure. In addition to having unwanted eyes on us, we have to get this puzzle in place, fast."

I sent Brynn back to her desk with a short, but important, to-do list. Digging deeper into the gang violence theory to disprove it seemed like the best starting point. If the previous shooting locations were just as targeted as the Garfield Street overpass, we clearly had a sniper on our hands. And if Brynn could find me an expert on Chicago's current gang environment, I could verify CPD's premise, find out the source of tensions, discover which groups were battling for control.

The words of my mystery poet replayed in my head as they had since the first email. I opened my mail program and reread the message. Was I fabricating importance where there was none? Probably, but my gut was telling me to keep on this track. Convinced that keeping the guy on the hook was the right choice, I composed a couple of sentences.

My job is to report, not deceive. Who are they? What deception are you referring to? Are you saying you know who the sniper is? Can we meet?

I hesitated, then hit Send, wondering if I was engaging a nutjob or securing my future.

12

The large room hummed with the low murmur of staff members conducted the business of city government. Associates sat with phones suction-cupped to their heads while barely audible one-sided conversations played out. People flitted off to meetings or over to hit up coworkers with questions. The atmosphere was one of controlled purposeful intent. But underneath the surface calm, I sensed the rip current of those accustomed to going to the mattresses at a moment's notice. I was led across the carpeted space to a wood-paneled office, shown a chair, offered coffee, and told that Owen Platt would see me shortly.

I looked around at the memorabilia lining the bookcases. Framed photos of visiting dignitaries, inspirational business books, crystal awards commemorating moments in time. Political badges of honor, too, though honor wasn't the word that first came to mind when I thought of Platt. Charming, shrewd, cunning, manipulative—all far better word choices for the man responsible for Rendell's success. Chances were there were a few more adjectives I'd add to the list if I got to know him better. No, thanks.

"Andrea, thanks for rescheduling. So nice to see you again," Owen Platt said as he breezed into the room, a stunning brunette dressed in Armani at his arm. Platt extended his hand, clasping the other over mine in the way politicians do when they're shaking the trees for cash or favors. "Have you met my wife, Jenelle?"

"Only by reputation," I replied. "Nice to finally meet you. And congratulations on the Compass deal. I understand it was a tough fight."

Jenelle was the CEO of MarkSpot, a tech company that developed project management software for the manufacturing industry. The firm's recent acquisition of Compass Industries was their first, and it positioned them strategically for growth into an important industry of the future. Reportedly there had been stiff competition for Compass, which had patented a new 3-D printing machine for use with glass.

"Nothing I'd want to repeat. It was a rough slog, but I'm thrilled that we can bring so many jobs to Chicago," she said, her smile gracious. "I've followed your work since the deli case." Seeing that I was disconcerted by the comment, she added, "I make a point of keeping up with the careers of strong women on the forefront. And anyone who can hold her own in the State's Attorney's Office with Denton can hold her own with the best of them."

She carried herself with the confidence of someone accustomed to the world of handshake deals and midnight negotiations. Yet there was a warmth about her, putting me immediately at ease.

"Darling, stop with the false modesty. There aren't many poetry majors who can say they've led hundred-million-dollar companies." He turned to me. "She may look like a kitten, but trust me, those claws can do damage."

"That's a woman's secret weapon. We're underestimated."

She smiled at me and winked. "I have a lunch appointment. Andrea, I hope we can find time for coffee one of these days."

"I'd love to."

She gave Platt a quick peck on the cheek. "Don't forget dinner at seven thirty with the Hindmans," she reminded him, and left.

Platt motioned for me to sit before taking the club chair to my left.

"This is your show. Please, jump right in," Platt said, leaning back and draping his arms over the armrests.

"You don't mind if I tape this, do you?" I tapped on my phone, opening my recording app. He shook his head, but a bit of his smile faded for just a second. "We hear that Mayor Rendell intends to challenge the governor. Can you confirm?"

"Yes, the mayor intends to make a formal announcement at eight a.m. tomorrow morning. Given our relationship with Erik, we're giving this to Link-Media first." The Cheshire cat smile was back. The one intended to lure you into a false sense of security before you became lunch.

That explained where Erik was getting his information. Was I supposed to be kissing Platt's feet because he and Erik were chummy? I knew they'd had business dealings back in the early days of EMco, and that relationship had continued over the years, but I was starting to feel like there was more subtext than that. Or was my legal history making me paranoid? I couldn't seem to get used to the political quid pro quo environment. Not that the legal profession was above that—far from it—but within the Cook County State's Attorney's Office, we were conditioned for constant propriety. Government seemed conditioned just for the appearance part.

"Does the mayor intend to resign to dedicate himself to the campaign?"

"At the present time, no. The mayor intends to continue with his agenda of job creation and strengthening Chicago's economy. There has been tremendous progress during his term, but he is relentless in his commitment to furthering that goal. There are no resign-to-run laws in Illinois, so we're free to continue our work here in Chicago. We feel that the mayor and his campaign staff are capable of addressing the demands of both. Of course, we'll evaluate that along the way."

Platt seemed in his element, relaxed, in control. Trotting out the approved response to questions he'd anticipated. Was that why Erik had been so eager for me to handle the story? He must have assumed I'd be so thrilled to be the one breaking the news that I'd take what I was given and not ask tough questions.

"Do you have a successor in mind?"

My question seemed to shift something in him, and he took the moment to reach down and adjust his tie. When he looked back up, there was a slight steeliness in his gaze, despite the lingering smile. My years as a prosecutor had taught me to watch for the tell, the moment when I was getting under someone's skin. The more accomplished the liar, the more subtle that moment was. And was there anyone more practiced in the art of deception than a politician? I also knew that was the moment to increase the heat.

"Let's be clear, the mayor isn't soliciting candidates. If an endorsement is appropriate once candidates come forth, he'll make that decision at a later date. We will not repeat the practice of handing positions to the highest bidder that this city has witnessed with previous administrations."

Something about the change in his eyes made me question his response.

"Do you have any interest yourself in the position? After all, as deputy mayor, you would be the logical choice."

"My interests remain the best interests for the city of Chicago." The line came out as if he'd said it a thousand times.

"Mayor Rendell has an excellent record of accomplishment. Job creation, lowered unemployment numbers, increased tourism that brings millions of dollars a year to our economy, including a booming convention business. McCormick Place—the largest convention center in North America, by the way—brings in over two million visitors a year. Stop and see my assistant before you leave for the most up-to-date statistics. We wouldn't want you to use old data, would we?" He chuckled as if we were both in on some joke.

Platt had just given me a natural segue.

"How will the mayor respond to criticism about the current rash of highway shootings that have happened under his watch? I understand that McCormick has received cancellations from three major conventions and that tourism has been slipping. The shootings are making national news. And there is a growing call in the local press for him to resign based on his handling of these incidents."

He stared at me, contemplating the questions. Or perhaps my gall in asking them. His eyes were flat, but the slight smile stayed frozen on his face, as if there were an on/off button he pressed whenever he was in the public eye so he didn't have to remember.

"I'm sorry, Andrea, I wish we could finish this up, but I have another meeting," he said, getting to his feet. "It was such a pleasure to speak with you. Say hello to Erik for me. And don't forget to stop by Jessica's desk on your way out for those stats."

Guess he hadn't liked my question. His evasion felt oddly satisfying.

13

"This is garbage," I said to myself as I stabbed at my keyboard, deleting yet another line of text that read as stilted and amateurish. I'd been back at my desk for forty minutes trying to get something salvageable out of my meeting with Platt, and all I could come up with was drivel that even my grandmother wouldn't commend me for. A week ago I would have been thrilled to be the journalist with the inside story on the mayor's run for governor. A week ago I would have believed I was covering this story because I deserved it. Today I knew I had been assigned to the story because Erik thought I would regurgitate his buddy Platt's press release and put my name on it.

Platt clearly wanted to gloss over Rendell's handling of the highway shootings, but if I ignored that subject completely, the piece would scream paid advertising. Screw it—ignoring the elephant in the room never worked.

I attacked my draft with renewed vigor, adding balanced commentary on Rendell's accomplishments and failures, including the highway shootings. This gubernatorial run would add new pressure on the search for the killer or killers. The success of his campaign would hinge on having a suspect in custody. These cases had the ability to scar the solid track record currently defining his candidacy. I wrapped up, but knew it needed one more read in case I had been overly zealous. Stepping away for a few minutes would help me bring back my professional eyes.

I grabbed my phone and scrolled through email. Still no response from my anonymous emailer. He'd wanted my attention; now he had it. So why the silence? I contemplated sending another email. Would that move him into gear or push him back like a spider into a crevice? I did know someone who could do a trace on the email address. It was pricey, but… What was I thinking? Again I was letting personal pressure control me. I stashed the phone back in my bag. *Get a grip. It hasn't even been half a day.*

I took a sip of my Pellegrino and a few deep breaths and got back to the story, freshly committed to balanced reporting. If Erik wanted to airbrush Rendell's history, that was on him. I could only write the truth. It wasn't in me to do anything less.

"You ready for a first pass?" Brynn was at the doorway. "Gang experts?" she said, noting the confusion in my face. I motioned her in.

She handed me a couple printouts as she flopped into the seat.

"First up is Father Luke Brogan. Religious community bigwig in Englewood. He runs several programs for teens, trying to keep them out of gangs. Staged a sit-in four years ago in front of City Hall when former Mayor Schiffer closed a mental health facility in the neighborhood." She reached across the desk and flipped to the next page. "Remember last August, when the cops shot and killed that seventeen-year-old kid with a cell phone in his hand? Said they thought it was a gun? Well, Brogan was also the guy who kept the peace when events almost spun out of control."

"Yes, of course. We haven't met, but I know his name." I thought back to the news coverage of a neighborhood almost brought to a boil by extreme emotions and extreme heat. The incident, although unfortunate, could have been disastrous. Father Brogan had been instrumental in facilitating rational dialogue between the community and CPD, resulting in a strained but peaceful outcome. "He has tremendous influence, not only in Englewood, but also with other neighborhood community leaders."

"Then we have Professor Edwin Larsson, at UIC. He's published three books thus far: one on the history of gangs; one on symbolism and groupthink, that compares gangs to sports teams, for some odd reason; and his most recent fantastical idea, the suggestion that gang structure is actually beneficial for society—they're just misunderstood."

"Larsson sounds like he might be an admirer," I said, confused by the idea of a professor touting drug dealing and violence.

"He sounds like an academic afraid to get his hands dirty, studying what intrigues him rather than living it." Brynn's voice dripped with disgust. "Fantasy is better than reality for some people."

Brynn's show of emotion caught me by surprise. I sensed a backstory but didn't pry. She'd volunteered little of her personal life, but every now and then, I'd picked up an edge, as if there were trauma in her past. With my own life far more exposed and vulnerable than I cared for it to be, I wasn't going to push. It was hers to share or not as she saw fit.

"This is a great start. I'll get on the phone, see what I can set up. Can you also get me the locations of the first two shootings? I want to know exactly where they happened, down to the position of the shooter."

"You got it. I'll have it for you in the morning." She grabbed her now-empty coffee mug and returned to her desk.

Flipping through Brynn's documents, I highlighted a few areas of interest, made some margin notes, then picked up the phone to call Father Brogan. We made an appointment to meet in the morning, and I moved to the next call. Professor Larsson's voice mail indicated he was away on sabbatical and only checking messages infrequently over the summer. I left one anyway.

I glanced at the clock: 3:30 p.m. Rendell's announcement needed to be in to Erik by 5:00 p.m. Now that I was no longer pussyfooting around the highway shootings and Platt's ego, the revision began to flow more smoothly, and the piece took on a reasonable structure with only a few tweaks.

As I wrote, Cai's revelation of gang payoffs slid back into my head. I searched Karl Janek's name, looking for information on the allegations. After ten minutes of digging, the bulk of what I had found was cursory coverage of the investigation. Without Cai's information, I probably would have glossed right over the stories. However, an anonymous blogger who called himself CopOut and claimed to be ex-CPD went deeper. His posts seemed to align with what I had heard from my own sources, but for all I knew, he was a fourteen-year-old kid with a vivid imagination.

CopOut alleged that two years earlier, a lieutenant in the Gangster Disciples had been indicted for drug trafficking when he'd attempted to recruit undercover cops for a satellite operation in the western suburb of Oak Park. The lieutenant had tried to take care of the situation by throwing money at the detectives. Unfortunately for him, the detectives didn't bite. Based on the lieutenant's readiness to open his wallet, the cops figured he'd pulled this move in the past and pushed him for more dirt. One chief of police talked to another, and before long, Internal

Affairs was up everyone's ass. Janek, being head of the gang unit, had a bullseye on his forehead.

CopOut hinted at other officers being involved as well. In true media fashion, none of his follow-up posts indicated that Janek had been cleared. Dubicki's name wasn't even mentioned. Nothing I didn't already know. Aside from the blog, I found no other coverage. Maybe Brynn could work some magic. The indictment of the gang member was easy enough to verify but didn't prove anything. Perhaps I could get Cai to spill a little more. She might know who represented Dubicki or could find out. I picked up the phone. As usual, her cell went directly to voice mail. I left a detailed message, knowing I'd hear from her shortly.

"Are you sure Rendell's a dead end? The funky money, I mean." Erik stood in the doorway, his face a mix of emotions I couldn't interpret. Sheepish, annoyed, distracted—I couldn't tell anymore. Whatever radar I had in the past for reading his moods had been seriously faulty.

"As I said in my email, there's nothing there. Just a former employee pissed off after getting fired." I shifted my eyes back to my screen. I was still annoyed over the morning's tussle and not looking for a replay. He, however, was making no effort to leave. I lifted my head and looked up at him over my computer screen. "Was there something else?"

"Can I give you a ride home tonight?" he asked, fussing with his watchband instead of looking at me. "I know it's early, but you really should be getting more rest. You've been pushing yourself hard this week, harder than I imagine your doctor would want you to. I'll need fifteen minutes and then we can leave."

Twelve possible responses darted through my mind starting with "fuck no" and moving downhill from there. Before I could say anything, my cell phone rang. Cai, returning my call, saving me from another "it's really over" conversation. Mindful of the paycheck I still needed, I shifted my attitude closer to neutral. "I'll grab a cab, but thanks for the offer," I said, then took the call.

Erik nodded as he left, his eyes filled with hurt at the rejection. At least he didn't argue.

"Hey, you there? Am I catching you in the middle of something?" Cai asked, hearing the pause after I picked up the phone.

"Sorry, Cai. Just chatting with the boss," I said, grateful for the interruption.

"Oh. Is he still pleading? Wants you to take him back? He's now a reformed man, shocked into honorability after nearly losing you, and can't imagine anyone else tucking him into bed at night."

"We do occasionally have to talk about work, but in this case, you're right. He hinted about nursing me back to health."

"Let me guess—a sponge bath is going to make you all better." She chuckled. "I gotta give him credit; when he wants something, he doesn't let up."

"And that's exactly the problem. He's like a kid who hasn't learned to delay gratification."

"Please no more details on your sex life—that's just too much information."

"You forget that I no longer have one, so we'll have to talk about yours."

"I couldn't do that to you. It would be too cruel to share all the juicy details when you aren't gettin' any. Might make you want to hop in the sack with Erik just to work it out of your system."

"Don't make me laugh, my bruises haven't healed yet."

"Then get the hell out of the office, go home, and get some

rest! Hey, I'm meeting this guy for a drink at Fig and Olive. Do you want me to bring you some tuna carpaccio?"

Cai worked almost as hard on her social life as she did on her day job. Not that it was difficult. Men tripped over themselves to meet her, but she never kept any of them around long enough to move into relationship territory. Boredom was always her excuse. In my opinion, she just hadn't found a male version of herself. But relationship coaching wasn't my forte these days.

"I don't want to ruin your chance at a sweaty liaison. Couldn't have that on my conscience, although I'm wildly jealous."

She laughed. "Trust me, no hot sex with this guy. A coworker has been trying to fix me up with her brother, the CPA, for months, and I've run out of excuses. Meeting him for a drink, period. You'd give me a reason to split. Gotta tend to my invalid friend."

"Thanks, but I think I'll just order sushi, take a long hot bath, and go to bed early."

"All right, have it your way, but text me if you change your mind. So, on to the other purpose of my call. You wanted to know who represented Matt Dubicki in his defense against the bribery accusations. Well, I did a little digging and found something interesting. He was exonerated."

"Yeah, I knew that."

"But you didn't know that he was represented by Blasik, Cameron, and Lord. Apparently, old man Cameron handled the case himself," Cai said, satisfaction ringing in her voice.

"Why would a top corporate law firm handle a case like that? Criminal law isn't their specialty." Alarm bells were clanging. Why would Dubicki have chosen that firm?

"More importantly, where did a cop get a thousand dollars an hour to pay for that legal talent?"

14

I pulled the replacement Audi I'd picked up last night into an open parking spot in front of St. Joseph's Catholic Church, told Siri to end directions, and stashed the phone back in my bag. Englewood was largely unfamiliar to me, known only through media coverage. I looked around at the mix of two- and three-story homes—some tidy, some rundown, others boarded up and abandoned. Empty lots dotted the landscape; whatever homes had once stood on these spots were now just ghostly memories. The neighborhood seemed to teeter between a distant past of middle-class success and a troubled future.

A text flashed on my phone, confirming that my story on Rendell's gubernatorial announcement had gone live. What kind of butchering had Erik done? I clicked through. Absent was any mention of the highway shootings and their potential impact on the election or Rendell's legacy. I shook my head and swallowed my pride. At least it was a byline.

Flipping through the notes Brynn had prepared for my meeting with Father Brogan, I fought the voice in my head that told me I shouldn't be here. This wasn't my story. Pursuing it could leave me exposed and more vulnerable than I had been at any point in my life. This move was flat-out insubordination, and Erik would spit rocks if he found out. Was it ego that had me here overstepping boundaries, or instinct? Or a desire to prove to Erik that I had the chops, that whatever he threw at me wouldn't break me?

The view across the expressway I had seen two days ago as I'd stood against the chain-link fence, in the very spot the shooter had stood, once again filled my mind. It sent shivers up my back. I felt as if CPD was being intentionally vague in their details of the shootings, possibly to ferret out the killer. Or perhaps intentionally evasive because gang violence was easier to explain than having no idea what was really going on. Regardless, there was no doubt in my mind a sniper was at work. But why? In my gut, I was having a hard time seeing these killings as some extended initiation rite.

Of course CPD was trying to downplay the incidents in order to manage the city's fear, as was State's Attorney Denton Tierney. A single unknown sniper wasn't a tidy explanation. It required getting into the psyche of an unknown killer and anticipating what was next. Gangs, on the other hand, required little additional commentary. Drugs and territory were stories we'd all heard before. The public didn't really care about the what or why of hoodlums as long as the violence was kept contained. Gangs gave CPD a convenient story—as long as people like me didn't lift up the veil. I took a deep breath and finished perusing my notes.

Father Brogan, a native of Chicago's South Side, had been with this parish for twelve years. Opinionated and controversial, he had shown few reservations for bending lines that religious purists saw as ramrod straight. He had argued for women in the clergy. He'd adopted a child. He used his voice and his clout to move his congregation to engage politically when he thought doing so was right.

And that right thing always involved being an advocate for those who didn't have a voice themselves. He worked tirelessly to provide services for the poor, whether that meant a soup kitchen at the church or fighting with city government over funding for mental health, affordable housing, and job training. But his primary interest was trying to prevent the ravages of gangs on his community. I hoped he would be a source of information as I tried to understand the framework of the territorial feud CPD described.

The church was a squat red brick building. Its original function was indefinite, seemingly retrofitted for its new purpose. It sprawled, as though added onto over and over as the congregation grew. The heavy carved wooden doors seemed out of place given the utilitarian nature of the structure. Even more awkward was the stained-glass depiction of the Resurrection squeezed in above. The grounds were well kept, but the vegetation sparse, with only a handful of red impatiens lining the concrete walk.

Uncomfortable teenage memories bubbled to the surface. Religion and I hadn't gotten along since my mother's death. I had rebelled against its demands for blind faith and logic-defying beliefs.

I followed the cracked concrete walkway around the corner of the building where a colorful hand-lettered sign announced the presence of the St. Joseph's Community Center. Children's watercolor paintings hung in the windows along with signs touting "respect" and "love." Graffiti had recently been scrubbed off the brick below, reinforcing the message. As I walked, my eyes stopped on a man across the street leaning against a parked Lexus. A baseball cap hid all but the whiteness of his strong jaw and neck as he stood engrossed in his phone. His starched striped dress shirt hung untucked but wrinkled, as if he'd just yanked it out of his pants. He looked about as out of place here as I did.

I was met with a cacophony of childish laughter and shouts as I pulled open the doors to the center. Groups of kids of varying ages sat at stations throughout the room for the after-school programs. They gathered around games, art projects, and computers. A random collection of mismatched donations and carefully repurposed furniture filled the space, yet everything was clean and in good repair. Someone cared.

In the far-right corner, doors opened to another room, and I could see a priest in his collar and black shirt, and a crowd of teens bent excitedly over a foosball table.

I nodded hello at the desk attendant. "Is that Father Brogan in the back room?"

"Yeah, just follow the hoots and howls." The large round woman chuckled and tilted her head toward the back.

"Man, I can't believe ya missed that shot! That was a complete gimme, Jamal," one of the young men in the crowd around the table called out in frustration as I entered.

"Well, if you all would back up and give me some elbow room, maybe I could hit them points," the player shot back, struggling against the butt-kicking he was getting. He looked to be all of fourteen, tall, with caramel skin—gangly, but already sporting chiseled cheekbones and a proud forehead below his close-cropped hair. He played with intensity, seeming to appreciate the competition despite the impending loss.

Father Brogan wasn't much taller than me. He was slender, and clearly comfortable in his body in the fourth decade of life. His thin brown hair was combed straight back, and wire-rimmed aviator eyeglasses hung by a chain around his neck, flapping with each jab. The crinkles around his soft green eyes brightened his pallid skin and spoke of humor and compassion.

I watched until the final shot and then the match broke up. Brogan came around the table to give Jamal a hug and a pat on the back.

"Thanks for letting the old man win this time. I was starting to feel a little insecure after you trounced me last week."

"Hey, Father B, you gonna let me beat you tomorrow?" one of the other boys called out.

"You're on! Although don't count on a win. I'm on a hot streak," Brogan laughed, then said his goodbyes.

"Father, I'm Andrea Kellner. Thanks for meeting with me." I held out my hand, which he took gently in both of his.

"Certainly. Let's go somewhere where it's a little quieter."

I followed him down the hall to a small office in the back.

"I'll clear a spot." Lifting a stack of papers from one of the chairs, he moved it to a shaky folding table, seemingly ready to buckle under the weight. "My secretary calls this her happy mess. She has a system in here somewhere. I don't dare try to intervene." He took a seat at the desk and motioned for me to take the empty seat across from him.

The priest had an easy laugh and an even easier smile. I could see how the kids could trust him.

"You indicated on the phone that you wanted to talk about kids and gangs in Englewood," he said, shifting the conversation quickly from small talk to the purpose of my visit.

"I'm doing some investigation into the highway shootings, and I'd like to discuss the impact of these crimes on the Englewood community. To approach the story from a more personal point of view," I said. It wasn't an exaggeration exactly, just a softer starting point to the conversation. I pulled out my phone. "Would it be all right to record this?"

He nodded, but his eyes were guarded.

"Exploring the impact of gang violence on young lives and families would go a long way toward helping Chicago understand how complex these issues are. Issues that, I believe, have been glossed over in the media coverage of these events. I believe that the story needs context. You, more than most of us, see the impact on Englewood, and I was hoping you'd speak to me about how these kids get roped into gangs in the first place."

Father Brogan's face had changed to one of cool calculation while I spoke, as if he had been suddenly reminded of something unpleasant but familiar. I wasn't sure what I had said, but something was giving him pause.

"When we set up this meeting, it wasn't clear that you were working on the highway shootings. Quite frankly, if I'd known that, I wouldn't have agreed to meet with you."

I quickly switched off the recorder, placing the phone back in my bag before responding. Unless I could establish trust in the next couple of minutes, I was going to lose him, and I had no idea why.

"Father Brogan, I'm sure you're tired of the negative publicity these terrible incidents have brought to Englewood," I said, grasping at the first logical thought for his hesitation. "The coverage has been sensationalized and stereotypical. I can assure you that my piece will focus on the issues that create a breeding ground for gangs to take hold. I want to put a human face on the media coverage, a story of humanity. I want to tell a story about the challenges these young people face."

I could hear the hint of pleading in my voice, but I hoped the sincerity I felt was also coming through. Father Brogan's cooperation could go a long way in opening avenues of information.

"Humanity," Father Brogan said, letting the word hang in the air. "What an interesting choice of words. Do you mean humanity of the kind shown to Damon Wilkins?"

My breath stuck in my chest. Damon Wilkins was a name I hadn't heard spoken in over a year, but it was a name that haunted me. And for the second time this week, I was being reminded of the vigilante deli owner case I had worked two years earlier, the most painful case of my legal career.

"I didn't make the connection initially, as you identified

yourself as a reporter. When I consented to this interview, I wasn't expecting to be meeting with the prosecutor responsible for Damon Wilkins's death."

His words were like a knife in my side. Granted, a knife that I had inserted myself many times over, but it had been several years since anyone else had made that accusation. Obviously Father Brogan's qualms about this conversation had nothing to do with his mistrust of the media, but with his mistrust of me. I didn't blame him.

At the time, the case had seemed straightforward enough. A South Side deli owner had become incensed by repeated robberies at the hands of the neighborhood gangbangers and the failure of law enforcement to end them. Pushed beyond his breaking point, the deli owner had armed himself, ready to take on the next thug that crossed his threshold.

Damon Wilkins had that honor. Just shy of eighteen, Wilkins had a history of petty theft and running with a crowd of low-level drug dealers who worked the corner near the deli. One sweltering August evening, Wilkins walked into the shop for Gatorade and some smokes, pocketing a bag of Skittles in the process. He was confronted by the owner and accused of theft. The dispute went south quickly. The deli owner managed to get his hands on his gun and, in their struggle, was shot and killed with his own weapon.

And I'd nailed the kid. That was my job. I painted a picture of a young man whose best buds were goons terrorizing customers and nearly bringing local businesses to bankruptcy. This was a kid who'd also been seen on the deli security cameras during a prior robbery. So what if he wasn't the one toting the gun?

I had no hard proof the kid had intent to commit a crime, beyond pickpocketing candy, or even that he was a gang member. But if it looked like a duck and quacked like a duck, I made it one. A law-abiding man was dead. Aggressively, I pushed the jury to see this kid as a punk without regard for the life of a hardworking shop owner. *Anyone of you could have been on the wrong side of that confrontation.*

Wilkins was tried as an adult and convicted of second-degree murder. His sentence was fifteen years. I had won.

Two months in, Wilkins hung himself in his cell on his eighteenth birthday.

"Father Brogan, with all due respect, that's a harsh accusation. Damon's suicide was horribly tragic, but the decisions he made about his life were his alone. I don't see how you can hold me responsible," I said with more conviction than I felt.

"He was a seventeen-year-old kid with only minor history. Your culpability lies in lack of perspective. You were rash. Your desire for your own success painted him with a broad brush and ignored the nuance of his circumstance. He was backed into a corner without hope."

Father Brogan's eyes cut deep into my core, bearing the sorrow of years' worth of heartache. I looked at the clock behind his head, the floor, anything but straight at him, fighting the guilt that had haunted me in the middle of the night ever since. I lifted my head and looked deep into Father Brogan's eyes, trying to process my emotions. Intellectually, I knew I had done my job and done it well, but had I allowed stereotypes and my own ambitions to influence my handling of the case? Did I have a hand in pushing Damon Wilkins to his death?

Father Brogan's voice broke the silence. "Is this case still as straightforward to you as it was two years ago?" His eyes had softened, and he looked at me expectantly.

I shook my head and leaned forward, clasping my hands on his desk. "The prosecutor in me has a hard time admitting this, but time has allowed me to see nuance. It was my job to present a case that had as few shades of gray as possible." I could hear my voice wobble as I spoke, feeling emotion tighten my chest. "While the state's attorney may not agree, in hindsight, I believe I should have made room for a bigger box of crayons."

He laid his hand on mine and said, "In that case, perhaps you've become the right person to tell this story. Where do we start?"

15

I felt the years of self-flagellation begin to drain from my body, wondering if this was what confession felt like for believers. I gave Father Brogan a small smile as relief washed over me, then reached again to turn on the phone recorder, noticing four new emails had come in. Had my anonymous emailer responded? Frustration and impatience had taken over last night, and I'd sent a second email, requesting a meeting. No reply. The screen tempted me, but given how close I'd come to blowing it, I couldn't chance offending Father Brogan any more than I had.

The urge to ask him flat out what he thought of CPD's assessment of the shootings tugged at me, but my training as a prosecutor held me in check.

"Why don't we start with the kids here at the center? Are any of these young people involved in gangs?" I asked.

"We have our share of baby gangsters, sometimes as young as eight or nine," he said, a pained expression creasing his eyes.

"Eight?" It was inconceivable to me. I stared back at Father Brogan, unable to wrap my head around the idea. "I had no idea it could start so young. What roles do children that age play?"

"They're lookouts, runners, whatever odd jobs an older member wants to throw at them. This is the stage where they flirt with the idea but haven't moved to a point of no return. Trying it on, seeing if it fits, if you will. Often they're simply too young to know any better. Or they're following an older sibling into the life. This entry point is the most vulnerable stage, but also the stage where we can have the most influence." He leaned forward, placing his elbows on the desk. "Look, these are kids just trying to belong somewhere. Children need structure, community, family. If they don't have that in other parts of their lives, street gangs become a substitute. If we lose them at that stage, they become insulated by the gang, and it's hard to undo that loyalty."

"Eight-year-olds should be in Little League, playing video games. It's hard to fathom," I said.

"Yes, it is, for someone who hasn't been exposed. I suspect it's a very different life from what you grew up in. Parents here are struggling. Addiction, jail, lack of education, lack of jobs. The layers of complexity are endless."

Father Brogan continued to answer my questions, speaking in depth on the family situations and economic realities of life in the poorest neighborhood in Chicago, before I moved the conversation again toward the highway shootings.

"How has the Englewood neighborhood responded to being in the crossfire of the shootings?"

"This community has been in the crossfire for decades. And gangs are winning the war. We do what we can as a community center, but our resources are few. The problems are simply too entrenched for one group to tackle in any lasting way. All I can hope for is individual successes. Frankly, the only reason people like you are paying attention now is because middle-class white people are involved." He said this without judgment, only sadness in his voice. "I'm long past any naive notions of outrage. It's painful to say, but we must speak the truth."

Unfortunately, I knew he was right.

"The police have explained the incidents as a territory dispute between the Black Disciples and the Black P Stones. Would I be correct in assuming this has something to do with control of the drug market at the Garfield L stop?"

"It's possible, but the Gangster Disciples have had control of that area for the past three years. They took out a key P Stone minister, which rattled the structure of that organization enough to solidify their control of the drug trade. I haven't heard any rumblings about their position being challenged."

"And this wouldn't be news to CPD?"

I was choosing my words more carefully now, conscious of the precarious start of our conversation and wanting Father Brogan to be unencumbered in his response. But my mind was racing ahead, questioning CPD's theory.

"No, it wouldn't." He laughed and pulled his aviators up onto his head. "That situation got bloody. In my experience, law enforcement is quite happy when one gangbanger takes out a comrade. Appears as another win in their war against drugs. I even recall reading the press release praising Detective Janek and his team."

Janek? He would have been heading Gang Enforcement at the time. Was he harboring a grudge because of the damage done to his career? Was bias misleading him about the cause of the shootings? I stopped myself. I was already drawing conclusions that it was too early to infer.

"Can you think of any reason CPD would believe that tensions have been reignited?"

"CPD has identified these shootings as possible initiation rites. A proof of loyalty if you will. Three shootings are not something I've heard of in this context, and the idea is concerning. One pull of the trigger proves your commitment, so my question would be, is this one shooter or three? What point would three deaths make that one doesn't? Loyalty has been established." He paused, thinking for a moment before continuing. "Another option comes to mind. I've heard a few rumors about some friction. I don't have a name, but there's a Gangster Disciple who's a bit of a lone wolf. He's ex-military. An agitator. I hear he's itching for a bigger role and not getting support from the leadership. He could be trying to make a statement. Prove himself as a tough guy."

"But you don't know who he is."

"No. That information wouldn't necessarily come my way."

"Thank you, Father Brogan. You've been very helpful. I appreciate this." My mind was already taking flight with the lone-wolf theory. What was the intended message? Intimidation? Diversion? To transfer blame onto someone else in order to open up a seat at the table?

"You're welcome, Ms. Kellner. I'm glad to see that there's more to you than what I saw on the surface when you were a prosecutor. But that's true of most situations, isn't it? I suspect that the answer to solving the highway shootings lies in your willingness to look past the obvious, as well." He looked down at his hands and shook his head. "I hope the Chicago Police Department is willing to do the same."

Thoughts exploded in my head as I left Father Brogan and returned to my car. CPD's rival gang theory was now even shakier. A text pinged through: Brynn sending locations for shootings one and two.

Looking up from my phone, I was surprised to see Mr. Baseball Hat still there, but now surrounded by a handful of teens all proudly wearing their gang colors of black and blue. Jamal, the young foosball player, was one of them. What were they doing engaged in conversation with a middle-aged white man who didn't seem to belong to this neighborhood? Baseball Hat shot his cold, penetrating gaze right at me, and I could see the set of his jaw, the nose flattened across the bridge from some fight in his distant past. He seemed familiar somehow, but I couldn't imagine why.

Mind your own damn business, his expression seemed to be saying. Or was I allowing my imagination to run off-leash? Yet, I caught myself questioning the group.

I broke the staring contest and headed to my car. Whatever was going on wasn't my concern today.

Father Brogan's statement about hoping the Chicago Police Department was willing to question assumptions was still on my mind as I stashed my phone in the cup holder and started my drive north toward the office. The priest didn't seem any more convinced by the current explanation for these shootings than I was. If warring gang factions were at the heart of these incidents, why hadn't Father Brogan heard something?

Another text popped up, and I glanced down at the screen. Borkowski. I didn't bother to read further. Whatever he wanted could wait.

Hold on. That was it. *That's* why Baseball Hat had looked familiar. He was the fourth guy at Gibsons with Borkowski, Ramirez, and Langston! Who the hell was this guy?

16

Coincidence? Not part of my belief system. Maybe it was my jaded lawyer eyes, but seeing this guy twice in just a few days rattled me. Why was someone friendly with aldermen and major business leaders hanging with teenage boys in Englewood? What business could he have with them? Discomfort washed over me. My instincts, the little voices that tickled the pit of my stomach, had proven useful, even reliable, in the past. I had learned to trust them, even when I couldn't define what they were telling me. Sooner or later, it would become clear.

Instead of continuing my drive, I pulled over to the curb and reread the text from Brynn. The first shooting had occurred fewer than ten blocks from where I was now and just a few blocks south of shooting number three. Why not? I put my car into gear, abandoning my plan to return to the office. I zigzagged south to 63rd Street, which crossed over the Dan Ryan, bisecting the neighborhood. I cruised the streets parallel to Wentworth to get a feel for the area before moving toward my destination. There seemed to be numerous For Sale signs around.

As I neared the location, my own run-in with the highway

shooter suddenly surged at me. The sharpness of the impact, the sound of the gun, the dead man's blood, all rushed back, and I felt my chest tighten and blood pulse in my ears. I became overconscious of the bruises still glowing yellow-green on my chest and forehead. Sweat was now beading on the back of my neck despite the air conditioning.

I pulled my car to the curb and parked, catching my breath and feeling my pulse slow. I looked up at the midsized building, locating the street number. The red brick building dominated this segment of the street. It was three stories tall with rows of caged windows lining each level. It must have housed a small manufacturing company at some point but appeared long vacant. Scanning the façade, I found the words Lambert Brush etched into the granite above the door—a marker of its original function as a paintbrush factory.

To the right of the door, a faded Temple Realty sign covered the window. A Sold sticker had recently been slapped on its face. Immediately adjacent on the south side sat a ramshackle auto body shop. It too sported a For Sale sign by the same realty company, with a Sold sticker over it. Highway traffic whooshed behind me as I surveyed the rest of the street. A few cars parked here and four blocks farther north, a city bus. There wasn't a person in sight. This area wasn't exactly on *Chicago Magazine's* hot neighborhood list. What was up with all the real estate activity?

A stretch of vacant land, overgrown and strewn with trash, ran for maybe forty yards along the north side of the building. Across the street, a chain-link fence bordered the expressway, leaving only a three-foot-wide easement. I crossed over to the fence. As with the Garfield location, there was just enough room for a sniper to crouch and shoot through the couplings. Easy line of sight to the vehicles below and deserted enough that getting off a round wouldn't be difficult.

Or had the sniper utilized the cover of the vacant building? I walked back, tested the locked front door, then stood on my toes along the crumbling sidewalk to peek through the window. The concrete was chipped away from neglect, and I was about an inch too short to see in clearly. I stepped to my left to gain more stable footing on a rock next to the foundation and stretched. It still wasn't enough to see through the grime. Back on firm ground, I scanned the face of the building, looking for a secondary door or a lower window. Nothing. So I followed the edge of the building around to the north corner, where I saw a rusted steel door. Bingo! It opened with a light push. Tentatively, I swung the door open and peered inside. Footprints made a path in the dust. Even in the dim light, I could tell they marked multiple individuals.

The room was large and completely open, with a ceiling that rose at least twelve feet. It was empty except for a few discarded machine parts scattered around. I followed the trail to a doorway, then into a hallway and up a set of stairs to the second floor. Sunshine didn't make it this far into the building, and the air was stale but cool. It was easy to imagine all manner of nefarious activity occurring in the shadows. My eyes swept the corners and up to the top of the stairs for movement, and I stepped slowly to minimize the echo of my footsteps as I climbed. One traumatic encounter this week was more than enough. I followed the disturbed grime as it led me to windows on the west side of the building overlooking the Dan Ryan.

Beyond enough dust to give the entire city of Chicago asthma, the large room was empty. The same gang markings I had seen at the Garfield Street L platform decorated the walls, as did a gallery of elaborate graffiti art. I walked to the area along the windows, where the foot traffic had been heaviest. Scanning the floor and the windowsills, I saw black smudges dotting the window sash and that a windowpane that had been smashed out. Finger print powder mixed with the years of accumulated dirt. CPD had been here.

Broken glass crunched under my feet as I surveyed the roadway below. I tried to re-create the incident in my mind. Plotted out the position of the vehicle, the shooter. I imagined the incident as the shooter took aim. From this distance and given the highway speed, it was hard to imagine this as an accident. It would have taken skill and precision. Was the shooter lying in wait for a specific person? Or was the target random?

And the question remained, why?

The angle and the distance meant that the shooter was experienced. I pulled my phone out of my bag to snap a few photos when the clomp of feet on stairs stopped me. I had company. Cops back to review the scene? The shooter returning for an encore? My eyes bounced around the room looking for another exit, but I saw nothing. I wasn't going to be able to avoid my visitors.

"Who are you?"

A young man had stopped at the top of the stairs and was shouting at me, apparently just as surprised to see me as I was him. Tossing his large backpack on the floor, he hiked up his pants and glowered at me like I'd invaded his private space. Uncertain of what I was dealing with, I stood silent, trying to get a read on the kid. He was probably sixteen and about my height, but all muscle and sinew. Tattoos trailed down the right side of his neck, under the strap on his tank top, and along his bicep. His mahogany skin glistened with sweat as if he had just been running.

"Jam, we got us an audience," he yelled over his shoulder as a second teen appeared in the door.

The tattooed kid sauntered over to me, obstructing my line of sight to his partner. My fingers gripped the phone tighter, ready to dial for help if needed. He tilted his head to the side, clocking the iPhone in my hand.

"I asked who you be?" He took another step closer, his eyes boring into mine.

"No one." I shook my head. "I was just leaving." Sweat dampened my neck, causing my shirt to cling to my back. I scanned the room once more, not knowing his intent. A quick exit was the best I could hope for. I started toward the doorway, now able to see the second boy. It was Jamal, the foosball player from Father Brogan's community center, staring back at me in confusion, a can of spray paint in his hand.

As I stepped past the tattooed kid, his hand gripped my wrist, pulling me back.

"Lemme see yer phone," the kid demanded, fingers digging into my flesh.

I turned to face him, and his eyes challenged me, but I didn't budge. It was only a piece of hardware, I wasn't going to be stupid, but handing the phone over just because he thought he was a tough guy would only make me look vulnerable. And who knew what ideas that would inspire? Jamal was now moving toward us, and I turned my head toward him, trying to read his face. Did he remember me from the center?

"Deon, back off. She's cool," Jamal said, encouraging his friend to release my arm.

"You know this bitch with the fine phone?" Deon raised his eyebrows but maintained his grip.

My eyes sought Jamal's, hoping for an ally.

"She hangs with Father B," he said. "Come on, we came here to tag. I don't need no priest on my ass." Jamal gave Deon's shoulder a slight shove and cocked his head toward the far wall.

Deon smirked at me, then tossed my wrist to the side and walked away. I mouthed my thanks to Jamal and was out of the building before his friend had a change of mood.

As I exited through the heavy metal door, I saw a man, his back to me, crouched at the corner of the building near the sidewalk. He was setting up equipment of some kind, consulting his laptop periodically as he worked. A truck was parked on the street in front of my car. An enormous drill and core sampler were mounted on its large bed.

The technician stood and turned toward me, surprised by my arrival. He nodded, then continued to punch into his computer. The large red logo of Delgado Engineering embellished the doors of the truck. Why was that name familiar? I hustled to my car, anxious to be back in its relative safety. As I slid into the Audi, I pulled out my phone and punched in the name. Two pages in, I found it. Delgado Engineering had employed the engineer who'd buried the toxic sludge reports for Rami Concrete.

Why were they testing here, and what were they testing for? And if Rami was involved in redevelopment of this property, that meant its owner, Nelson Ramirez, was still in bed with Alderman Langston.

17

What was going on?

How many engineering companies in the Chicago metro area did soil testing? Dozens? More? Yet the one company mixed up with falsifying data was working across the street from the shooting. Seemed odd, but I couldn't imagine how there could be a connection.

I leaned forward, resting my elbows on my desk and rubbed the back of my neck. Luckily the bruises on my forehead and chest were no longer painful. Digging around the fringes of the highway shootings, I couldn't see anything but endless questions with no answers. The location of the second shooting had been just a hundred yards north of the first, and he'd again chosen cover along the chain-link fence. Pushing myself upright, I scrolled through my email again, hoping for a response from Anonymous. I was again disappointed.

Damn, I needed a massage.

"Don't you respond to texts anymore?" Borkowski stood in front of my desk, arms crossed like a parent chastising his teenage daughter for not making curfew.

I grabbed my phone and scrolled to his message. "Call me"

was all it said. I held up the screen and looked up at him, unable to resist the eye roll that accompanied it. "I was driving. What is it that you wanted to discuss? You didn't exactly give me much context." I kept my tone neutral, but only because I didn't have the energy to get testy.

"You have an administrative contact at CPD, don't you?"

"Hold on," I said, distracted by a news flash that popped up on my phone screen. "Damn! Platt just announced his candidacy for mayor. I asked the man flat out if he wanted to run. Why didn't I get a call?"

"What? You expected an engraved invitation?" he said, snorting and shaking his head. "Someone else's turn for a favor. Don't take it personally. You just haven't accrued enough points in your special favors account yet. It's give, give, get. Can't expect him to put you on speed dial if you haven't tossed a little love in his direction. Platt knows everything that happens in this city long before the rest of us do. He's got an underground information network that rivals the NSA. How do you think that happens? It ain't benevolence. Now, that source?"

"Yes, I have someone. Why?" I responded cautiously, wondering where he was going with this and irritated that my impatience was being thrown back at me. From day one, I had found Borkowski arrogant and of the opinion that a couple of journalism awards entitled him to kiss-my-ass status. Now that I had seen him chummy with insiders, suspicious had been added to the attribute list. What was *that* backstory?

"I need someone inside. Can you give me a name?"

"Excuse me? You want me to hand over a relationship I've cultivated since I was first hired as an ASA just because you ask? Why would I risk exposing my source for you? Call the Office of News Affairs."

He shifted his weight to the other foot and huffed. "I thought you were dying to be involved in the highway shooting story?

I've got some information I need to confirm and can't wait for some PR wonk. I'd go to my own source, but he unfortunately had a heart attack last week, so I'm SOL. Now do you have a name for me or not?"

I contemplated his request. What did he have? There had to be some way to use this situation. I got to my feet, matching his posture.

"I'm not giving up my contact," I said. A pinched expression crossed his face, and he turned to leave. "But what I will do is check it out for you." He stopped at the door, his face crunched as if he'd just gotten a whiff of midsummer garbage. "Tell me what you've got. I'll run it by my guy and let you know if it's legit."

He clenched and released his fist as he stared at the floor, evaluating the barrel I had him over. Tough call. His pride or his story. He lifted his head.

"I hear that the first victim, Velasquez, had a history. Used to go by King Angel. Was hooked up with the Latin Kings about ten years ago," he said, each word delivered like he was swallowing a nail. "See if CPD will confirm. Might be an old grudge or score being settled that goes to motive."

A decade-old grievance? Would that explain the other victims? I nodded as Borkowski slunk back to his office, pleased to have an official reason to ask questions, then fished around in my bag for a business card I had tucked into an inside pocket. Might as well go right to the source. I dialed Michael Hewitt, smiling as I heard his voice come on the line.

"I've been wanting to call you," he said. "But I couldn't come up with a legitimate reason."

"Do you need one?"

The silence was rich with nervous energy. We were both feeling awkward, skirting around our mutual attraction. As a prosecutor, cops were definitely off-limits in the romantic department, not that I'd been in the market. As a journalist, the rules were blurry, but no cop was ready to defend pillow talk with a reporter, at least not to the public.

"I'm glad your friend didn't show up," he said, his voice soft. "I know I'm supposed to play it cool, but I enjoyed spending time with you."

"I did as well. First time I've enjoyed being stood up." I wanted to say more, to ask if I could see him again, to... *Stop.* I already had one work entanglement; I didn't need another. "Actually, I'm calling for professional reasons. We hear that the victim in the first highway shooting, Angel Velasquez, was a former member of the Latin Kings. Went by the handle King Angel. Can you confirm that?"

"I think I like how the conversation started better." He laughed. "Where'd you get that information?"

"Can you confirm, Detective Hewitt?" I wasn't about to fess up to doing Borkowski's bidding.

"What I can confirm is that Mr. Velasquez had a prior association with the Latin Kings as a teenager." His voice was crisp, all business now. Too bad. The soft voice was far sexier. "We believe his association with the group ended years ago."

"Was he targeted because of this association?"

"There is no reason to believe that he was known to the shooter or specifically targeted."

"Can I quote you on that?"

"No, but you can reference the official press release that went out about two minutes ago." He laughed. "Since we're in work mode, how is your story going? The puzzle piece? You seemed concerned by the email you got while we were at MK."

"I see your detective instincts were at work even on a night off." It sounded like he was fishing for information.

"Sorry, habit. It's not something I can control. Just how my brain works after all these years. I've been told that I cross over into interrogation mode occasionally, but since we're sharing...," he said.

"I've received some of the same constructive criticism myself." I laughed. "Actually, I was intrigued by the email more so than concerned," I said, deciding to open that door a crack. "I'm playing a little cat-and-mouse with a source, and right now he has all the cheese."

Again, I had the urge to tell all. There was something about Michael that made me trust him. Yet the complications of our respective careers were impossible to overlook. Perhaps just a toe in the water.

"I've received an anonymous email," I said. "An individual who is suggesting that he, or she, has some information. I'm struggling to decipher his messages." I was intentionally vague, wanting to see how the volleying played out between us. Would Michael be a cop in his personal life, too?

"Why do you have to decipher it?"

"He's communicating in poetry."

"Poetry? As in Wordsworth?"

"Far less eloquent." I laughed. "But that's the general idea."

"Try me. Maybe I can unlock a clue. I'm pretty experienced with puzzles."

I hesitated, sensing that he, too, was torn between personal and professional interest and not sure which direction to go.

"I'd like to talk about it with you. But the boundaries between our work and personal lives are murky. I don't know how to approach that. The last thing I want to do is put you in a compromising position." I said, voicing the reality that we both knew. "Besides, I'm still trying to figure out if this email is even worth my energy. It could just be some bored teenager with too much time on his hands."

"Andrea, I respect that, but I need you to be straight with me. Is this associated with the highway shooting story?"

I took a deep breath. "I'm not certain, but that's my suspicion."

Dead silence on the other end of the phone.

"Michael?"

"Sent to personal or work email?"

"Work."

"Did he ask to meet?"

"No." I held back, not adding that I was the one pushing for a meeting.

"Send it to me."

"Michael, your partner made it very clear that CPD wasn't interested in collaborating."

"You have to understand what you're stepping in the middle of. You've seen the murder stats. It's gang warfare. We have flat-out hand-to-hand combat going on down in Englewood, and you could be involving yourself in something that isn't safe."

"I understand what you're saying. But at this point, I don't know that this email has anything to do with the highway shootings. It's just a hunch. I want to play it out for a while. If there's anything halfway solid, we can talk. But if I involve you now, before I'm certain, your relationship with Janek could be compromised, as will my source."

"Send me the email, Andrea. Janek won't matter if you're injured or dead."

18

A soft rubber mat cushioned my head as I lay prone on the floor, eyes closed, listening to the melodic voice of Tara, my yoga instructor. She spoke softly over the gentle harmony of her vinyasa playlist.

"Let the tension leave your body with each deep, cleansing breath," she cooed.

Not happening. While the workout had moved my body to a state of limber relaxation and eased the tension that remained from the accident, my mind was another story. Bouncing from detail to detail, question to question, I couldn't get close to clearing my head. And I didn't have a clue how I was going to excavate the truth behind these highway shootings. Lying still to deepen the yoga afterglow wasn't working for me this morning; impatience crept in instead. Gingerly I got to my knees and silently rolled up my matt. I tiptoed out of the dark room, leaving twelve other women to explore their bliss before morning coffee.

As I hit the sidewalk, the rising sun cast a beautiful amber glow over the lake, creating a halo around the Hancock Building. It was too early for the Michigan Avenue tourists, so I easily rattled through my to-do list without having to take evasive maneuvers. The short five-block walk back to my co-op moved me full-on back into work mode. Investigating the drilling company and the sale of the paintbrush factory were first on the list. Could the sale of this property be relevant to the highway shootings? I couldn't imagine how it would be tied in.

Returning to my apartment, I showered, dressed, gave Walter some love, then parked myself back in the pitifully ugly and decidedly uncomfortable folding chair that graced my dining table. With the renovation underway, functional office space was a luxury I didn't have for the time being. With construction dust and floors yet to be refinished, major furniture investments didn't make sense. I pulled back the coverings on my dining table, which sat draped in protective blankets and fenced by crates of kitchen cabinets, releasing a cloud of drywall dust, exposing the beautiful veining of a prized possession underneath: an Arabescato marble Saarinen table. I had scrimped and saved for three years in the early part of my career to pay for it. My contractor had been threatened with bodily harm if so much as a tiny scratch occurred during his watch.

I set up my laptop, dug out the research materials I had pulled from the office, and then got to work organizing the documents into neat piles, adding a map of yellow Post-its to the opposite wall. Taking a sip of tea and tossing back a couple of raspberries, I powered up the computer and logged into my email account, hoping to see a response from Sgnt1764. Nada. Damn. This was getting stupid. Why the hell had he emailed me if he didn't want to talk? I opened his email. Although I nearly had the thing memorized by now, I read it again, trying to figure out if I was missing something. The words "blight," "injustice," and "discarded" seemed to suggest the "throwaway people" were the poor or some other downtrodden group. Was he making a political statement about urban poverty? His subject line, "Killer or Thief", kept pulling me back. As did his reference to greed.

Despite my urge to prod, emailing again would only paint me as pathetic and desperate. Both were true at this point, but letting him know that wasn't going to be helpful. I'd end up with a source expecting to be paid for information. I pulled up the website for Delgado Engineering. The phone rang as I began reading. Brynn. Hmm, 7:15 a.m. on her day off?

"Hi, Andrea, I hope it's not too early to call," she said. "You normally get going at the crack of dawn, so I thought I'd give it a try. Didn't want you to have to wait until Monday."

"Of course I'm up. Working at home this morning. What's going on?"

"Well, after you emailed me last night about that paintbrush factory sale, I took a look."

"Great, what did you find?" I asked, pulling over a notepad, once again impressed with her dedication. I would need to find a way to protect her job, or help her find a new one if things got ugly at Link-Media.

"The property was owned by a guy named Anthony Bonilla. Well, I should say owned by his estate. He was the founder's grandson—died about two years ago. Apparently, Bonilla had been in poor health for years and the property sat vacant after he couldn't manage the business any longer. Anyway, they've been trying to sell the thing ever since. A half dozen agents and just as many price cuts."

"The recession can't have been helpful, but it doesn't sound like the estate was greedy, sitting on an unrealistic price."

"As of the contract date, it was listed at forty percent of the original ask. The final selling price hasn't made it into the public domain yet."

"Who's the executor?" I could hear the rustle of paper on the other end of the line.

"Ah, here it is. A Jerome Finkleman, Esquire."

I jotted down the name. It didn't ring any bells. "And the purchaser?"

"Hold on. The Orton Group, LLC. Coincidentally, they also purchased the neighboring building."

"That means they want to develop the property." I ran back through images of the surrounding mix of homes and commercial properties, trying to figure out what might be planned. "The paintbrush factory had to be about forty thousand square feet. The second, was maybe three thousand," I said. "I wonder if they plan a teardown? Just buying for the land?"

"It gets better. I just sent you an email. There's some data you should see."

I clicked back in. "Got it." I scanned the spreadsheet, getting a read on the information. "Looks like transaction history for the area."

"Exactly. The first sheet lists all the completed transactions in the 60621 zip code for the past year."

"I see the two properties on Wentworth marked as pending. What caught your attention?"

"Take a look at the totals, lower right. Total closed sales of fifty-one. Now scroll to the next page. See the total for the previous year?"

I scrolled down. "Huh, a thirty percent increase this past year," I said, mulling over the number. "The economy is reasonably strong. Prices bottomed out eighteen months ago. I would expect improvement, although thirty percent seems high."

"You have to put it into context. That zip code has pretty consistently averaged thirty-five to forty sales a year. Even in 2008, during the worst of the recession, there were thirty-one sales. Granted, it's very low compared to most of Chicago, but the numbers have always been consistent until this year —fifty-one."

"So what's causing the sudden interest in Englewood?"

"Seems like the right question to ask, particularly after I looked at the monthly breakdown. Here's the kicker—forty percent of the sales have occurred in just the last three months."

"Hold on a second." I pulled up a zip code map, Garfield to 76th, State to Racine. The For Sale signs I'd seen flashed back into my head. "That zip code, 60621, is Englewood, but the majority of the district is west of the Dan Ryan. Do we have a way to segment those sales that are east of the expressway?"

"I'll have to do it manually, but I can isolate that sector."

"Let me poke around a bit with this. We can talk about a deeper dive on Monday. Brynn, thank you."

"You got it. Send me a text if you need me over the weekend."

I ended the call and went back to my laptop, fingers flying over the keyboard. Line by line, I matched each transaction with the Cook County Recorder of Deeds, working back to March, when the pattern had shifted.

Noting purchasers, pricing, and addresses, I worked through the sales list. Click after click, a pattern started to come into focus. I stared at the notes in front of me, running through the data one more time to assure myself I wasn't mistaken. One company had their eyes on Englewood and was aggressively claiming a stake in real estate. But for what purpose?

I looked at my watch—it was all of 8:30 a.m.—then phoned Platt. Too early for his gatekeeper, he answered himself on the third ring.

"Good morning, Owen. It's Andrea Kellner."

"What a delightful surprise. A call from a beautiful woman is not how my mornings generally begin. What can I do for you?"

I nearly gagged at the sexist schmoozing, but knew any response would be perceived as engaging in the flirtation. And encouraging that behavior was the last thing I wanted to do with a man like Platt, unless it had a purpose.

"I'm following up on yesterday's mayoral announcement. I understand congratulations are in order. It seems there have been some changes since we last spoke. I'd love to sit down and discuss your campaign and your position on the issues," I said, glossing over his previous denial of intent to run just hours before the news broke.

"I'll have Jessica get you on the schedule. As you can imagine, the calendar has gotten quite tight. I'm sure you understand." His voice had taken on that man-of-the-people tone politicians seemed to use when they wanted to avoid something.

"Yes, of course. I'll follow up with her," I said, playing along. "Since I have you on the phone, do you care to comment on the information CPD released yesterday that the first victim of the highway sniper was a former gang member?" I had no intention of dragging the victim through the mud, but I wanted to know how quickly the Mayor's Office would jump on the information to play up the gang theory.

"I'll leave the official comment for Superintendent Wachowski, but, Andrea, I take issue with your continued use of the word *sniper*. That is highly irresponsible and inflammatory language. I need to caution you against journalistic sensationalism. You may be new to this industry, but your prior career should have taught you proper protocol," he added, his voice now grave. "CPD has shared their evaluation of the gang situation, and this victim's connections confirm that is exactly what we're dealing with. Inserting your own language won't change the facts."

I listened to his monologue, thanked him for his time, and ended the call. Experience had taught me that when people were intent on delivering a tirade, let them. It often revealed interesting information. And the question here was why was

Platt trying so hard to control the message? There was always an underlying objective behind the actions of a man like Platt. I just needed to figure out what it was.

My phone rang seconds later. I answered, noting the "unknown" caller ID and expecting Platt to be calling back from a private line.

"Stay out of Englewood," a male voice growled into my ear. "Or you won't walk away from the next accident."

19

The midday sun hit my face as I stepped off the curb at Superior and Wells, but I could only feel the icy chill that remained from the threatening phone call I'd received. I wasn't sure what I'd done, but I was making someone nervous. All the more reason to press forward.

Neither the beautiful weather nor the walk could improve my mood. My eyes jumped, hyperaware of my surroundings, wondering how real the threat was. Time was pressing on me. If I didn't find a way to take control of this story, I'd be relegated to covering the St. Patrick's Day parade and new exhibits at the Field Museum—provided I still had a job after Erik brought in a new partner. Questions bounced through my head, all of which lacked answers. What was motivating the shooter? What connected the victims? And who was I pissing off?

Turning south on Clark, I dodged the tourists flocking into Portillo's for a Chicago-style dog and lined up on the sidewalk outside the rock 'n' roll McDonald's for the Untouchables tour. I was on my way to meet an old colleague, Toby Rodale, from my ASA days. Recently retired, Toby had been a reporter for the *Chicago Tribune,* known for his integrity, persistence, and balanced reporting. In that capacity, he had attempted to insert himself into any prominent case that fell into my hands. He'd needled me for behind-the-scenes dirt, and I had given him all the pre-scripted lines. Occasionally, we'd tossed each other a tidbit out of mutual respect—nothing that moved the needle dramatically, but being the first to know had its value. Toby had also been at the *Trib* with Borkowski during the Nelson Ramirez trial, and I wanted to know how far back their relationship extended.

It might have been a coincidence that Delgado Engineering, the soil-testing company Ramirez had bribed, was working at the scene of one of the shootings. And that Borkowski was buddies with Ramirez. Maybe. But something deep in my brain was whispering. Toby could give me the parts of that old story that had ended up on the editing floor.

I pushed through the door at Eataly, snaked my way through the crowd waiting for gelato and espresso, then climbed the stairs to the second floor. Toby was seated at the far end of the Le Verdure counter. Even with his back to me, there was no mistaking that mop of unruly white hair.

"Did you order one of those for me?" I asked, nodding at the red wine in front of him.

He held up his glass to the light, as if not sure what to make of it. "This was Plan B, after I found out I was at the wrong station to get a beer," he laughed. "It was a nice surprise to get a lunch invitation from you, but what's up with the vegetable bar?"

I laughed. "Trust me, the grilled bitter greens will change your life."

"Hmm, bitter greens. Sounds yummy." He grimaced.

I sat down on the stool beside him and ordered a glass of Nebbiolo.

"Don't worry, I won't let you leave hungry. We'll move over to the salumi bar after this course, and you can gorge yourself on all the pork fat you want."

He shifted in his seat, but a small smile turned up the corner of his mouth. "I hear you're the competition these days. What's that all about? The attorney wardrobe getting too boring?" he said, looking at my twisted knit Rick Owens dress and platform sandals.

"Someone had to fill the journalistic void that opened when you retired last year. But I can't say I miss gray pantsuits." I tucked my hair behind my ears and raised my glass in acknowledgment.

A waiter appeared to top off our water glasses, and I placed an order of grilled greens and cauliflower cannelloni for us to share. Then we spent a few minutes catching each other up on life and mutual acquaintances before I eased into the real purpose of our meeting.

"Your old friend Art Borkowski has joined Link-Media. Had you heard?"

"Yeah, the word had gotten all the way to my ears," Toby said, looking at me sideways, as if he felt sorry for me. "But I'm not sure what you'd want with that old hack."

"Hack? Isn't he Chicago's godfather of investigative journalism? I assumed there was a shrine dedicated to his exploits over at the *Trib*. That's why Erik stole him away."

Toby took another drink of his wine and showed a sudden interest in the shishito peppers being blistered on the grill. "Good luck to you," he said after an uncomfortable pause.

Interesting. I hadn't considered the possibility that Toby might not be a fan. Given Borkowski's reputation, I'd assumed he had earned his respect. And that he treated me like crap because he was offended by how I'd gotten my job. Hmm, perhaps I'd been wrong.

"Look, Toby, I'm going to be straight with you. I don't kiss

Borkowski's ring. And based on the tone of your voice, I'd say you don't either."

He turned toward me, his face expectant, but not ready to volunteer anything.

"I'm working on a story, and as I dig into it, a few old familiar names are popping up. Names that create some questions about associations Borkowski may have, or may have had in the past. I don't know how to interpret the connections. I asked you here because I need help figuring out if I have anything to be concerned about."

Toby was still making up his mind whether to trust me. He wasn't the type to disparage anyone without a damn good reason, but I could see that he knew something, something he wasn't sure was worth the risk. He looked off over my shoulder, his eyes dark with some unpleasant memory of their past—perhaps an old grudge still smoldering. I waited, trying to read him, but I couldn't decipher what I saw in his face.

"If it helps, I'm distressed by some friendships that might interfere with Borkowski's journalistic integrity."

Nothing pissed off Toby like slimy journalists. If he was going to talk, this would unlock the door.

"So, you're seeing the asshole behind the accolades. The Art Borkowski I came to know and hate," he said, tearing off a piece of bread and dunking it in rich green olive oil. "Gimme the names." He smiled.

"Rami Construction and Delgado Engineering."

Toby's eyes got dark again, and he shook his head. "You're bringing back bad dreams. I assume you know the basics."

I nodded. "Nelson Ramirez paid to have toxic sludge erased from an engineering report. He got caught. Did some jail time."

"And Borkowski wrote the award-winning story of his fall from grace. Yada, yada, yada. You've read the piece?"

I nodded again. Toby's voice dripped with sarcasm and

resentment. As though he didn't believe Borkowski deserved the kudos. Professional jealousy? Competition? I hadn't considered the possibility that Toby might not be a fan. Opening the wound could work in my favor.

"I take it you weren't impressed."

"It was a half-assed story." He ran his hands through his hair. His eyes followed a waitress, delivering fresh focaccia to the other end of the counter.

"Come on, Toby. Why do you say 'half-assed'? I can see there's something more. Were you involved in the story? You sound resentful."

"Yeah, I am resentful. I resent the hell out of lazy journalism. I resent taxpayers getting fucked over by corrupt businessmen. I resent colleagues who lose sight of their objectivity and allow themselves to be compromised, and then bullshit their way into an award. So yeah, resentful is an understatement."

"What happened? Talk to me."

"Borkowski had dirt on Ramirez. He had a doctored soil test dated two years earlier than the one that sent Ramirez to jail. I saw it myself on his desk. I don't know where he got it, but he didn't use it. Didn't turn it in to the prosecutor, didn't mention it in his story. If the court had been aware of the past behavior, Ramirez would've been sent to the farm for a hell of a lot longer than eighteen months. How many other toxic dumps are buried under our buildings because this guy got a hand slap instead of the root canal he deserved?"

"Why would Borkowski bury incriminating evidence? What journalist would walk away from a major headline?"

"Exactly! I cornered him one day. Told him I'd seen the report and wanted to know what happened to it. He said I should get my eyes checked and suggested I'd had a few too many martinis at lunch. Asshole!" Toby pounded his fist on the counter before continuing. "I ran it up to the editor, but

Borkowski was their star. He pushed back, kept at the drinking on the job angle. Pissed me off. What reporter ignores something that big? Right? Especially the great man himself with over two decades of journalistic integrity behind him."

"So what do you think now?" I said. "That you were mistaken?"

"Fuck no! He buried it. I just don't know why. Unless he'd developed selective Alzheimer's, it was a financially motivated decision. I can't think of any other plausible reason. There was a lot of money on the line for someone like Ramirez. If those lucrative contracts were to dry up, where would that leave his company? What's a little cash to keep one reporter from a tell-all, when you've been paying off engineers for years? The bones of the incident were undeniable. Ramirez wasn't going to get off scot-free, but eighteen months ain't the five to ten he could have gotten. Financial win-win. Hell, Borkowski even got the glory from writing the partial story."

"Proof?"

"Not a damn thing. Just my gut talking."

I watched the kitchen staff on the grill, considering this new information. It was plausible. The Toby I knew wasn't inclined toward revenge or petty jealously. If he said he had seen he report, I believed him. If Borkowski had been paid off to keep quiet, that was interesting, and it meant my instinct not to trust him was justified. The image of Ramirez, Langston, Borkowski, and the mystery man filled my mind. Was this a simple dinner or a meeting of cohorts? Was there something still going on with these guys?

"Can you think of any reason Borkowski would still have contact with Nelson Ramirez?"

He gave me a smug smile and leaned in close. "I can think of sixty-four million reasons."

20

With Rami Concrete valued at sixty-four million dollars, and seriously in bed with the city, Toby was right—there was ample motivation to keep the contracts flowing and Nelson Ramirez's reputation as untarnished as possible. The possibilities for collusion preoccupied my thoughts as I returned to the office. But what was Borkowski's motivation? Was it lucrative enough to be a retirement plan if things went south? Because if there was any truth to this, and it went public, his thirty years of hard-won reputation would be reduced to rubble. The intimate group of men I'd seen earlier in the week at Gibsons flashed in my mind. Suddenly their meeting felt like something more than dinner.

What about Alderman Langston? The toxic soil test that had put Ramirez away had occurred in Langston's ward. Bribery was commonplace in the offices of aldermen—any of them. Hell, in Chicago, a project without payola was a project that never saw the light of day. It wasn't as crass as envelopes of cash being bandied about, but everyone had an uncle, cousin, or girlfriend who needed a job or a jumpstart to a small business.

As the city's legislative branch, aldermen influenced or

controlled zoning, permits, city contracts, and licensing within their wards. They operated as individual fiefdoms, and the opportunity for graft and corruption was as easy as scoring a Chicago parking ticket. Layer in the lack of policing, and you were left with the Chicago Way. One-third of the city's elected aldermen had been convicted of corruption charges over the past forty-five years. And that was only the guys who got caught.

Or maybe I was just predisposed to assume devious intent because I thought Borkowski was a dick?

Once back in the office, I put in the call to my attorney I'd been avoiding and updated him on the possibility of a new financial development at Link-Media. I'd held off, hoping that Erik might say something or that I'd realize I'd been mistaken about what I'd heard. Nope, it was time to share, although the lawyer agreed that this was a wait-and-see situation for now. I jotted a few notes for Brynn, then picked up the phone to see if I could get someone at Delgado Engineering to talk to me about their work at the paintbrush factory.

As the receptionist came on the line, Erik brushed past my doorway and roared, "In my office, now!" I hung up promptly, wondering what had set him off. I sighed, grabbed my water bottle, and trotted down the hall after him, feeling like a five-year-old being called out by her parents. I imagined that was his intent.

Erik's door was closed when I got there. I rapped gently on the glass, let out a deep breath, and entered. He stood next to the window, arms crossed, face prepped for battle.

"What were you thinking, going after Platt?" he shot at me before I'd fully passed the threshold. I closed the door and walked over to face him.

"What are you talking about?" The confusion that must have been written on my face only seemed to aggravate him more. He paced the length of the credenza as I watched, baffled. "I spoke to him about the mayor's announcement. I was doing my job, Erik. What's got you so wired?"

"No. You weren't 'doing your job,' you were harassing a well-connected individual simply because your imagination and conspiracy theories have gotten out of control."

"Harassing? I asked a few questions. How is that harassment?" I stood open-mouthed, stunned by the accusation, playing the conversation over in my mind. Had Platt described our interaction as harassment? Obviously I'd irritated him enough to pick up the phone. "Would it piss you off if Borkowski tried to shoulder his way into a story? Or is it that I didn't wait my turn?"

As I said the words, it became clear. I knew what had happened. Platt had phoned Erik when I hadn't kept to the expected script, and Erik had gotten an earful from his powerful friend. My head had been so wrapped up in the jigsaw puzzle of the shootings that it hadn't crossed my mind that Platt would report back directly to Erik. But it shouldn't have mattered—Erik should have been on my side.

"It's not your story," he said, his voice glacial. "You keep reminding me to treat you like an employee and not my wife, so act like it. Your boss—that's me—gave you another assignment. And even then, you had to sneak in a dig at the mayor's reputation by bringing these damn shootings into it." His jaw was locked tight with controlled rage. "The highway shootings aren't yours. Back off and let Art do his job. Or do you need a refresher on the concept of insubordination?"

"What's the real problem here? That I went after what I wanted?" I felt my restraint starting to slip away.

"Don't push me, Andrea."

"Don't push you?" Anger was roiling inside me. Anger that my professional life and my personal life had twisted into one big red ball of twine. And I could no longer find the end to untangle it. "Are you saying I shouldn't push for what I want? Well, we certainly know you've had no problem seeing that your wants were taken care of!"

I felt myself on the verge of another meltdown, another painful rant that would offer only the briefest moment of release before the grief, anger, and hurt swallowed me whole. How was this ever going to work? Every time I looked at Erik, the wound was ripped open again.

"You can't throw my past in my face every time you don't get your way. I've paid enough."

"Is that what you're calling it now?" I said, unable to keep the sarcasm out of my voice.

"We're done here!" he exploded, flailing his arms at me. "This isn't working. I'm probably buying my attorney another Mercedes with this, but I can't function this way. You're fired!"

Fired? We stared at each other, not saying another word, but every drop of the pain of the last six months was seared across our faces. This moment was an inevitable outcome to our sad, twisted story. I dug deep, somewhere into my gut, to a place underneath the pain, pulled out my impassive lawyer façade, and walked out.

Hold it together, I repeated silently as I shoved papers in my tote bag. I could still feel the sting from Erik's look as I worked over my desk. Don't cry. Don't yell. Don't fall apart. Don't let anyone see you lose control. Get the important stuff, the stuff I didn't want Borkowski to pick over while he did a happy dance on my grave. I grabbed the research on the highway shootings and got the hell out.

21

Too angry to think, I barreled out of the building and stormed down the sidewalk. The art gallery windows and modern furniture stores that typically beckoned to me didn't even make it into my peripheral vision as I walked. People on the sidewalk were simply obstacles to avoid, their conversations nothing but the buzz of mosquitoes. I pounded forward, not having a destination, my feet taking the lead because my brain couldn't.

The L rumbled overhead, moving north on Franklin, shaking me into awareness of my surroundings. I was too incensed to go home and lick my wounds, and too agitated to do anything productive. I spotted a Starbucks half a block north on the corner of Franklin and Chicago. A cup of tea and a chair should buy me a few minutes to regroup before I did anything I'd regret tomorrow.

A cardboard cup in hand, I sank into an upholstered chair in the corner. Resting my head against the chair, I dipped my tea bag and fought to control my emotions. I didn't know who I was angrier with, Erik or myself. How had I let this happen? More important, what the hell was I going to do about it?

Go back and apologize? Beg for my job back? Even if it worked, Erik would lord it over me with the satisfaction of a child toying with a grasshopper before he killed it. I could call Tierney, do my penance, and pretend to be happy there. Not appealing, but an option. And options were what I needed right now. I sipped my tea and stared at the bag of files at my feet. If I didn't press forward on this story, would anyone?

The balances in my bank accounts flashed in my mind. I had some time—not an indefinite amount, but enough of a cushion to play this out if I was careful. If I could prove something else was going on, that CPD's assessment wasn't the full story, and could get to the bottom of it, I could convince the *Tribune* to run it. Maybe even a national. No one would turn down a freelance writer breaking a story this big. And if I couldn't? If Erik was right, if everything CPD said was already the full truth, and I was just someone with an overly active imagination rushing to a conclusion, Tierney would still be an option.

I grabbed my cup and walked out to the corner to flag a cab. A fleeting desire to enjoy the leisurely Friday afternoon flickered on the edges of my brain. A walk on the lake path, a glass of wine at an outdoor cafe, anything to distract me. I shut the thought down. There would be time for relaxation after I nailed this story.

As the taxi eased through the backed-up traffic moving south on Wells, my mind rumbled through real estate scenarios. My digging had revealed that the Orton Group, formed only six months earlier, had not only purchased the two properties, but seventeen others as well. Why the land grab? And who was behind them?

I jumped out of the cab when we caught the red light at Clark and Wacker, then walked around the corner to a neighboring highrise. I glanced at my watch: 3:15 p.m. Lane would still be in her office, attending to last-minute prep for her weekend open house, the only time I could reliably expect to find her behind a desk instead of behind the steering wheel of her car. Lane's database meant she could access information on the transactions that Brynn couldn't. After signing in with security, I rode the elevator to the fourteenth floor.

"Hi, Rachel," I said to the firm's long-time receptionist. "Is she in?"

"Sure is. Go on back. Don't mind the closed door. She's just holed up in there with her music."

I walked past the warren of cubicles, then rapped lightly on the door, but didn't wait for a response. Tim McGraw's melodic voice played at concert volume as I stepped in, wincing at the volume and the harshness of the fluorescent light in the windowless room.

"Have you ever considered headphones?" I yelled, a headache already starting to form behind my eyes.

"Your country-western music bias has no place here. Do what you want in your office. Here I control the playlist," she said, but turned the volume down anyway. "Quite frankly, I don't understand your problem. Have you seen McGraw? He could sing me the Constitution and I'd be drooling."

"Great way to judge musical talent." I slipped into the chair in front of her. "How do you work in here without any natural light?" The room sent quivers—not the good kind—racing up my back every time I was here.

"Did you drop in just to give me advice on office acoustics?" She tugged on the neckline of the knit top threatening to fall off her shoulder, then pushed her purple reading glasses to the top of her head. "Functional is all I need. You know I don't spend much time in the office. The address on my business card should read, 'black Mercedes, C-Class,' and my license plate number. That's where the real work is done."

Lane rambled on, her speech playing at double speed. She

was typing with one hand and pawing through papers on her desk with the other. Some would compliment her multitasking skills or praise her obsessive, one-dimensional focus on the deal. But I knew firsthand how easily her frenetic side could spill over the edge.

"Hey, I meant to call you," she said, not looking up. "That unit in your building just went into contract. Twenty-five percent appreciation in two years. Let me know when your reno's wrapped and I'll get yours listed."

"You want two commissions from me in one year?" I laughed. "Lane, I'm not flipping my co-op. We've been through this before. I'm staying put for a very long time. Renovating to my tastes, not to the market's."

"I just thought with the divorce and all, you could've changed your mind. Might want something smaller. It's just you rambling around in there. Why do you need three thousand square feet? What about investing in a three-flat? I've got a new listing on Sedgwick with great cash flow." She looked at me for a reaction, didn't get the one she wanted, huffed, and turned back to her screen.

"No, I don't need all that space, but I'm not selling." I wasn't ready to tell Lane I'd lost my job, not today. Couldn't face the questions, the "you shouldn't have left him" rant, the "I told you it was a bad idea to change careers" rant, which were really all about her. There'd be time for that later. "My renovation is all the real estate activity I can handle right now. I came over because I need your database." I pulled Brynn's spreadsheet out of the bag at my feet and passed it across the desk.

She scanned the top sheet for a moment, then flipped to the subsequent pages. "That's a lot of movement. What is this?" She turned to the large map on the left wall, the room's only piece of pseudo decoration. "Englewood. Not my territory, but looks like things are heating up. Hmm."

"Have you heard any rumors about development? Tax incentives? Anything that might spur activity?"

"News to me. The demographics down there are tough. You can't do residential, unless it's low-income rental, and private developers aren't touching that segment of the market," she mused.

She swung her chair back to face her monitor and hit a few keys. Pulling her glasses back down to her nose, I watched her eyes run down the screen. Listened to the clicks of her keyboard as she worked, her head slowly shaking side to side as she read the screen.

"Nothing that I'm finding." She looked up at me, then picked up the documents again. "Why? Are you thinking development?"

I handed her a slip of paper. "Does this name ring any bells? They've closed nearly twenty deals in the last three months."

Lane stopped typing and looked at me, eyes wide. "Never heard of them, but I'm not up on the commercial developers." Again back to the screen. Again a shake of the head as she contemplated the information she was seeing.

She looked at me, brow furrowed, but I had her full attention. "What is this all about?"

"I'm not sure yet." My mind ran through options, trying to connect the dots. Opportunistic buyers? My gut said no. No one buys twenty properties without a plan.

Lane watched me, uncharacteristically quiet, trying to see where I was taking this. Most likely gauging whether there was an opportunity to make a buck.

"What can you access for me on pricing trends? I'm looking for comps. Unusual spikes in pricing. Anything that feels out of the ordinary."

"Are you going to tell me what this is about? 'Cause I'm not the research library. I do have two open houses this weekend I'm trying to prepare for."

"Just run the report, please."

She rolled her eyes, but her fingers slid over the keyboard.

"It would be helpful if you gave me some idea of what you're looking for. I don't have all day to devote to your pet projects."

"Short memory, Lane." I couldn't keep the irritation out of my voice. "Do I really need to remind you of how often I've been the one you called when your credit card bill was two months overdue? Hell, I practically run a finance company devoted to your overspending. Don't you dare give me grief." We glowered at each other for a moment. For once, Lane had the good sense to keep quiet, so I proceeded. "I'm not sure what I'm looking for. These guys are buying for a reason, and I need to know why. Look at the data and tell me what feels odd."

Lane swung back to her desk and thumped on the keys in irritation. *Too bad,* I thought. She owed me, and I needed her database.

"Okay, here it is." She pulled a document off the printer and pushed it in my direction. "Prices are flat to last year. Now can I get on with my work?"

"Wait." I stood and walked around the desk to the map on the wall. "Zip 60621 runs from roughly State Street west to Racine. Is there any additional segmenting you can do that would isolate the area closest to the highway? Say the eastern third of the zip code?"

Lane snatched the printout from my hand, muttering. "Payback's a bitch."

"Don't start," I said. "Your balance sheet is so deep in the red it's bleeding. Can you segment it?"

She held her tongue but continued to type.

As she worked, my eyes rolled over the sparse room. Engraved crystal plaques filled her desk, touting her sales prowess: 10 Million Dollar Club, Top Producer Award, Top Listing Agent. A powerhouse in her professional life, a frickin' mess in her personal one. I never knew when the next swindling deadbeat boyfriend, overdue debt, or drunken fender bender would pop out of the mayhem that was Lane's life. Inevitably her problems became mine when she needed help extracting herself from one mess or another. The phone call would come, and she'd need money, my car, a bed for a few days. It had been that way since our mother's death back when we were teens and would most likely remain that way. My sense of obligation ran too deep.

"I've divided the area into thirds. East, middle, west." She laid another printout on the desk in front of me. "You're on your own from here. I have to go pick up my brochures before the printer closes at five." She lifted her hands and shooed me out of the office.

"Hold on." I read through the numbers, thoughts ricocheting in my head. "This says prices have declined twenty-eight percent since the shootings began, but only east of the highway." Maybe that was the point.

22

Five a.m. and sleep continued to elude me. My email called to me like a drug, as it had been doing since I'd asked for a meeting with my anonymous writer. I reached across the bed for my phone, willing a response from Sgnt1764 to be waiting for me. Telepathy failed me again, and the mailbox remained as empty as it had been the last 147 times I'd checked.

Walter stared up at me through half-opened eyes from his perch at the end of the bed. "It's still dark out there, dummy. Go back to sleep," his lazy gaze seemed to say.

Impossible. I dragged over a pillow that had been flung in my late-night tossing and turning and placed it behind my head. Then I pulled the linen duvet up closer to my chin and traced the city lights and shadows that fell across my ceiling through the open drapes.

Why? Why? Why? reverberated in my head. Why was the Orton Group buying property? I had no information that said these land purchases were connected in any way to the highway shootings, so why was my radar beeping at me? Being threatened with bodily harm did that, I guessed.

After a quick shower, I threw on a simple cotton wrap dress, made tea, scooped some yogurt and fruit into a bowl, and sat down to get to work just as the rising sun was lighting up the Hancock Building in a blaze of orange outside my windows.

I started with the pile of documents related to Rami Concrete. Their list of contracts extended throughout the state, many of them governmental. They had nearly three thousand employees at four locations. The company was privately held, so confirming Toby's estimate of Ramirez's net worth would take more time and creativity, but projected revenue for Rami Construction was in the just-shy-of-a-billion range according to *Crain's*. The Chicago projects alone showed that Rami had gotten their hands deep in nearly every large-scale construction project for the last twenty years.

All that proved was that Ramirez had enough money to shut Borkowski up. Hell, he could probably shut almost anyone up. Who else might he want silenced? Or need favors from? An interesting thought.

I took another sip of tea and considered the possibilities. Politicians, developers, any number of business types could be susceptible to financial arm-twisting. But so what? That didn't mean there was a connection to the highway shootings. The image of Nelson Ramirez and Alderman Anthony Langston at Gibsons popped back into my head. I wondered if Rami Concrete had done any projects in Langston's district. Another project for Brynn. Oh right, no more Brynn. I made a note to myself to give her a call later; she'd already left for the day when things had blown up, and I wanted her to hear the news from me.

I reached for a copy of the story that had convinced Toby of Borkowski's loose ethics. Was this a pattern? I tapped the keyboard again and scrolled, looking for any additional stories Borkowski had written on Rami Concrete or Alderman

Langston. A sixteen-month-old softball piece about Langston approving a zoning change for a liquor store popped up. The only unusual aspect was that Borkowski had neglected to mention the community outrage over the backdoor fast-tracking when every other journalist had hit that hard.

Where is that email?

I picked up the phone and stared at the text Michael Hewitt had just sent, then placed it back on the dining table without responding. This was his second request for a copy of the emails from Sgnt1764, and it made me squirm. Was he asking me as a cop? Did I want him to? The voice of the man who had threatened me popped back into my mind.

I sipped my tea and stared at the screen. Sharing the information with Michael would be a gamble. On the plus side, I might be able to win his help resetting the story. The downside was that it would also mean Janek would be pulled in. Hard to imagine that going well. Janek would prefer a dental extraction to working with me. But was trusting Michael smart? I wasn't certain. Images of a CPD-supplied body guard came to mind. Goodbye, story.

No, until I knew more, involving Michael had more risk than reward. I slid the phone back across the table, opting for avoidance.

Victims, locations, real estate data, all the known facts. I wrote them all on Post-its and added them to those already gracing the dining room wall. Then I moved on to unknowns and did the same. The soil-testing company at the shooter's location. The connection between Nelson Ramirez, Anthony Langston, and Art Borkowski. The Orton Group. Father Brogan's lone wolf. Any bit of information that seemed odd or had a possible association, I placed on the wall.

Standing back, I surveyed my work, hoping the visual map

would help me see connections and holes to fill. I rearranged a few of the notes and stared at it some more.

The soil-testing company had come up twice now. Coincidence? Unlikely. I returned to my laptop and reopened their website, scanning the company information. Delgado Engineering was also privately held, run by Colin Delgado, the eldest son of its founder, Charles Delgado. A sweep through the listing of services did little to enlighten me on what might have been occurring at the paintbrush factory. Hazardous waste? Soil stability? Maybe the buyer just wanted to build an addition. I didn't know enough about the process to come up with options.

Where were these guys? I clicked on the contact page. LaSalle and Hubbard. Maybe I could find someone in the office to enlighten me. I grabbed my bag, threw on a linen jacket to tighten up my casual attire, then headed downstairs to hail a cab.

Delgado Engineering occupied space in a bland mid-rise on the west side of LaSalle. The utilitarian brick and a no-frills entrance seemed appropriate for a business that dealt in dirt. The outer doors were unlocked. That was a good sign, but the glass on the other side of the vestibule stopped my progress. No front desk and, therefore, no attendant to let me in.

I located an electronic directory on the wall to my right, stepped over, and paged through to the listing. Delgado Engineering—Room 807. I punched in the code and listened to the phone buzz seven floors above. As I waited for a response, the door behind me opened. A bookish-looking man stepped to the sensor, flashed his badge, and pulled on the door as the buzzer sounded. Perfect. I smiled at him and hustled in after.

The elevators were straight ahead. The car opened immediately, and we stepped inside.

"What floor?" I asked.

"Eight," he replied.

"Me too." His brightly colored plaid pants and lime green polo shirt suggested either a short work day or colorblindness. "Tough day to be stuck in the office. Looks like you'd rather be on the course."

He smiled and gave a little chuckle. A thin clump of strawberry blond hair fell over his wire-rimmed glasses, and he pushed it back over his thinning crown.

"Vacation interruptus. Just have to file a report, then I'm off to chase a little white ball, not that I'm very good at catching it."

The doors opened, and he motioned for me to exit. Pausing to glance at the signage, I saw that 807 was just to my right. My elevator companion was already walking in that direction, his hand on the doorknob. He looked at me quizzically as I approached, but said nothing as I followed him into the office.

"Good morning, Patrick," the receptionist said, contemplating me oddly, as if visitors were a rare event. "Sorry to drag you in here on a Saturday. Kristoff made a bloody mess of the Schiffer report. It's on your desk. All the data formatting is off. Can't make heads or tails of it. Of course it was supposed to have gone out last night. The big guy is screaming."

"Don't worry about it, Darlene. I'll get it straightened out, but I'm getting tired of this. That kid needs to learn the software or move on to gentler pastures. I don't care who his daddy plays nice with around here."

Patrick nodded at me, then continued past the reception desk and down the narrow corridor. Darlene looked at me over the top of her glasses.

"What can I help you with?" she asked. Her tone told me I had better not be there to complicate her day further.

"I'm a reporter with Link-Media." I handed her my business card. "I'm doing some background research on a story, and I was hoping to speak with someone who could answer a few questions about soil testing."

She tugged on a small pearl that dangled from a chain around her neck as she contemplated my card.

"And you thought you'd just sashay in here, without an appointment, on a Saturday no less, and we'd drop everything to help you out?" Her long auburn bob swayed as she scolded me.

"I was in the area, so I thought I would take a chance." I smiled back. "If I could just ask a couple of basic questions? Then I'll make an appointment to come back if I need more detail."

Patrick was back, now standing behind the desk, a thick stack of papers in hand, listening to the exchange.

"I've never heard of Link-Media," my inquisitor said. "Waltzing in here unannounced like this is some *60 Minutes* segment ain't going to work. If you want to interview someone, you need to have an appointment like everyone else." She tilted her head back to her computer screen. "The boss will decide if he wants to speak with you. I'm not going out on that limb."

I looked at Patrick and smiled hopefully, directing my plea at him. "Five minutes. I promise."

He hesitated, then said, "My program will take about that long to cycle. We can talk until then, but if it finishes faster, I'm going to cut you off. I'm not going to miss my tee time."

After handing the document he was holding to Darlene with a few words of instruction, he motioned for me to follow. Darlene scowled at me over her monitor.

His janitor closet of an office was at the end of the hall. My chest tightened immediately at seeing the pressing tower of books, binders, and charts that formed a chaotic mess in the small room. A tiny sliver of a window faced the brick of the building next door, adding to the gloom. Patrick flicked a light switch, giving the room the harsh glow from a fluorescent pendant overhead, then stepped over a stack of files.

We took seats at his metal desk, the brown enamel chipped

and scratched with decades of use. He tapped a few keys on his PC, looked at his watch, then over to me.

"So what is it that you want to know?"

"Why don't we start with an overview of the services your firm provides?" I had no idea what I was looking for, simply hoping that throwing out questions might spark an idea or lead me down a new path.

"Our services are very focused. As you know, we test soil. Pure and simple. Composition, chemical analysis, thermal resistance, contaminants, structure, compaction, the full gamut."

"Are you hired by individual land owners or by commercial enterprises?"

"Both, but our emphasis is on corporate work. An individual might hire us to investigate contamination from buried oil tanks on their property, for example. Our corporate work spans a broader range. Environmental issues, of course, are a big part of the business. Regulations have changed substantially over the last fifty years, and remediation can be an enormous expense. Not that lawyers have made that any easier."

By the tone of his voice, I suspected he'd had an unpleasant run-in with an aggressive litigator. The image of the paintbrush factory pushed into my mind, as did the falsified report that had sent Nelson Ramirez to jail. Was the brush factory a toxic site?

"How are these samples obtained?"

"Each situation dictates the number of samples, the depth, and method by which we obtain them. There is no answer to that question without understanding the objective of the test."

On the wall to the right of Patrick's head, in a patchwork of paper pinned to the bulletin board, was a photo of a man standing against the type of truck I had seen at the factory.

"Is that the type of equipment you would use to obtain samples for environmental testing?" I nodded at the image of the truck with the monster drill.

Patrick turned his head and squinted at the wall. He got to his feet and pointed to the photo. "Are you looking at this vehicle?"

"Yes, the truck with the large drill."

"No, that's used for taking core samples. We use that when a client needs foundation testing."

"Can you explain what you mean by that?"

"In simple terms, it's the ability of the soil to hold weight. Structural integrity to support a building of considerable size."

"Like a high-rise?"

He looked at his computer screen and typed. "Not in this case. I'd say a commercial complex of some kind. Four stories max."

"I was at one of your test sites recently." He raised a brow. "What can you tell me about testing at this address?" I scribbled the address of the paintbrush factory on a piece of paper and handed it to him.

He looked at the address, then back at me contemplating my request. After a couple keystrokes, he scrunched his eyes and said, "I don't know what you're getting at with these questions. The one thing I will tell you is that we've been contracted to perform that same testing on three additional locations within a thousand yards of that site. So like I said, I'm thinking a complex."

23

I slipped back into the folding chair at my dining table, a Pellegrino in my left hand and a thick falafel sandwich wrapped in aluminum foil in my right. As tahini threatened to drip down my hand, I powered up my computer and dug into the pita before I had a soggy mess of garbanzo beans on my hands.

Who was behind the Orton Group? A couple of minutes on the Secretary of State's website and I had the barebones basics. The LLC had been formed six months earlier. The registered agent was Gabriel Abascal with Abascal Services. It sounded like a service provider—one of those business mills that does all the filing for you, serving as a required local contact and mailing address and nothing more. There'd be no association with the business beyond an annual invoice. Completely legal, but was the service being used for convenience or camouflage? Regardless, it made it harder to track down the guys behind the scene.

I plowed on, using my full repertoire of search tricks to find out more about the business. Nothing. Not only was there nothing of substance on the purchaser, but Abascal Services seemed ignored by Google as well. Who operates a business without a web presence when any ten-year-old could design a rudimentary site?

Brynn could dig. If there were a live link buried somewhere deep on a server in Russia, she'd locate it. I opened the French doors to the terrace and picked up my phone to call her, parking myself on a chaise before delivering the news.

"Sorry to interrupt your Saturday, but I wanted you to know that yesterday after you left, Erik fired me."

"What? He can't do that."

"Yeah, he can. Apparently, he disagreed with how I handled Platt. The timing isn't ideal, but we were on this path one way or another."

"What happens to the highway story?" she asked, and then, her voice softer, "What happens to me?"

"I'm not sure." It seemed unlikely that Borkowski would pick up the story and even more unlikely that Brynn would be given a shot at stepping beyond administrative work. "I wish I could give you some assurances."

"Don't worry about me, I'll figure something out. But this story will get buried if you walk away. Whatever you need, I'll be there. You've gotta find a way to get at the truth or we'll never know why these people were killed."

I'd already come to the same conclusion. I promised Brynn I'd be in touch and ended the call.

The warmth of the sun felt magnificent as I leaned back on the chaise and surveyed the terrace that wrapped three sides of the apartment. I'd fallen in love with the luxury of the large outdoor space the moment I'd seen the apartment. Now sporting slate tile, lushly planted boxes, and a smattering of comfortable furniture, it had been my first renovation priority. A grand lady who had been loved and then neglected, the co-op had been quietly begging to be made beautiful again. I had thought I was the one to restore her plaster walls, coffered ceilings, and inlaid flooring. But after yesterday, would someone else have to do the honors? Would I lose my cherished home along with my job and my marriage?

I stared at the skyline, hoping for a flash of genius to strike. Instead there was a ping as an email came in on my phone. A response from Sgnt1764. I bolted upright and read. Thank God Erik hadn't cut off my account access yet.

Illusion and mirrors. Deception and lies. What is the goal? What is the prize?

Have you asked the right questions? Can you see through the haze? Are you up to the task or lost in the maze?

Who stands to profit? What's the secret within?

Killer or thief, the goal is the same.

I Know Who He Is!

Heat flushed the back of my neck. The highway sniper. This guy knew the highway sniper. I read the note again. *Deception. Goal. Prize.* He was telling me the cops had it wrong—that there was more to the story, just as I suspected. And for the second time, he'd used the word profit.

"When can we meet?" I immediately shot back. I stared at my inbox, willing him to be patiently waiting, ready to give me an instantaneous response.

Deception. Were the shootings being credited to the wrong people? My initial instinct had been targeted hits, not random stray shots. But the victims had checked out. Average joes with average lives, going about their business. Michael had dismissed Angel Velasquez's past gang association as a motive. Maybe random was the point? What's more frightening than a sniper on the loose with no rhyme or reason to his targets? Any one of us could be next. What did the sniper want us afraid of? Gangs were obvious. Was that the deception—a misdirection?

Or was that the distraction? If so, what was the goal, other than fear? What was the prize? Location? Were the shootings tied to the real estate activity? If so, that explained his reference to profit.

Giddy with new purpose, I returned to the dining table.

It had to be the location. I pulled a map out of my folder and spread it out on the table. Brynn had already marked the shooting locations in red. I added a blue dot at the paintbrush factory and another for the neighboring building to signify the sales. Rifling through my tote bag, I pulled the transaction list out of the file folder and started working down chronologically, marking each sale on the map.

"Botox won't take care of a saggy neck, so I'd give more thought to your posture if I were you. Chin up, honey. Keep it taut."

I'd been so engrossed in my work, I hadn't noticed Lane standing in the center of my living room. Once again, I'd forgotten to latch the door.

"The doorman is supposed call before sending anyone up," I said, folding up the map and sliding it back into the folder.

"Norman and I are buds. He knew you were home, so—"

"If you've stopped to buy me lunch, I've already eaten. I'll take a rain check, though."

The dig slipped out before I could catch myself. Her indebtedness had gotten so out of control that three years ago, I'd set up a spreadsheet to track my contributions to the Lane Kellner emergency fund. She was always just one more big deal away from settling up. Maybe when pigs flew, or it snowed in July, or I just stopped feeling like a guilty shmuck.

She plopped into the chair across the table, her bleached hair blown out too big, her tight red crepe skirt too short, her print blouse one size too small, and one too many buttons undone. I guess we both broke the conservative Midwestern dress rules. The gray and navy pantsuits of my legal career had quickly been replaced by a curated selection of architecturally inspired wardrobe basics.

"You know me, Diet Coke and a Clif Bar get me through the day." She flipped a loose strand of hair out of her eyes and wiggled in her seat like a kid about to get the super-sized hot fudge sundae. "I've got a proposal. An amazing deal, actually. It's time you start thinking about what's next, don't you think? Your financial next. Life post-Erik. Invest some of that divorce dough. Protect yourself."

She leaned over, fishing around for something in her bag.

"Lane, please! Flashing me your boobs isn't going to get me to do anything but run screaming from the room. Button it back up."

"When did you become a prude?"

"Hardly. But getting a peek at my sister's nipple is not in my top five good surprises."

She humphed and straightened up. And, thankfully, adjusted the gapping silk.

"I think you're on to something with your tip on Englewood. It's been a while since I've been ready to invest myself, but I looked at the market conditions, and I can see a tremendous upside."

Her sales voice was switched on, and I knew already that I wasn't going to like what came next. She shoved a couple of documents across at me as I waited for the pitch.

"I talked to one of my banking contacts. It's not official yet, but this could be solid." She tapped her finger on the page. "Said he hasn't talked to anyone else, but the deal won't last. There are two conjoining properties."

"What are you talking about? What properties?"

"Right here." She moved the document closer to me. "About a block east from that factory you talked about, marching fast toward bankruptcy, and we have the inside scoop. I figure we can get in for about a hundred and thirty thousand dollars, might go as high as a hundred and forty-five, each. We do a quick clean and paint, contact the boys who bought the factory, then flip the suckers for twice what we paid within six months. Or sit on the sidelines for the cash flow."

I felt my jaw clench and my head swing side to side. I should have known my questions would light up the greed region in her cerebral cortex—"Deal, deal, deal!" in flashing red lights. And I was supposed to be the finance guy.

"We? I can guess what that means," I said, unable to keep my tone neutral. "Do you really think I need to complicate my life any more than it is already? You want me scrubbing floors and wielding a paint roller as I field calls from divorce attorneys, and —by the way—try to do my job?"

"You're being dramatic again," she said, inspecting the gold bangle on her wrist and shifting in the rickety chair. "I know people. We hire out. This is what I do, remember? I promise you wouldn't even chip your manicure in the process. You'd be the silent partner."

"You mean I'd be the banker." I pushed the document back at her.

With a sigh she flopped back in the chair, and shook her head. As if this were merely Monopoly money and a damn good deal obvious to anyone smart enough to see it.

"Lane, don't go there. You're into me for a solid twenty grand right now. I'm not your damn bookie."

"I'm not asking for a loan," she shot back. "I brought an investment opportunity to my sister. You know, even if you do get alimony, it won't last forever. Think about it. You've got adjustments to make. Your salary isn't going to fill the gap between the lifestyle you've been accustomed to and your new reality. Renovation costs, new furniture, and the monthly HOAs on this place aren't exactly cheap. I'm not saying you're going to be left with a beans-and-rice budget; your attorney's no novice. But if it were me, I would've gone with more of the pit bull type. Bury Erik in subpoenas and see when he plays chicken."

"Thanks for the divorce strategy advice, but I don't want to hear it. Backseat driving isn't helpful. Surprising, I know, but I'd prefer not to hate my ex-husband."

"Okay, okay. Touchy subject. I'm just looking out for you." She laid an MLS printout on the table, tapping her finger on the two properties. "Honey, it's time to get smart. Think about it."

I was getting smart all right. Smart to Lane's schemes. I tried to push the truth of my financial vulnerability to the background. Reality could wait.

Divorce attorneys had a way of taking what seemed simple, straightforward, and twisting it into some Rubik's cube. Pre-divorce assets. Marital assets. Depositions. Motions. Was that stupid, god-awful ugly ruby necklace he gave me eight years ago a gift, or something to add to the balance sheet? And that didn't even factor in my current employment status.

A ball of foil gum wrapper bounced off my forehead and pulled me back to the here and now.

"You with me? Or did you shift off into dreamland?"

More like a waking nightmare. I glared at her. How could she even bring a real estate purchase up right now? "Lane, I can't go there. It may be a good investment, but I just can't cope." I turned back to my computer, ready for this conversation to be over.

She sighed one more time, then grabbed her notes.

"All right, but you're missing a great deal. I thought I should make the offer, sister to sister, but I'll move on to someone else."

"How about putting a dent in what you owe me before you move on?"

Again, the jab came out before I could stop it, but this one I didn't regret. I was frustrated. I was angry. I was hurt. And if

Lane was going to be the one to turn the knife, she should expect whatever venom spewed out.

She smiled sweetly as she stood, yanking her skirt back into place.

"Got a sale closing next week. I'll send you a check off the top."

"Sure," I said, not looking up from my laptop. Been there. Done that. Got the stupid T-shirt. And didn't have the energy to remind her of any of it.

She swung her purse over her shoulder and headed off to look for a more gullible partner, while I turned my attention back to my computer and forced back the tears. Damn it! Why was I crying? Was it the truth of Lane's financial warning, the continuing agony of Erik's betrayal, or the endless responsibility I felt for Lane?

I wiped my eyes, took in a deep breath and shut everything out of my mind, everything except the shootings.

24

Cai sat at a small table on the outdoor patio at Nico next to a lushly planted box of herbs and trailing vines. A burgundy slip dress accented her pale, delicate skin. Her wineglass was half-empty, and her thumbs were rapidly tapping out a message. Quintessential Cai. An alpha girl who never squandered idle minutes.

"Sorry I'm late." I maneuvered between the tables and around the plants, then leaned in for a quick hug before taking the seat across from her. "Lane hijacked me this afternoon. Took me down another rat hole and I lost track of time."

My eyes followed pedestrians as I settled in, conscious of any gaze that lingered, anyone who seemed to hover expectantly. A man leaned against a lamppost thirty yards south, a Cubs hat blocking his face as he tapped into his phone. Was he the guy? I hadn't been able to shake my discomfort since the threatening phone call. I knew I should tell Michael, but I'd held back.

"Anything good? Or just her usual plea to have you play mommy?" Cai asked. She inhaled the rich aroma of her cabernet and took a sip, my answer a foregone conclusion.

"She's considering buying some investment property. Wants

me to come on board. You know Lane, always looking for a quick buck."

"And you're the ATM. I assume your response had something to do with hell no."

"And hell freezing over." I signaled the waiter to bring two glasses of whatever Cai was drinking. We both knew the wine menu at Nico well enough that favorites had been established. "I also got fired yesterday, so even if my resolve were weak, the bank account is a good deterrent."

"What? Wait a minute. Erik fired you?" Her glass came back to the table, and she leaned forward, her eyes round. "What happened?"

"I made the mistake of challenging the male ego. Pushed ahead on the highway shootings even though it wasn't my turf. I defended my right to keep the story and got canned for it." I raised my glass in mock salute.

"In other words, insubordination. That is, if you're female. A man would be called tough. Well, that should add an interesting new layer to your divorce. Have you talked to counsel yet?"

"Yesterday, but about another issue. My list seems to grow daily."

"There's more?"

I sighed, feeling the emotion of the last twenty-four hours draining me. "I overheard a phone call earlier this week. It sounded like the business might be in financial trouble. I think Erik's looking for a partner."

"Lawyer up, honey, lawyer up. This could leave you holding the bag, as in a bag of shit. Employed or not, Link-Media is a marital asset. If he dilutes that asset through investment or debt—"

"I know. I'm screwed any way I turn."

"So what are you going to do? Keep feeling beaten down and sorry for yourself? Or come out swinging?"

Cai looked at me, her eyes full of challenge. Prodding me to shed the hurt and the pain. Knowing the questions that were forming in my mind.

"Can't I have the weekend to wallow in self-pity and failure?"

"Self-pity is boring. Honey, it's time for some tough love. You've grieved enough already over Erik, the jackass. Time to shake it off, move on. It's time for offensive maneuvers. Start by running a credit check on both Erik and the business. See if he's hiding anything. I'll email you the contact info for that PI I've used. I know you haven't wanted to go that route, but you might want to reconsider under the circumstances. This guy can dig so deep Erik will feel like he's had a colonic with a fire hose. Hell, I'll even foot the bill if I can be there to see the look on his face when a judge slaps him upside the head for lying, via his bank account."

"Can I finish my wine first?" I laughed awkwardly, emotionally exhausted. I was letting Erik control the situation, allowing my future to be defined by a man who treated me badly. I knew Cai was right. It was time to shake this off.

"Cheers," I said, raising my glass. "Thanks for the reality check."

"That's me, here to kick your ass anytime. And I expect the same in return."

"Actually," I started, "if I put aside this most recent setback, the way out of this mess hasn't changed. My probing is making someone uncomfortable. I have to keep on this."

"What are you saying? Uncomfortable how?"

"I got a phone call. Some guy warning me away."

"A threat! Andrea, who have you told?"

"I'm being careful. Look, I need this story. I need to find out who's behind these highway shootings, what's really happening. That's a story I can sell. Right?"

My cell pinged me with a new email, and I pounced.

Tonight. 7:00 Corner of Cermak and Wentworth. Bring company and I'm gone. Sgnt1764, yes!

"*I'll be there,*" I typed back. My shoulders relaxed, and I let out what felt like the first full breath of air in days. Finally, a break.

"A smile. I hope someone sent you a naughty text, because you're making me nervous with this talk about crazy phone calls."

I glanced at the clock on my phone—6:15—calculating how long it would take me to get to my car and then to the meeting location.

"Something better. I'm going to run. Wine's on me," I said, throwing a couple of twenties on the table. "I have a source who's been sending me emails. I think he knows who the sniper is. He wants to meet tonight." I grabbed my phone. "I'm sending you a text with the location of the meet and the guy's email address."

"Wait," Cai said, putting her hand on my arm, her voice filled with alarm. "Are you going alone? You can't be serious. Someone's threatened you. This isn't smart."

I smiled and squeezed her hand hoping to reassure her and myself. "If you don't hear from me by ten, call Michael Hewitt and tell him where I went."

THE STREET TEEMED with visitors ogling the hanging duck carcasses and mooncakes artfully displayed in the Chinatown shop windows. The dinner parade was as much a part of the experience as chopsticks and menus with pictures. I stood, my back against the brick wall of a gift shop at the intersection of Cermak and Wentworth, listening to the screech of the Red Line train and smelling the garlic and deep-fried fish that emanated from the restaurants around me. Locals hurried home with bags full of bok choy and long beans, while tourists swung their heads from sight to sight, in awe of the foreignness of it all. I scanned faces, watching for a gaze that hung on a bit too long, a subtle nod of acknowledgment. Nothing.

Had I missed an email? A change of time or place? I pulled out my phone. Nothing. Twenty-five minutes past our meeting time and counting. How long should I wait? Or was this just some stupid game? I shifted my weight from right foot to left and wiggled my toes, trying to relieve the pinch. The shop-keeper inside had now poked her head out to look at me for the third time, probably starting to wonder if I was a working girl. With nothing else to do, I scrolled my email and continued to scan the street, craving an order of vegetable pot stickers.

After another half hour and another fifteen checks of the phone, I finally decided the guy was a no-show. If he was trying to test my patience, he'd won. It was nearly 8:00 p.m. I was tired and hungry, and my shoes were meant for dating, not stalking. I should have called Lao Tse Chen and had food delivered to my corner forty-five minutes ago. I sent Cai a text that the meet had been a bust, I was fine, and I'd call her when I got home. I took one more look at the busy sidewalks, then turned and headed west on Cermak toward my car.

I rounded the corner at Archer, bypassing the opportunity for takeout. Surely there were some salad fixings in the fridge I could throw together before a hot bath, a trashy novel, and an early bedtime.

A man dashed across the street in front of me as I reached my car. Wait, a Cubs hat? Was this the same guy I'd seen at Nico?

I flung myself into my car and tapped the lock. My heart pounding, I watched as he disappeared into a dumpling shop. I was letting paranoia get the better of me. I closed my eyes and let out a breath, feeling my body relax. When I opened my eyes,

I noticed a flyer had been tucked under my windshield blocking my view. Probably a menu for a new restaurant with a shoestring marketing budget. I opened the door and tugged it out, tossing the flyer on top of my bag. A handwritten note scrawled on the back caught my eye, and I plucked the paper back.

Pull back the layers. Expose the lies. Who stands to profit? Who sits on the side? I know who they are!

Sgnt1764 had been here at my car. I swung around, scrutinizing every person on the street. Was he watching me now? Why hadn't he identified himself? What did this mean? I flipped over the flyer. It was a notice for a community meeting. Alderman Langston's meeting. Tonight, starting in two minutes. I shoved the car in gear and flew.

25

Cars lined the street around St. Joseph's Catholic Church. Finding a spot two blocks south, I parked and scurried into the community center nearly fifteen minutes into the meeting. Had I missed whatever Sgnt1764 had wanted me to see? Why the games? Was there a reason I had needed to stand on a street corner in Chinatown for an hour?

Windows glowed in the waning light of the evening, and I could hear a man's voice, loud and commanding, resonating through the open windows. I gently opened the doors, careful not to let them slam shut, and tiptoed in. The large central room that had been filled with children when I'd met with Father Brogan earlier in the week was now a sea of folding chairs. The small tables and toys and easels had been pushed to the side. Thirty, maybe forty adults sat with their backs to me. Some were slumped in their chairs like high school kids listening to a lecture on ancient Greece, others tried to distract young children they'd dragged along, and an eager handful listened with rapt attention.

Alderman Anthony Langston stood at the front of the room.

His makeshift dais was a portable wood podium stacked on top of a folding table, with a microphone at his side. He hunched over it awkwardly, the height too low to stand, too tall to sit, as he attempted to pacify a resident angry over the recent addition of parking meters to the street in front of his apartment. Surely that wasn't what I was here to listen to. Two men in navy business suits sat to Langston's left, looking every inch as out of place as I was in this room of tank tops and basketball shorts.

Langston's complexion seemed to flare red as he spoke, as if the effort were causing all the blood to his rush to his head. With his bulbous face and equally round body, I pictured his head deflating like a balloon when he removed his tie.

I took an empty seat in the back row, hoping to be inconspicuous. Unfortunately, as one of only three white faces in the room, blending in was impossible. Father Brogan sat in the first row in front of the suits. He turned when I entered, then smiled and nodded. As the annoyed resident reiterated his belief that he should have special immunity from the new expense, I scanned the faces in attendance. Was Sgnt1764 in the room?

Was it the man in the second row, around twenty-five, small gold hoop in his ear, orange polo? Or the forty-year-old one row in front of me with the close-cropped afro with a *Semper Fi* tattoo on his forearm? Why was I even assuming it was a man?

I watched the group, attentive to any looks in my direction that hung on too long. I also had the opportunity to observe Langston as he smoothly steered the complaints lobbed at him into vague, meaningless political language. I hung onto every word and the unspoken messages between them. There was something I was supposed to see or learn.

Fighting impatience, I sat through conversations on parking meters, nuisance dogs, inconsistent trash pickup, and rat infestations, waiting for the bolt of lightning that would explain my presence. The last item on the meeting agenda was a discussion on a proposed zoning change for a plot of land, currently zoned residential, whose new owners wanted changed to commercial. Largely a moot point—aldermen didn't need community approval for small zoning changes. The conversation was simply an attempt to put a good face on one of Chicago's dirty secrets—aldermanic rule resembled dictatorship more than democracy.

As Langston ran down the highlights, the two suits perked to attention. Were these guys the new owners? The request seemed straightforward. The owners of the property were requesting a change to a strict commercial zone with no housing. Langston was effervescent in his enthusiasm for the change, touting the job-creation opportunities.

Nods of approval flowed around the room, but one man stood up. He was around fifty, with a Santa Claus body and long gray hair slicked back into a braid.

"You know this ain't no different than the last switch they pulled on us," he said to the group. "You all forget the childcare center we got promised? Ain't no daycare in that CVS got built instead." He turned toward Langston. "You wanna tell us what they really goin' to do?"

"Sir, please, I assure you there is no alternative story," Langston said, smiling like he was talking to an elderly uncle. "Job creation is my top priority."

"Then what they building? How many jobs they creating on a lot that ain't half an acre? We all know that this already worked out. Why you bother talkin' 'bout it as if we got any say?"

Langston gestured to the well-dressed man seated immediately to his left. He stood, buttoned his suit jacket and scrutinized the residents. His stance registered control, arrogance, and a touch of superiority.

"Thank you for your questions," he said, nodding to the

speaker. "My name is Porter Gladwyn. I'm an attorney representing the parties who've purchased this parcel."

An attorney? The resident humphed but took his seat.

"The intent is to build an office building. The tenants are unknown at this time, as are the number of jobs they would bring in. These issues are subject to the leasing conditions at completion. But we can safely project in excess of twenty positions."

The dialogue continued, but in typical legal fashion, Gladwyn used a lot of big words chosen to make him sound smart. After about ten minutes, Langston adjourned the meeting and citizens began to depart, some huddling to share their disappointment.

Why send an attorney to seal the deal for twenty jobs? I reached over and picked up a meeting agenda that had been left on the seat next to me. The property address was listed with the agenda item, so I grabbed my phone and pulled up a map.

Damn, my battery was almost drained.

"Hello, Andrea. This is a nice surprise." Father Brogan was at my side along with an African American man in his midthirties. "I'm thrilled that you are being so thorough in your work."

He'd assumed this was a get-to-know-the-neighbors visit. I didn't explain further—my eyes were following the man with the dissenting voice who was speaking with another attendee.

"Your timing is fortuitous. I have someone I'd like you to meet. This is Quincy Harris—you met his nephew Jamal the other day."

"Yes, it's lovely to meet you. Jamal seems like a really good kid," I said as I shook his hand, the incident at the paintbrush factory fresh in my mind. I recognized Jamal's chiseled features in Quincy's face, despite the thirty-pound difference in their weight.

"I raised him since he was ten, when his mama died. It's been tough for us. He's smart, does real good in school." Quincy looked at Father Brogan, who nodded as if to say, "Go ahead." "Father B. says you're a reporter and a lawyer. Says maybe you could help me out."

"What's the issue?" I asked, still glancing occasionally at the man who had challenged the zoning, wanting to speak with him before he left.

"Well, my house got stolen."

"Stolen?"

"See, I got a little behind on my payments. Broke my arm and couldn't work for two months. Anyway, this man comes to my door one day. Said his company, they help people goin' through a rough patch. Said they could take care of me, talk to the bank, get them to reduce my payments till I got square. Few days later, his boss came. Told me I wouldn't even have to pay the late fees the bank wanted. That they help lotsa people round here. So I signed up. That was four months ago."

"What happened from there?"

"I get home from work, and there this letter on my door. Says my house don't belong to me. Locks been changed."

"Did you speak with the bank?" I asked, suspecting that Quincy had been a victim of one of the insidious housing scammers who preyed on the financially desperate.

"I went right over. They say they been sending me letters 'bout foreclosure and shit. I got 'em but I don't have the money to pay all at once. And then they add on all these penalties. Didn't know what I was supposed to do."

"They weren't willing to adjust your loan."

Quincy grunted and shoved his hands into his pockets. "Got told I don't own the house no more. Some company do. Said I signed papers. I didn't sign no papers that gave away my house.

And this company s'posed to help me, their phone been disconnected. Didn't help me. They robbed me."

Father Brogan and I exchanged a glance, knowing that Quincy had likely signed away his home to a financial predator. I straightened up. My target was on the move.

"Quincy, if you could pull together copies of the paperwork you signed, any documents, notes, contact info. Whatever you have. I'd be happy to take a look." I placed a hand on his arm and handed him my card. "Give me a call. I'll see what I can do."

I said goodbye to Father Brogan and Quincy, then scurried out. The man was heading west, his short legs moving at a pace that surprised me.

"Excuse me, sir," I called after him.

He turned at my voice as I caught up with him.

"Could I speak with you a minute about your comments inside?"

He looked me up and down, eyeing me like the outsider I was. "What about?"

"I'm a journalist." I handed him a business card and he looked at it carefully, turning toward the single streetlight. "You seem to have concerns that the developers aren't being truthful. Why is that?"

"Developer ain't honest. Langston ain't honest. We seen this before. They just puttin' on a show, think we too stupid to care. He switched up plans before. Langston already worked this all out. Done it already. No reason to talk about it like it matters. Nothin' matters but Langston's pockets and his friends."

"Do you have any ideas on why they'd be secretive? Why they'd lie about their intentions for the property?"

He shifted his weight and glanced at a woman leaving the meeting before answering.

"That's the right question, ain't it? Guess they don't think we'd like the truth if we heard it. Easier to apologize later. You have a good night, miss."

He turned and I watched his back as he headed home. It was exactly the right question. I smiled. Sending an attorney was the red flag. I pulled out my phone to get back to the map, zooming in on the small screen. *Come on, don't die on me yet. Got it!* The property on the agenda was on Garfield just east of Wentworth—across the street from where the shooter had been positioned in the third incident.

It was the land! It had to be tied to the shootings. I ran to my car.

Darkness was descending as I approached the plot. I parked, then stood next to the curb surveying the landscape. It was a double lot, vacant except for a small shed abutting the neighboring greystone on the eastern perimeter. Weeds grew two feet high and a scraggly buckthorn tree invaded the corner closest to Wentworth. An office building? Maybe. I looked around. The Garfield L was only a hundred yards to the west, as was the Dan Ryan exit, but unless they had a wildly creative architect lined up, parking wasn't part of the plan. To the east and across the street, a spotty mix of vacant land and more three-flats.

A sign had been tacked to the tree. I walked to the corner, hoping to get a closer look, but the streetlamp was out. Steeling myself against my spider repulsion, I stepped into the overgrowth and felt my way forward, my phone lighting a path. A faded hardware store For Sale sign was on the other end. As I squinted to read the contact information, a rush of movement distracted me. Before I could turn, my body was slammed into the tree, knocking my phone from my hand and my breath from my chest.

"You aren't very good at listening," a male voice snarled. His hands gripped my shoulders, digging into my bare flesh and pressing me into the rough bark.

I froze, knowing instantly that this was the man who'd threatened me. He must have been watching, following me from the community center. How had been so stupid to lose sight of my surroundings? Perspiration dripped down the side of my neck as I tried to come up with a plan.

"Last warning."

With that, he tossed me to the ground and disappeared.

26

An insistent pounding on my apartment door interrupted me as I poured kibble in Walter's bowl early Sunday morning. I was still shaken from last night's encounter, and sleep had only come in fits and starts. Walter looked up at me and yowled, impatient for his breakfast, unconcerned about my state of mind. I put the bowl on the floor and padded over, feet bare, my hair tied back, wearing only a short strappy, silk nightgown. Please, not Lane again. I really needed to speak to the doorman about sending people up without a phone call. Michael Hewitt stood on the other side of the open door. His face was unshaven, his hair a tangle of misdirected strands. He was dressed casually, wearing jeans and a Cubs T-shirt.

"Hi," I said, pleased to see him, but also confused about why he was here looking as if he'd just rolled out of bed.

"You're okay?" He searched my face and ran his eyes over my body before looking past me into my apartment.

Walter mewed at my feet, rubbing his head against my ankle.

"He doesn't like it when his breakfast routine is disturbed," I said, scooping up the cat. "Come on in."

I trotted back to the kitchen as my teakettle hissed. Michael closed the door and followed.

"Don't take this the wrong way," I said. "It's nice to see you, but why are you at my apartment at eight a.m. on a Sunday morning? Shouldn't you be home, leisurely reading the paper in your jammies?"

Michael looked around, his face a mixture of confusion and curiosity.

"You're not answering your phone."

"And this makes you run over here to check on me?"

"Your friend Cai called. Said you didn't check in with her last night after sending a text that you were on your way home. She got worried, said that you were meeting some source, and that you gave her instructions to call me if something happened. So she called half an hour ago."

Oh no! After I'd visited the property on Garfield last night, I had forgotten not only to call Cai, but also to charge my phone.

"I'm so sorry," I said, pressing my hands to my temples, embarrassed at the concern I'd caused. "I did tell her I'd call last night but got distracted and forgot. I didn't mean to worry her. It was nothing worth dragging you over here for." I smiled as his shoulders relaxed. "I'm sorry I interrupted your morning. It was very kind of you to come. Just a false alarm, I'm fine."

"Wait a minute. You think after you scared your friend, and me, that you can get away with being evasive? No chance. Talk. What were you doing that I became the emergency backup plan? And what's this about someone threatening you?"

I should have known being vague wasn't going to work. I looked at him, debating my next move: continued evasion or spill all. By the look on his face, option one wouldn't be well received.

"Fair enough. Since you came all the way over here, you deserve an explanation. Let's at least sit down. The water is hot.

Would you like a cup of tea? I don't keep coffee in the house, I'm afraid."

He shook his head. I dunked a tea bag, stirred in some honey, then led him over to the sofa, suddenly aware how short my nightgown was.

"Just let me plug this in and send Cai a text."

I could read the impatience in his face. I wasn't stalling, just needed a few minutes to figure out how deep to go. As I settled into the sofa, I could feel his eyes on me. His nearness confused me, my professional and personal needs were clashing. I pulled a cashmere throw off the back of the sofa and covering my bareness, pulling my legs up under me for good measure.

"You met with that person who emailed you, didn't you? The poetry guy," he said, no longer willing to wait. His professional voice was back—controlled, no hint of emotion or judgment. But I sensed the concern under the surface. Could see the change in his eyes.

"Not exactly. We arranged a meet, but he didn't show up." I reached for my tea, stalling as Michael's jaw got tight. "Let me back up. I've been receiving emails from someone who's suggested that he has information about the identity of the highway sniper. And that the situation is not what it seems. I, too, am convinced that other things are at play, so I asked to meet. That's where I went last night, but he didn't show up."

"Do you have any idea how fucking stupid that was?" The vehemence in his voice startled me.

"The meet was set up for a very public location in Chinatown," I continued, trying my best to dial down his emotion with calm logic. "I didn't climb into a stranger's car. I didn't go into a building alone. If this guy knows who the sniper is, it was worth the risk."

"So he didn't show, and you came home, forgetting that you

had promised to check in with your friend?" The sarcasm came at me like a wave, as if my veracity were being questioned.

"No. When I returned to my car, someone had slipped a flyer under my wiper blade." I pushed off the throw and walked over to my purse, pulled out the flyer and handed it to Michael.

"And?"

"And more poetry. Look." I pointed to the writing on the back. "The guy didn't show, but this was his personal invitation to the meeting."

"And you went?"

I nodded, watching Michael's face as he reread the words scrawled on the page. Waiting to see the flicker of comprehension that would tell me he was drawing the same conclusion that I had.

"All the emails have been like this. They suggest that the shootings are not what they seem." I could feel myself getting excited, my hesitation over pulling Michael into my world dissipating as I spoke. Was it the idea of having a partner on this investigation, or that I wanted to chip away at his veneer? "The thing about this note that's different is one simple word. *They.* In his previous emails, he always said 'I know who *he* is.' Look at those words. They were chosen deliberately. So yes, you bet I went to that meeting."

"And was this mystery bard present?"

"If he was, he didn't identify himself. The meeting was routine stuff except for one agenda item, discussion about a zoning change. In any other context, it, too, would have appeared routine. The new owner wants commercial zoning."

"So what's the context that makes this important?" Michael leaned forward, elbows on his knees. I could see that I hadn't fully convinced him.

"Two things. The owner lawyered up. Sent a high-priced legal shark to represent him over an empty lot barely big enough to build a three-flat. I drove over after the meeting. And that lot is owned by a corporation that is buying up everything in Englewood east of the expressway."

I paused, watching Michael's face as he processed what I was saying. A little Googling last night after I'd gotten home had given me Porter Gladwyn's bio. For the life of me, I couldn't conceive of any reason he should have been a logical choice for a piddly-ass real estate transaction... other than it wasn't a piddly-ass deal. The owner, the Orton Group, had a plan. A big one. But who were they? People were dead. How could that have anything to do with a real estate play?

"So let me get this straight. You're suggesting that these shootings are occurring because someone wants to make a few bucks investing in Englewood? What? They're killing the competition over a chunk of dirt or a shabby rental building? Do you have any idea how crazy that sounds? People die over dumb things all the time, but you're reaching here." His eyes softened. "Look, Andrea, I know you're just trying to do your job, but concocting some fairy tale isn't helpful. There is a story. The story is children, neighborhoods, being eviscerated by gangs and greed and poverty. Write about that. We're on this. I can't give you details, but we—"

"What if it's a cover? What if these assumptions about gang violence are being used, manipulated to hide another agenda?"

The questions tumbled out. I wanted—no, needed—Michael to hear me. To consider what I was saying.

"What agenda would that be?"

"I don't know yet." I shook my head, aware that everything fell flat without a motive. "What I do know is that this company is gobbling up land in Englewood as fast as they can. A company didn't exist six months ago, and they're making efforts to conceal ownership. Someone wants me frightened enough to walk away. That means something."

My voice grew pleading and I realized how much I wanted Michael to get it, to jump on board and support my theory.

Michael pressed me for details, his face grave with concern as I spoke. When I finished, he said, "I don't understand how shooting people would further any kind of acquisition goal, but I do understand that your life has been threatened. That changes everything. You have to stop with this foolishness." He stood. "If you hear from him again or you see anyone that makes you nervous, call me, call 9-1-1. I'll help as much as I can."

I followed him as he walked to the door. We stood in the open doorway, eyes fixed on each other. Conscious of the closeness of our bodies, my bareness. Unsaid words hung over us, daring to escape. I leaned against the door frame, afraid that if he stayed a second longer, I'd do something foolish.

"You can't help if you don't believe me," I said softly, feeling the gulf between us.

Michael laid his hand on my shoulder and his touch sent a flutter of desire down my body. As we stood, inches apart, he trailed a finger across my shoulder and over my clavicle as if memorizing the feel of my skin. The heat of his hand rekindled embers long cold, and I stood locked in his gaze. Seeing the longing in his face matching mine. As his finger traced the curve of my neck, his phone rang, jarring us both.

He stepped away from me, breaking our connection, and took the call. A few monosyllabic words later, he ended it. "That was Janek. We have the shooter in custody."

27

"Is that what you're wearing? First you scare me last night, now this?" Cai stood in my doorway, looking at me like I'd just come in from mowing the lawn and had dirt smeared across my face. Her silk blouse was perfectly steamed, a jacket thrown over shoulders, her Prada heels a mile high. "I know I said casual, but what is this?" Her hand fluttered up and down in disgust. "If you're not feeling well, you could have called. It's just brunch."

I shook my head, knowing I was on the verge of tears. "I'm not sick."

"This is, I don't know, scrub-the-toilet attire? I can't remember seeing you without makeup. Ever. Raggedy leggings and Erik's old shirt? What gives?"

I motioned her in, closing the door behind her and following her over to the sofa. Cai laid her jacket over the arm, then sat waiting for me to speak.

If CPD had a shooter in custody, my story was done. Everything was crashing down on me. My failed marriage. Financial fears. My career gone in six months before I'd ever gotten it off the ground. Too little, too late. Everyone would have this story.

An also-ran wasn't good enough. I'd simply be regurgitating facts that had already been reported. No story meant no career, and meant I'd be reduced to groveling for Tierney to take me back, my tail between my legs and failure branded on my forehead in big, bold letters.

Frustration won out, and tears pooled in my eyes, threatening to spill. I opened my mouth to tell her about the arrest, and it all came pouring out, raw and disorderly. The pain, the fears, the defeat I felt. I let it flow, not caring about anything other than release.

Cai sat patiently, her face a model of concern as I blathered on. At one point, she grabbed a full box of tissues out of the bathroom to help me mop up. When there was nothing left to say, I leaned back, sinking into the downy cushions. I wanted to curl up and not leave this spot for a week.

"Are you done? Is the feeling sorry for yourself over, now that you've had a good cry?" She leaned in and put a hand on my knee. "Life has been shitty lately. So what? Kick it in the balls and fight back. Or are you going to let Erik win? Are you going to hide in a corner and be a girl, let the boys take this from you because it's easier to give up than to fight?"

I scrunched my eyes tightly closed, trying to summon Cai's courage, trying to remember what had happened to mine. Taking a deep breath, I looked up at Cai. "When will it be over? When will I stop hurting?" I asked, my voice quavering.

She squeezed my knee again. "When you get off your ass and take control of the situation. When you start behaving like the strong, confident, kick-ass woman you were a year ago before the asshole you married tore your heart out. Now go take a shower, throw that ensemble in the trash, and let's go have brunch. You need a cocktail."

Two mimosas and a veggie omelet later, I was back in my co-op with a substantially improved attitude. My confidence was still in the toilet, but I no longer had the urge to hide in a cave and lick my wounds for a month, thanks to Cai's jolt to my backside. I sat on the sofa and pulled my laptop onto my knees, scrolling for coverage of the arrest. "Chicago police have arrested Lashan Nash, 31, an Army veteran and reputed member of the Gangster Disciples, for the three shooting deaths on the Dan Ryan." Nothing about motive. Why would he do it? Was this the lone wolf Father Brogan had spoken of?

I sent a text to Michael, doubting that he'd engage in any more detailed dialogue with me. But what the hell. Maybe Tierney would? He might be inclined to speak to me privately before the PR machine took over. Once I'd figured out how to manage his bark, we'd had a good relationship. I left a message on his cell, knowing that I was likely just one of over a hundred in the queue.

Now what? I pushed myself up from the sofa, slipped my phone into my pocket, and headed to the terrace. Maybe deadheading the geraniums trailing over their planter boxes would provide some inspiration. I snipped the spent blooms, inhaled their fragrance, and loosened the soil as I contemplated what to do next, forcing my insecurity back into the pit of my stomach each time it took hold of my chest.

It had to be the land.

My cell rang as I doused the pots with water. I jabbed the trowel in the dirt and set down the can before glancing at the screen. Not a familiar number.

"Ah, Miss Kellner?" a male voice on the other end of the phone asked. "This is Quincy. Jamal's uncle. Father B. introduced us yesterday. You said it was okay to give you a call 'bout my house."

"Yes, of course, Quincy. I remember you." Pro bono legal advice wasn't where my head was at the moment, but I owed the priest. "Were you able to able to find the documents we discussed?"

"I just sent them to your email. The one on the card you gave me."

"Hold on a minute while I pull them up." I traipsed back inside, located the message, opened the attachments, and quickly scanned the documents. "Okay, I've got them. Now tell me in detail what your understanding was of what LRM Property Holdings was going to provide for you."

"Like I said, things been tough. I got a few months behind in my house payments. One day I get a call from this guy, says his company helps people like me. Helped a lot of people 'round here. Said he can work out a plan with the bank to make my payments smaller and take away all the late fees. Help me get through this rough patch. Sounds good, right? The supervisor, he says they can cut my payments in half. So I say sure. Next thing I know, all my stuff is in the yard, and I got new locks on my door."

"And the representative from LRM asked you to sign some paperwork related to your agreement. Is that correct?" I clicked through the contract, homing in on the details buried deep in the pages of legal jargon, already knowing that there was little I could say that would comfort Quincy. The final page bore an unreadable scrawled signature. "Is that your signature on the final page?"

"Yeah, I signed it, but I didn't sign nothin' givin' my house away."

"And your bank, were they contacted by LRM?"

"Said no one talked to them 'bout my payments. I got no home, but the bank, they still want their money. How I supposed to pay them? I can't afford no lawyers. Me and Jamal stayin' with my cousin. Sleepin' on the damn couch. Ain't no way to live. Ain't right."

"I'm so sorry, Quincy. No, it isn't right. In fact, it's illegal. You've been a victim of a predatory real estate scheme. The document you signed does in fact transfer ownership to LRM Property Holdings, but it didn't transfer the loan obligation. That was not the scenario presented to you. You were not given the opportunity to consult an attorney. And most important, you received no compensation for the transfer. I suspect that LRM is what's known as a shell company, set up to hide the identity of the people behind it. It's hard to take legal action against people you can't identify. That's why the phone number they gave you is disconnected. The office address is likely fake as well."

"So that means I'm screwed 'cause I signed them false papers? Two of my neighbors, they signed too. So we all got played."

"No. You were swindled. It's different. Companies like this target individuals in your situation. They're playing the odds that you won't understand the contract or won't consult with a lawyer prior to signing the documents. You have recourse, but I have to tell you, it won't be fast or easy to get this resolved."

I didn't want to tell him that it could take years to bring this to closure and that banks were rarely empathic.

"What am I supposed to do? Can you fix this? I still got my job. I can pay you a little bit every month."

"You don't have to pay me. I'm going to contact the state's attorney personally. I used to work for him. He'll be very interested in taking this on, particularly if LRM is targeting your neighborhood. You mentioned that there were others. Talk to them, ask them to get in touch with me right away. I can't make promises about the outcome, but I will get your case to the right people. Be patient and follow the legal advice you're given. I know that's a lot to ask, but have faith. I'll check in with you soon. It'll take time, but they won't get away with it. I promise."

I didn't hold out much hope that Quincy would be back in

his home anytime soon. Predators like this were motivated only by cash. They'd be flipping or pulling in a renter almost immediately. Structured to obscure ownership, the shell companies were hard to break. Tierney had done it before, but the position on his priority list would dictate the resources he'd throw behind it. More victims would help. I tapped a few keys. How many layers of muck hid the ownership of LRM Property Holdings?

I stared at the screen, a small smile forming as a familiar name glowed back at me. Abascal Services.

28

I pulled open the door to the four-story walk-up at the corner of Diversey and Lincoln first thing Monday morning, located my target on the short list of tenants labeled on the mailboxes, and headed up. As I climbed the stairs, a Taylor Swift tune crooned at me over the hum of blow dryers from the second-floor salon. Abascal Services, the firm listed as the managing agent for the Orton Group, was nestled in the back end of the fourth floor. Its gray metal door was marked simply with an engraved plastic sign. A flotilla of Valpaks, Chinese takeout menus, and cheap oil change coupons littered the floor.

I glanced at my watch, hoping this guy was the early-riser type. I knocked lightly and got no response, so I tested the door. Finding it unlocked, I entered.

A man sat hunched over a small desk in front of me. A stringy ponytail bobbed along with whatever was pumping through his massive red Beats headphones. Running my eyes around the twelve-foot-by-twelve-foot space, I saw little more than his desk, a couple of file cabinets that were ready for the local salvage yard, and towering piles of manila folders fencing the room. Guess all his money had gone toward the expensive ear candy.

I closed the door and took two steps forward before the movement caught his attention. His No. 2 pencil drumstick went flying, as did the contents of the Dunkin' Donuts cup at his elbow.

"Aw shit! I didn't hear you come in," he said, jumping to his feet and dabbing at the puddle of coffee before yanking the hardware from his ears. "What can I help you with?"

Pink sunburned skin flushed at the collar of his blue button-down oxford, magnifying the acne that dotted his lower face. He pushed a hank of greasy brown hair behind an ear and shuffled from foot to foot as if unsure of the social requirements for the situation. I guessed walk-ins weren't a usual thing.

"Are you looking for the graphic designer?" he asked, assuming my appearance in his office was purely accidental. "She moved out a couple months back. Took a space in the West Loop, I think. Landlord should know. His number is downstairs by the mailboxes." He folded himself back into his seat, content that I'd thank him and be on my way. Not so fast.

"Are you Gabriel Abascal?"

He nodded at me blankly.

"And you provide business registration services? LLC formation, etc.?"

The gears clicked in his mind as he realized he might have a live client on his hands. Pulling himself back up to his feet, he jammed an untucked hem into his jeans and extended a hand.

"Sorry. Clients usually contact me by phone or email. You threw me off. Please have a seat."

He reached across the desk and pulled over a folding chair, then turned to a file drawer at his knees. I parked myself on the plastic seat and watched him stab through. Locating whatever it was that he was searching for, he pulled out a couple sheets of paper, placed them on the desk, then settled back down.

"Okay, so you're looking to form an LLC. Excellent choice. Cost-effective, great options for pass-through taxation, and of course, much safer for protecting your assets. So, have you decided on a name?" He grabbed a pen, ready to sign me up.

"Give me a primer on how all this works," I said, playing along. "You handle all the filing paperwork, right?"

The real purpose of my unannounced visit could wait. Let the guy talk. See where assumptions could get me.

"That's exactly right. I'm an incorporation agent. Depending on your business structure, we can do the EIN, the LLC, any of the official stuff. Why spend your valuable time trying to understand complicated legalese when I can do it in a quarter of the time? You've got serious start-up work to do. Staff to hire, space to lease, marketing plans to develop. Smart businesspeople know how to use their resources. It just makes sense—time and money sense—to hire that out."

"And if I don't have a business address yet?"

"To form an LLC, you need a managing agent, that's me, with a local address. Your business can be based anywhere. As far as the requirements go, *we* are your business location."

My mind drifted to the possibilities that provided. Talk about a needle in a haystack. How was I going to learn who controlled Orton if they could hide behind a guy like Abascal?

"Don't let that scare you," he said, mistaking the expression on my face. "I assure you the only authority that grants me is the ability to receive mail on your behalf. So, what do you say—can I sign you up?"

"I understand you're the managing agent for the Orton Group."

Might as well throw the question out there and see where it

led. LRM Properties seemed to operate by another playbook, so I kept that out of the conversation for now.

"Oh! Porter sent you. You should have said something. I wouldn't have acted like such a buffoon when you walked in. He's always sending business my way. Smart guy. Now, there's someone who knows how to make a buck or two."

Porter? I replayed the name several times, drilling it into my consciousness. First name or last? I kept my face neutral. My attorney face. But something familiar pinged in my brain. Porter Gladwyn from the community meeting. Could he be representing both companies?

"How do you know each other?" I played along, hoping to keep him talking.

"We worked together back when I was with Blasik. He was my first client when I started up."

His hands flashed outward, indicating the expanse of his domain, and my mind raced. Gladwyn worked at Blasik, Cameron, and Lord, the same firm that had represented Karl Janek's ex-partner, Matt Dubicki. At Rendell's press conference, I'd run into my cop buddy, Coogin, who'd said Dubicki now headed security for a real estate developer. Was it possible that Gladwyn was representing that same developer? I made a mental note to find out who Dubicki worked for.

"Anyway, I'll need about fifteen minutes of your time and we can have you up and running and officially filed." He picked up the pen again and got ready to write. "It'll take two to three weeks for the paperwork to come back, but it gets you started."

Time to make an exit before I had to face some tough questions, like my name. "I should give this a little more thought."

I reached across his desk and grabbed a business card, waving it in his direction as if I would call soon.

"You've been quite helpful," I said, getting to my feet as Gabriel

Abascal scrambled for his sales pitch. He'd blown the close and was trying to recover, but I was out the door in four steps. *Buddy, you have no idea how helpful.* I now had a name I could associate with Orton, and I knew he worked at Blasik, Cameron, and Lord.

I had a call in to Cai before hitting the landing on the second floor. "Please be at your desk," I muttered to myself as the phone buzzed in my ear.

"You're not getting intimate with an EMT again, are you?"

"One incident and you assume incurring bodily harm is a weekly event?" I laughed. "What happened to 'Hello'? 'How's your day'? Even, 'I was just going to call you.' You remember those classic social graces, don't you?"

"Honey, neither one of us is the classic type or we'd never have been friends this long. Since you're obviously alive and your normal sassy self, what's up?"

"Are you at work?"

"No, I'm at the Ritz, waiting for my hot stone massage," Cai responded with her usual snark. "It's nine fifteen a.m. on a Monday. Where else would I be?"

"I know you're working. I meant are you at your desk?"

"I am, but since you're having a rare moment of not getting to the point, why don't you tell me what's got your head in the clouds, and we can start over?"

"I need you to log into Westlaw. Blasik, Cameron and Lord. Look up an associate named Porter Gladwyn."

"What's the matter? Erik too cheap to pay for the service? Oh right, you don't have access anymore."

"Do you have it pulled up?" I asked, hearing the flatness in my voice.

"Geez, what happened to your sense of humor?" She sighed. "Okay, I see a Porter Gladwyn, forty-two, senior associate. Practice areas are construction, zoning, gaming, corporate, and real estate. That do it?"

"Fabulous. Now I need a current employer for a guy named Matt Dubicki. He's not an attorney and Google isn't giving me what I need." I hadn't had an opportunity to ask Officer Coogin which real estate developer had hired Dubicki.

I could hear a voice in the background as she typed.

"My next appointment is here. I don't have time to run a full background check for you."

"Can you get the employer before you go?" I pleaded.

She sighed yet again. "Okay, but I expect you to tell me what this is all about. Dinner tomorrow?"

"Sure. I'll even pay." I could hear the click of the keys as she searched the database.

"Dubicki is VP of security at Mezey Development. Been with them for almost two years. I'll let you research Mezey, although I imagine you already know the basics. I gotta run."

"Thanks. You're a doll."

"Don't tell anyone. Wouldn't want to destroy my reputation."

As I listened to Cai click off, I could feel the warmth of a smile wash over me. A connection. A name. Porter Gladwyn was representing the company that had purchased land near the shootings. He worked for the same law firm that had represented Matt Dubicki in his corruption trial, and Dubicki worked for one of the largest real estate developers in Chicago. This just couldn't be a coincidence.

But what did Mezey want with the land—and why hide their involvement? They had a role in nearly every significant development deal in the city and weren't shy about shouting their accomplishments. They'd advertise on the back of a hearse if anyone would let them.

29

Damn! Why was there never a cab when you needed one? I flailed my arms frantically until a cab barreled across two lanes and screeched to a halt in front of me. I had called Porter Gladwyn's office the second I'd ended my conversation with Cai, fabricating a story about an urgent real estate need. Having just taken a cancellation, the receptionist had plugged me in, provided I could get there in fifteen minutes. I promised the driver an extra twenty if he could get me to the Loop in ten.

One of the largest law firms in the city, Blasik, Cameron, and Lord occupied a million square feet of office space and employed more than 350 attorneys. Enough money had gone into law school debt in this building to fund a small country. I headed inside to the security desk where I presented my ID and then was directed to the proper elevator for access to the seventy-seventh floor.

The reception area displayed the pomp and circumstance that first-year law students dreamed of. Visions of prestige, big salaries, and the word "partner" in the job title that kept wannabe attorneys shackled to their desks in law school libraries until 2:00 a.m. It was those dreams that motivated the ones who made it through the bar exam until the reality of one-hundred-hour work weeks hit home.

I'd known my competitive instincts weren't honed enough for the contact sport of litigation, choosing instead a branch of law more akin to chess. But I did know the playbook, and I understood the species.

Gladwyn stepped toward me, hand outstretched. Close-cropped hair, toffee skin, ice-blue eyes that held me like a specimen. I stood, immediately sensing an undertow. A feeling that there was something cautionary underneath the dashing surface of his precisely chosen hand-tailored suit, Egyptian cotton two-ply shirting, and artfully folded silk jacquard pocket square.

Five thousand dollars' worth of wool, silk, and leather adorned his body, and he carried it like a billboard. It was hard to imagine what he and Abascal had in common.

"Nice to meet you," Gladwyn said. His grip on my hand held me as tightly as his eyes did. "I have a conference room reserved. Follow me. I only have a few minutes."

"Thank you for squeezing me in. I'm sure your schedule is quite full." And at eight hundred dollars an hour, he wasn't going to be spending a lot of time on a free consultation until he knew if it was worth his while.

As we moved down the hall of glass conference rooms, a tug of regret washed over me. Had I made a mistake leaving my position with the State's Attorney's Office? I tried to shake off the vulnerability of my current employment status by drawing on memories of an endless workload and victories that felt hollow.

Gladwyn led me into a room of glass, marble, and steel. A room designed to smack you in the face with success, to justify the billing rate, and to give off the impression that if the client chose them, they would somehow become successful, too.

"So what can I help you with, Ms. Kellner?" Gladwyn asked

as he settled into the chair across from me and dated the yellow legal pad on the table. "You indicated an interest in commercial real estate. It's one of my areas of specialization. There is a great deal we can do to structure purchases to present the most advantageous tax scenario. Smart of you to get legal advice prior to adding real estate to your investment portfolio."

"That's exactly what I came to discuss. I understand that some of your clients are investing in Englewood." I slid a business card across the table and watched a tiny ripple of emotion cross his eyes. A shift so subtle that it wouldn't have registered to anyone who hadn't been trained in this brand of poker. Discomfort. Interesting.

"What is this in reference to?"

"Perhaps we could discuss the parcel you want rezoned?" He didn't respond. "Alderman Langston's community meeting?"

"It's a simple rezone. We brought it before the community out of courtesy. As I'm sure you know, this is not the type of thing that requires a community referendum. Alderman Langston is dedicated to keeping his constituents involved and aware." A small robotic upturn of the mouth told me he'd recovered from whatever initial apprehension my agenda shift had caused. Let's see if I could loosen that control.

"I understand there are other parcels, beyond the one you identified, up for zoning changes. Do you care to comment?" I didn't, in fact, know that to be true, but I had to fish with whatever bait I had available. Getting a rise out of the guy would tell me if I was in the right pond.

"I'm not sure where you're getting your information, but you'll have to excuse me. I really don't have time for whatever this fantasy story is you're working on." He picked up my business card again, giving it another look. "And quite frankly, I didn't think sending in reporters under false pretenses was a tactic Link-Media endorsed. You'll have to excuse me."

He got to his feet. But I wasn't quite done with him.

"I'm aware that you've done some work with the Orton Group. Did that work include real estate transactions in Englewood?"

"I have no comment." He snatched up his legal pad and stepped toward the door.

"I understand that you can't discuss clients," I said, adjusting my approach. "Tell me in generic terms what you can do for a company. Tax abatements? Support from the city perhaps?"

"I'll need you to leave now." His voice was modulated in that ice-under-the-surface attorney tone that got played heavily in my own toolbox. He swung open the glass door and stepped into the hallway, waiting for me to follow.

Got it. Meeting over. Don't let the door slam you in the ass when you leave.

"Thank you for your time." Waste of time, more accurately. But I had gotten under his skin, and that meant something.

I trotted out behind him as he zoomed off to his next appointment. Despite his pace, he kept glancing back to make sure I hadn't stopped to go exploring, only relaxing once the hallway branched back to the reception area. I hadn't expected him to be a pushover, but the total stonewalling was an interesting response.

As I stepped out of reception toward the elevator, my phone rang. Michael.

"Can you meet me tonight?"

"Sure. What's up? You sound frazzled."

"I wanted you to hear this from me. There's been another shooting. We need to talk."

30

The tap, tap, tap of my heels on the polished marble floor of City Hall echoed louder and louder in my head as I marched down the central lobby. Each click was a reminder that time was pressing on me, that CPD had the wrong man and the shooter was still out there. The elegant neoclassical arches and barrel-vaulted ceilings of the stately 1911 building normally fascinated me, but today my thoughts were focused on images of less pristine real estate. And dead bodies.

I scrolled Link-Media's website as I walked, bringing myself up to speed on the details of the morning shooting. One man, thirty-five, dead from a gunshot wound to the head at 9:55 this morning on the same northbound stretch of the Dan Ryan. If I had screamed louder, pleaded harder with Michael, would the man be dead? My stomach twisted. I should have done more. I should have made Michael listen to me somehow.

Borkowski's byline tugged at me for a fraction of a second, but this wasn't the time for petty insecurity. I had to connect the shootings to the real estate before there was another victim. It wasn't just about me anymore. I couldn't let anyone else die. I'd lived with the guilt of Damon Wilkins's suicide. I couldn't live with more blood on my hands. My phone felt heavy in my hand, tempting me to text Michael, but he would be knee-deep in the investigation. He'd call when he could. But finally I had his attention, though it had come at a cost.

City Hall was home to the fifty Chicago aldermen, and considered by many to be one of the biggest white-collar crime scenes in the city. Statistically, Chicago was one of the most corrupt cities in the country, with a legacy extending long before its mob heyday. Malfeasance was the juice that had historically run this city.

After consulting with the officer at the information desk, I joined the fray of people at the elevator bank and crept up to the eleventh floor, home of Alderman Anthony Langston's office. Michael's words bounced around in my head. Another victim. My heart was heavy with the news. Was the suspect CPD had in custody the wrong man? Or did the shooter have an accomplice?

I pushed my way through the opaque glass door and found myself in a waiting room lined with convention hall chairs and Chicago propaganda posters. A construction type sitting on the right eyed me from head to hips as if I were a Chicago Red Hot on game day at Wrigley Field. I stepped past him to the receptionist before I had to watch him drool.

"Good morning. I'm Andrea Kellner, Link-Media," I said, laying a business card on the counter. Stretching the truth on my employment status wasn't going to work much longer, but for now I intended to keep the lie going as long as I could. "Is there someone I can speak to about development plans for a parcel in the alderman's ward?"

She stared back at me with a plastic smile and flat eyes. Years of public service to a constituency that was never satisfied could do that.

"Someone will be with you shortly. Please take a seat."

Her gray ringlets bounced slightly against her ample ebony cheeks as she spoke, but that was the only sign of life. I thanked her and settled into the last open chair. Lucky me, I was going to be able to watch Joe the Builder slobber after all.

I fished in my bag for my phone and distracted myself with email while I waited, occasionally looking up to watch the slice of humanity that pressed itself up against the gatekeeper. Most needed to be directed to yet another office, to yet another line, to yet another jaded government worker.

Forty-five minutes in and my patience was shot. The ripped plastic on my chair was scraping my back, and I hadn't eaten anything since an uninspired Caesar salad last night.

"Excuse me, is Alderman Langston available? Perhaps I could speak with him directly. Given the tragic recent shootings in the Twentieth Ward, I'm sure he'd like the chance to comment."

"I'm sorry, the alderman is unavailable." The corners of her mouth lifted slightly, but the rest was frozen in place. "I'm sure someone will be out shortly."

An automatic response. The gatekeeper wasn't budging. I returned to my uncomfortable throne and pushed aside my annoyance.

"Ms. Kellner?"

I looked up to see a tall young man standing next to the reception desk. He was fidgeting like a four-year-old who needed the toilet. His arms were inches too long for the sleeves of the navy blazer he wore, as if he were sprouting up so fast it didn't pay to shop. The pumpkin-colored locks surrounding his earnest, freckled white face screamed "intern." I wondered whose kid he was. They sure hadn't pulled this one from the ward.

I picked up my bag and followed him around the corner to a cramped hallway of a room, grateful to be moving. Four desks, seven people, and an assembly line of postcards being stickered and stamped. Howdy Doody led me to a chair out of the fray.

"I understand you have some questions about real estate in the Twentieth. How can I help?" he asked after settling into the chair next to mine, our knees nearly touching.

This kid, who belonged in an acne commercial, was supposed to be my source?

"Excuse me, but is Alderman Langston available?"

"Not at the moment, but I'm sure I can help. We have several wonderful brochures that explain our various housing programs. Was there a specific program you were interested in?"

He reached over and grabbed a pamphlet, flashing his Crest-strip smile as he handed it to me.

"Jim," I said, pulling from the pin on his lapel. "Is this your first summer with the alderman?"

"It is, and what an opportunity. I'm majoring in poli-sci at the University of Chicago and hope to represent the great city of Chicago myself someday."

Yep, I'd been shuffled off on an intern.

"The questions I have go a little deeper than a pamphlet can cover. I'd really like to speak with the alderman or someone who's a bit more conversant about future development in the ward." I flashed him a big-sister smile to see where playing nice would get me.

"Oh, yes, I understand. But everyone is in a strategy meeting. It's a busy week. I could get you on the calendar for the end of next week."

Not good enough. I needed another tactic.

"Do you have a database of pending building permits? Or requests for zoning changes?"

"Yes, but I'm not really trained on that system."

"Could we take a look? I'm curious about the process." I whipped out the sister smile again and tried to nail it home.

"I suppose it wouldn't hurt. I did get a demo last week, but I need a PIN number or a street address." He swung his body over to the ancient PC on the desk and logged in.

In all likelihood, the transaction was too recent to be pegged for zoning changes or permits, but maybe my friend had the magic touch. I read off the address of the paintbrush factory as he typed.

"Nothing in the pipeline on that address," he said.

As I read over his shoulder, trying to decipher the data on his screen, I wondered if my request was too narrow.

"The items listed on the bottom of the screen, are they properties up for zoning changes?"

"Yes. All the requests are entered in this system. The PIN number, the lot size, current zoning code, the requested change, etc. You know about PIN numbers, right?" he asked. "Each parcel of land has its own Property Index Number. It's the legal description of the land."

I nodded. "And this is sorted by request date?"

"I can sort by any qualifiers, but yes, what you see is chronological."

"Could you print that out for me?"

"Um, I don't know if I should. Like I said, I haven't been fully trained on the system," he said, squirming in his seat.

"I just want to understand the process. A visual reference helps me remember. I wouldn't want to be inaccurate in my article."

He shrugged. "No harm, I guess."

He pushed a key, and a printer on the next desk sprang to life. As he stepped over to retrieve the document, I turned toward the clamor at the far end of the room. Apparently, the strategy meeting was breaking. Alderman Langston and a handful of suits filed in.

Jim returned as I watched the group parade past the staff. Shoulders back, chests out, that special swagger men of a certain status seemed to possess. It seemed to be something handed out with club membership like tote bags. They were off to a luncheon of thick, rare porterhouse steaks and Glenlivet neat, no doubt. A dark-haired man at the back of the pack locked eyes with me as he passed, looking like he was searching his memory for a reference. Something about him was familiar. The squareness of his jaw? The wide bridge of his nose from an old break?

"Here's the printout," Jim said, handing me the document. "Although the property you asked about wasn't listed, I do see nearby parcels on the list." He pointed to the third line down.

"And how do you know that?" I asked, searching the page for whatever commonality he was seeing.

"Anyone who owns property in Cook County knows they have a PIN number that is unique to that parcel of land. It's on every tax bill."

"Yes, I'm aware of that."

"But what most people don't know is that the numbers have meaning. The PIN is always fourteen digits. The first two numbers specify area, the next two sub-area, then three digits for the block, and three for the specific parcel on that block."

I pulled the pages over and felt a smile wash over my face. "And looking at this, you could see that the address I asked about is on the same block as this parcel because the first seven numbers match." What I didn't comment on was the five other addresses that a quick glance also told me were also in the immediate area.

"Exactly. Cool, isn't it?" he said, thrilled to be able to show off his knowledge.

"This seems to be a pretty long list. Is this an unusually high number of zoning applications?"

"Well, I don't really know since I just started, but Doreen—she's the supervisor who trained me—seemed to think so. Said there hadn't been this much activity in the twelve years she's worked for the ward."

The group of men were moving past the reception area. My buddy who needed the nose job had turned and was still glowering in my direction as he rounded the corner. Why did this guy seem familiar? Given the look he was shooting at me, we weren't long-lost buds.

I thanked Jim for his help and exited with my new treasure. How many of the other recent purchases were on this list? I glanced down, running over PIN numbers. I needed to map this out. Needed to see if there were consistencies in the zoning changes. The Orton Group had some grand plan for the area. But what was it?

My mind sped through the options. Greed was driving this. It was one of the words my anonymous emailer had used. The potential for profit had to be so great that nothing else mattered. Was Mezey Development—Dubicki's employer—behind this? Were they behind the Orton Group? I shoved the documents in my bag and searched the Mezey website as I moved past reception and out of Alderman Langston's office.

Engrossed in the profile of Mezey's founder, I found myself inadvertently in the center of the group of men who had just left, now clustered in the hall outside. Their chatter ended, the way it did with men easily distracted by a pretty face. As they grinned their goofy grins and pretended they were gentlemen graciously allowing a lady to pass, I surveyed the faces like they were mug shots.

Langston stood in front of me, arms crossed over the round bulge of his stomach. His bloated face flushed with a web of red capillaries from nose to jowls, the way alcoholics deep into their disease presented. The rest were unknown to me. The man with the mangled nose was the only one who wasn't looking at me like he was a fourteen-year-old boy. Instead, his gaze cut deeply.

"Alderman Langston, I'm Andrea Kellner with Link-Media." I extended a hand, not about to waste an opportunity. "Do you have a moment? I was at your community meeting on Saturday evening." I doubted he'd engage in a conversation with his posse around, but I might not get another chance. "I was curious about the property on Garfield up for a zoning change. I understand there's a fair amount of real estate activity in Englewood currently. Do you have any development plans you'd care to announce?"

"So nice to see the media take note of good news now and then. Englewood has a real need for entrepreneurial office space. This project will be a great addition to our community and give our residents a much-needed resource for small business. We have a couple of dissenters who fear Englewood will discard its past and let gentrification change the flavor of the community. But they'll come around when we see the improvement in the unemployment rate." He laughed, but it was hollow and condescending.

"So you're saying there is no larger-scale development that you're prepared to announce?"

"I'm saying that this property on Garfield is one development project—an important one, but just one. It's a toe in the water. If it's successful, I'm sure we can count on more. Now if you'll excuse me, I have a situation to attend to. Gentlemen, go ahead. I'll join you shortly." With that, he stepped back into the sanctuary of his office.

I nodded and walked past the men toward the elevator, aware of the eyes on my backside and, more important, the fact that conversation had not resumed. As I stepped into the car and turned my focus back to my phone, a strobe went off in my head. The guy with the nose. He was the guy outside the community center. He was the guy at Gibsons having dinner with Langston, Ramirez, and Borkowski. Now he's attending strategy meetings with Langston? Who *was* this man?

31

The zoning printout, all five pages, lay spread out in front of me on the stained Formica table. My iPad, open to the Mezey Development website, sat propped up on my left, with a legal pad on my right. The chatter of the coffee shop crowd disappeared into the background as did the pedestrians who whirred by outside the window. The sweet scent of lightly crisped waffles drowning in maple syrup, on the other hand, made it through. Feeling my blood sugar rise just from the smell, I ordered a pot of tea and a fruit salad instead.

"Interesting zoning info you emailed me." Brynn stood tableside. The sleeves of her burgundy-striped oxford were rolled past her elbows; a slight sheen of sweat glistened on her forehead. I had phoned her as I'd left Langston's office and asked her to meet me with a parcel map and the sales data. "I'm so glad you called. Borkowski's got me pulling statistics on concrete usage in the city over the last fifteen years. I don't know which of us is going to slit our wrists first. Me because of the drudgery, or him because he's tired of my bitching about it," she said, sliding into the booth.

I flagged our waitress.

"A large coffee—actually, make it two, and a Reuben sandwich, heavy on the fries," she said to the server. "I know it's only eleven thirty, but this is my only shot at food," Brynn said as the woman left.

"I said I was buying. The German chocolate cake looks pretty decadent if the sandwich doesn't fill you up." Looking at the tiny bowl of overripe bananas slices and dried-out grapefruit in front of me, I might be fighting Brynn for her French fries.

A sly smile crossed Brynn's face as she pulled a file out of her backpack and laid it on a clear corner of the table.

"I took the lists you photographed from the zoning department and cross-referenced them against the list of properties sold over the last six months. I think I've got everything. Your photos were pretty clear." She opened the file and tapped on the papers to show me her spreadsheet. "Then I loaded the data into a parcel map." She pulled out two printouts gridded off to show property boundaries. "See these?" she asked, handing me a map and pointing at a cluster of red dots on the east side of the Dan Ryan. "All the properties with dots are owned by Orton. And all either currently have, or have submitted a request for, a zoning change to C3-3."

"All of them?" I had anticipated some correlation, but this was an all-out assault. And an aggressive one.

"Just about anything on Wentworth was already C3 commercial. Some needed a minor adjustment from C3-2 to C3-3. It's primarily the residential property to the east where the big changes are occurring. So what's going on? This is a lot of real estate."

"There are probably more. I have an MLS printout of active and pending properties, so I expect more in the pipeline soon," I said, wondering how many parcels were in their crosshairs. "And this map doesn't include parcels owned by LRM."

"LRM? Who are they?"

"A property company that's scamming people in Englewood out of their homes. Another shell company, but they might be connected to whatever Orton is doing."

Brynn took a long draw of her coffee and stared at the map. "Do you know what parcels they own?"

"Not yet." I picked up a red pen and dotted Quincy's address. "I just learned of this scam. Only one address confirmed. I'm expecting to hear from two others. I've got a call in to Tierney. I want to see if there's anything on his radar yet."

"The way the properties are clustered, it's clear these are targeted buys. So what do they want to build?" Brynn's mile-high sandwich had arrived, and she bit into the crispy toasted rye. Russian dressing dripped down her chin as she waited for me to answer.

"I don't know yet. Based on the parcel map, the potential here is for about ten acres of contiguous land before big obstacles, like the Norfolk Southern rail yard, slow them down. And it appears Orton's already acquired forty percent of that. There's an L stop at Garfield and at 63rd as well as highway access, so easy in and out," I said, trying to figure out the opportunities the location provided. I stared at the parcel map, moved the papers around like they were pieces to a puzzle, hoping that when arranged just right, I would see a clear path to follow. But it wasn't fitting. I couldn't see the picture yet.

"How could the real estate transactions be connected to the shootings?"

"I can't prove they are, but greed makes it possible to imagine anything. I need to find out what's motivating these sales. Hard to imagine that Langston is in the dark on a development project."

"Here's a thought. Could there be holdouts who are putting a damper on the project? People who don't want to sell? Maybe key pieces are contentious, so he doesn't want to go public."

"That's possible." I nodded. "Controlling the land would be key to getting a substantial development off the ground."

"Would the Mayor's Office would be aware of a project like that?"

"The developer would start with Langston. Without the alderman's buy-in, or payoff, the project would be dead in the water. But after that, yes, the next level is the Mayor's Office. They would partner in anything this big, eventually. For some reason, they're not talking yet. Maybe they don't own enough land for Langston to feel he can sell the project, and he's keeping it close to the vest until then. I hit him up about development this morning, but he's playing dumb."

"It might be interesting to speak with other property owners. See if anyone's been approaching them."

"Good idea. Let's divvy up the list. And I want to start talking to anyone hoping to sell as well." Brynn nodded as her jaw worked over the corned beef. I grabbed the plot map and divided the area into two segments. "We'll have to do lookups by address, so it'll be a bit tedious. You take the southern half of the area, I'll take the north."

"Could they be building a convention center?" Brynn asked.

"I doubt it. McCormick Place is only a few miles away."

"Housing?"

"Given the size of the parcel, that would make sense, but the developer would need planned development zoning, PD instead of C3-3, commercial. In this area, housing would have to be low-to-middle income, and the Mayor's Office would want the victory dance. A large-scale development plan would certainly have city support," I said, thinking through how that could play out. "So why keep the project hush-hush? The city has to be involved in any PD approval. Maybe the developer can't push for planned development zoning until they own a bigger percentage of the land needed. It wouldn't be the first time entrenched homeowners upended a construction schedule. The developers might not want to start the buzz until a few more deals have been cut." I stared at the map. "This would also be a great location for some kind of entertainment complex or concert venue —size, access, cheap property. Rendell would give up a kidney for a feather like that in his cap before the next election season."

"Well, unless you need anything else, I'll let you decompress. Give me a buzz later, and we can compare notes. While you're here, take out your frustration on a piece of cheesecake or something," Brynn said.

"You think a sugar coma is going to help?"

Brynn laughed. "Can't hurt, can it? I'll talk to you later this afternoon."

Settling into my makeshift office, I passed on the cheesecake, ordered a chef's salad to round out the wimpy fruit salad, then sent Michael a text asking when we could talk.

Buried somewhere in my contact list was the name of a real estate attorney, Peter Retley, I'd met a few years ago. He called regularly, hoping he could get me into bed regardless of my marital status. Not what I had in mind, but he could order encumbrance reports. If there were mortgages involved in the Orton purchases, I'd have a money trail back to the owners. I made the call, explained what I needed, dodged committing to a meet-up, then emailed him a list of the properties after we hung up. And prayed that the limits of how far I was willing to go for a story weren't about to be tested.

32

I sat in the coffee shop long after Brynn had left, still staring at the map. The scale of this project meant money, serious money. If I was right and the shootings were tied to the real estate, the profit had to be massive. But what did killing accomplish?

Langston had to know the endgame. It was impossible for him to be in the dark, given the zoning requests. So if this was all legitimate why wasn't he talking?

Although not up for reelection this term, Langston had never been shy in front of the media. If there were a deal even halfway close to being wrapped, he'd be getting his mug out in front of any fool with a phone and a Facebook account—that meant the deal wasn't sealed or didn't have the proper momentum yet. Or maybe there was something to be gained by keeping quiet until it was too late for anyone to muck up the plans.

I made another call to Tierney, this time going straight to his executive assistant, Natalie. Unless he wanted to be totally off the grid, she'd be able to get me in to see him. A couple of well-placed questions about her three kids and within minutes I had half an hour on his calendar later today.

Gladwyn was the connector. But did he know the grand plan? Or was he simply executing and not bothering to ask questions? At the very least, I might be able to get a name out of him. If I knew who had hired him, I was another layer closer to identifying the structure that made up Orton and LRM.

Moving back to the list of property owners, I began the tedious work of matching properties with contact information. Nearly two dozen calls later, all I had to show for my time was one elderly-sounding man who went on a tirade about a door-to-door salesman offering to buy his house. He didn't remember any names and I couldn't tell what upset him more, the pushiness of the guy or that his nap had been interrupted.

I was about to punch in the next number on my list when my phoned beeped with another call.

"Are you okay?" Michael said when I answered. "I'm sorry I couldn't get to you sooner."

"It's good to hear your voice," I said, feeling myself relax. "I'm fine, just anxious to know what's happening."

"We had the wrong guy." I heard Michael sigh. "We off the record?"

"You forget I'm unemployed."

"Nash wasn't the shooter. We picked him up on a tip but it wasn't him. However, we think he knows who is. Nash runs with the Disciples. Says one of his crew has been bragging about making the hits. For all I know, Nash was handing him the ammo, but he has an outstanding warrant. We're hoping his attorney can knock some sense into him and we can get something useable." He paused. "Andrea, he's claiming this was a paid gig."

I leaned back against the vinyl booth, my head swimming with thoughts.

"Michael..."

"I know. Promise me you'll stay safe. I'll come see you tonight."

"Okay. Call me later."

A text from Retley popped up. "Can you be here in an hour?"

His office was only a ten-minute walk, so I agreed to meet and moved back to the call list. Nothing but voice mail or quick hang-ups once I explained who I was. As I prepared to dial the next number on the list, my phone rang with another call. The guy in the next booth gave me a dirty look, apparently annoyed with my temporary office. I flashed him a weak smile and looked at the screen. Link-Media. It wasn't Erik—his name would have come up—so I took the call.

"Andrea, it's Art Borkowski. I need to talk to you."

Borkowski? What in the world did he want? Other than to annoy me. "I'm sure Brynn can find whatever research notes you're looking for. Or are you working on getting her fired, too?"

The jab just tumbled out. And it felt good. Petty and childish, but I was so damn tired of condescending, arrogant men with personal agendas and egos the size of a goddamn Goodyear blimp. Well, my personal agenda was the only thing that mattered right now. Unless Borkowski had something for me, he could take a hike.

I heard him clear his throat on the other end of the line. "Okay, I deserved that," he said, a smattering of humility in his voice. "This isn't about Brynn. It's about the business." He paused, waiting for me to shut him down. When I didn't, he continued. "I got a call from an acquaintance, a hedge fund guy I use as a source now and then. I haven't spoken to him in over a year, but in my *Tribune* days I could always count on him when I needed finance geek language translated."

"Fascinating. Is there a point to this story?"

"I know you're not on the payroll any longer, but you are still a co-owner, right?"

"I own a very small percentage," I said. "What does that have to do with your friend?"

"Well, this guy starts asking about the staff. Who's good? Is there any room to cut back on personnel? Do I see myself here long-term? I answer a few questions, just surface level. Seemed innocent enough, but then he wants to dig into numbers. Is there any fluff in expenses? Could we kill the overhead and function with freelancers? And it's not feeling so innocent anymore."

"And what did you say?" I asked, but my head had already gone to the phone call I'd overheard. Erik was looking for money, and this guy was a potential investor doing his homework.

"I told him I had no plans to move on, but that he should speak with Erik directly if he needed anything. Like I said, I know the guy, and he was probably counting on me for payback, but hey, that's over the line."

"Erik could be doing some restructuring of his loans, or your money guy could be trolling for a competitor. Doesn't necessarily sound like anything to be concerned about," I said, fibbing like a five-year-old. "You were right to pass him off, but why aren't you asking Erik these questions?"

"So you're not aware of any financial changes in the business?" he asked, being evasive, trying to feel me out before he said anymore.

I told him I wasn't. The call I'd overheard wasn't definitive enough to draw that conclusion with certainty, and I wasn't about to share rumors with an employee, especially Borkowski, despite my suspicions.

Borkowski continued. "I'll be blunt. I owe you that. I did ask Erik if there was anything going on. Didn't tell him why I was asking. Essentially, he told me to go fuck myself. Look, I'm sorry to be the source, but according to my guy, Erik isn't restructuring the loan, he's selling off a percentage of the company, a big percentage. I didn't let on with Erik that I'd heard rumors of a sale. I'll leave that in your court if you want to push.

"Andrea, I know we never got off on the right foot. I can be a real jackass. My bullheadedness takes over and gets me in trouble. Despite how I came across, I never doubted your honesty or your commitment. I had a feeling Erik hadn't been straight with you. Divorce makes men real pricks," he said with regret in his voice, as if he knew this personally. "If there's some big shakeup coming, I'd like to know. The *Tribune* wants me back as managing editor. I'd hate to turn it down, then find out three months later that my paychecks are bouncing."

I thanked Borkowski for the heads-up and ended the call, my mind numb. I didn't know how to feel other than terrified that my financial future was dangling at the edge of a cliff. I opened my email and jotted off a note to my attorney, distracted by thoughts of castration. Any naive expectations I'd originally had for a quick and easy divorce were long gone, but this stunt was a new low. I glanced at my watch, threw money on the table, and headed out.

Retley's office was on the fourteenth floor of a 1930s high-rise on LaSalle, just south of Wacker. Tall ceilings, creaky elevator, carpet that hadn't been cleaned since 1965. I opened the door to his suite and the smell of fumigant hit me. A cute young thing with a silly bun on top of her head and earrings the size of pancakes greeted me. She offered me a seat, then phoned Retley. I looked around for a window, afraid my brain would get pickled if I didn't get some fresh air into my lungs.

A door opened on the left, and Retley stuck his head out, motioning me to come back.

"Good to see you, Andrea. Interesting stuff you sent my way. I knew you'd want to see this ASAP. Don't know what to make of it, but I guess that's your problem, ha." He pulled on his French cuffs and ran a hand over his slicked-back hair before walking over to a large white board on the right wall covered with scribbles.

"Okay, so, what we have here are the twenty properties you inquired about. All purchased within the last five months. Plus..." He paused. "There's another five that haven't hit the books yet. So, twenty-five in total between them. None of the properties are worth much individually; we're talking a hundred and twenty-five K to about two hundred K. Collectively it's near the four point three mark." He tapped his finger on the total, a gold chain bracelet clanking as he moved. "As I suspect you already know, it's the sum of the parts that makes this rich. Given the proximity, I'd bet it's a development play. But again, I imagine that's what has you interested."

I nodded. "Do you have any estimates on the value of that land if it were one parcel?"

"That's tough to gauge. Parcels that size, ten minutes from the Loop, are practically unheard of. But land value would conservatively have a thirty to fifty percent premium. Which doesn't suck, but the big money is in the redevelopment."

Retley was confirming my assumptions. But the question still remained—what were they planning?

"Now to the dollars," he said. "You were interested in who holds the paper. Before I get to that, some of these deals were financed, some all-cash. I was curious about that, so I sorted the data a few different ways. Turns out that the first five purchases were the all-cash deals. Maybe money got tight for some reason, maybe the plan changed, got bigger as things moved along, and they needed financing to keep going. Not sure it's relevant, but interesting, I think."

"Makes sense," I said. "The original investors might have realized they had a bigger opportunity than they first thought.

Needed to take it to another level. What did you learn about the mortgages?"

"Of the twenty properties being financed, we have three different financing companies involved. Two of the financing companies weren't familiar to me. One, I've dealt with before."

"If they're spreading the debt around, I'm not sure that helps me."

"Don't go crying in your beer just yet," he said. "I got a few more tidbits up my sleeve. That finance company is based in the Cayman Islands, land of the super-secret investment. Which is good news for you because a few years ago I had a client that, shall we say, needed to keep a low profile. I helped him stash some assets, and it just happens that I used the very same Blue Water Financial Group that your buddies here in Chicago are using. So, being the mensch that I am, I get my Cayman guy on the phone. And what do you know? I find out the two other lenders are subsidiaries of none other than Blue Water Financial Group."

A satisfied smile crossed his face as he waited for my reaction.

"Throwing another layer over their identity, is what they're doing. Makes it hard to track," I said.

"Bingo. And the guys in the Caymans are happy to play. You ready for a name?"

"A name? You've got a name?"

"Yep. Don't know how high up on the food chain, but I have a name."

"And..."

"All right, I'll stop torturing you. My contact deals with a guy named Porter Gladwyn. Mean anything to you?"

"Yes, it does." I couldn't hold back a smile. "Peter, you're incredible. Call me next week. We'll go have that dinner you've been asking about. I'm buying."

33

Gladwyn. There he was again, hovering around the fringes of these real estate deals. I snaked through the pedestrian traffic on LaSalle, dodging businesspeople and tourists alike, my normal swift pace ramped up a few notches by adrenaline. Was he just the legal talent executing the strategy, or did he have a hand in pulling the strings? My gut said he wasn't the lead. Not that attorneys weren't a greedy lot, but this scheme was too audacious. He didn't strike me as a man who wanted to get his hands dirty. He wouldn't have been the idea man, but he'd execute the plan like a good soldier. There would be layers and layers between his involvement and the alpha dog. So who had hired him? Could I get at his client list? I racked my brain for names of attorneys I might have met in my previous career who'd worked for Blasik.

Wait. Janek's former partner Matt Dubicki had been represented by Blasik, Cameron, and Lord in his corruption defense against bribery accusations. The same firm employed Gladwyn. And Dubicki now worked for a real estate developer. Could this be another connection?

As I walked the six blocks south from Retley's office to my meeting with Tierney, I phoned Cai.

"Hey, do you remember telling me about Janek's partner, Matt Dubicki, being represented by Blasik, Cameron, and Lord?"

"Yeah, sure. But why should I interrupt my day to think about the competition?"

"Because I'm the one that's asking. Is there a better reason?"

"You've become very needy since losing your job. I'm not sure it's a quality I like in you."

"Then help me get reemployed so I can stop bugging you during the day." I laughed, nearly bowling over a woman who had stopped dead in front of me to take a selfie.

"Ready to return to the world of motions to compel and understated wardrobes? I'm happy to pass your resume around."

"I'm not throwing in the towel yet. Dubicki. Tell me how you know he hired Blasik. Who else was on the legal team? What else do you know about the case?"

"You know I can't talk about that. What's this all about? You're moving into murky territory with these questions."

"Cai, I need a break on this story," I pleaded. "It's possible that one of the attorneys on Dubicki's case might also be involved in a suspiciously large number of real estate purchases in Englewood."

"Are you saying Dubicki is connected to these land deals or the attorney?" Her voice was hesitant, unsure of what picture I was painting.

"I don't know, but I haven't ruled anything out. This land is being purchased through a shell corporation, and the only name I can attach to them so far is an attorney at Blasik who has facilitated the corporate formation. At the very least, he's also a front man on some of the mortgages."

"The guy you asked me about? Gladwyn? I can't imagine anyone at one of the city's big-five firms taking a risk like that."

"As far as I know, Gladwyn has simply done the filing and helped arrange financing. He may not have the big picture. He may not be aware of any connection between the land deals and the shootings. But then again, maybe he is."

"You have some reason to be suspicious?"

"I went to see him. He shut me down the second I voiced the name of the company involved. Couldn't get me out of his office fast enough. It's not proof of anything, but it did set my alarm bells screeching. Now I'd love a look at his client list, but since I don't have an inside track to anyone with that information, I'm doing the next best thing I can think of—calling you.

"Dubicki's current employer is Mezey Development. As you know, they're one of the largest real estate development firms in the city. And Gladwyn is representing someone buying real estate in Englewood. It's a long shot, but what if they're both working for Mezey? If I can establish a connection between Dubicki and Gladwyn, I may have a path to finding out who is behind the transactions. Synergistic, don't you think?"

The line was silent as Cai struggled with her conscience. I was now standing in front of the State's Attorney's Office with only a minute to spare.

Cai wasn't budging, so I wedged the phone between my shoulder and my ear, then pulled out my iPad and punched in "Matt Dubicki + Mezey," hoping for a flash of brilliance to push Cai's decision making in my direction. A fuzzy series of images flashed across the top of the screen, distracting me for a moment with something vaguely familiar. I clicked over to Google Images. Staring back at me was a photo identifying Matt Dubicki, posed with a hard hat and shovel in hand, at the site of a ground breaking for a strip mall in Schaumburg. I hadn't seen a picture of him before now, but it was the same face I'd seen three times—at Gibsons, at the community center, and in Langston's office!

"I have to go," I said to Cai, my mind stumbling over the implications. "I'll call you later."

The roles were becoming clear. If Mezey was the force behind development plans for these parcels, the company's owner, Ty Mankoff, could coordinate the project, Gladwyn could handle the real estate acquisition, and Alderman Langston could handle the zoning and get mayoral buy-in when the time came. Dubicki had the gang connections, so he could act as an enforcer.

This was a goddamn org chart of coordinated greed under the pretense of business development. But where was the money coming from? Unlikely that this group alone had the millions of dollars needed to pull this off. Buying the land was simply phase one.

Could others be involved—like Nelson Ramirez, the owner of Rami Concrete? He had a history of corruption, access to cash, and was buddies with Langston. His concrete business would profit from a large-scale project. Made sense. But could I prove any of this? And I still didn't know their endgame, or how a sniper fit in.

All of these thoughts swirled in my head as I passed through security and rode the elevator to Tierney's office. I dialed Michael. My call went directly to voice mail.

As Natalie showed me into his office, Tierney was downloading instructions to an intimidated young associate with flop sweat staining the collar of his shirt. I took a seat, mouthing a heartfelt thank-you to her for getting me on the calendar. The young man hid his embarrassment in an averted gaze as he hustled out of the office. I remembered the feeling. It was like having your stomach turned inside out with a sledgehammer. Although I liked to think I hid it better.

Although the purpose of my meeting with Tierney was to discuss Quincy Harris's situation, and the broader issue of deed theft in Englewood by LRM, I was also hoping to plant a few well-placed questions in Tierney's mind about strange real estate activity. His own nose for bullshit would start connecting the deed theft with the high number of sales transaction. I just needed to get that door open. And right now, I needed someone else doubting CPD's explanation.

"Damn kids. Entire generation wants to pee their pants the minute they don't get a gold star for knowing the difference between a motion and a brief. Coddled group of brats, the lot of them. You don't have any, do you, Andrea?" Tierney asked. I shook my head. "Good, don't."

I sat quietly, waiting for him to finish his condemnation. I'd heard it all before. It was just part of being initiated into Tierney's world, a world that didn't suffer fools, failures, insecurities, or prima donnas. He took a seat and leaned back into his Eames executive chair, its espresso leather battered and worn to match his body like a vintage pair of Levi's. He'd carted that expensive piece of furniture with him from job to job for the past twenty-five years and would likely keep it twenty-five more.

"So, why the hell are you here? Looking for a favor? You know my policies on the media. If you've come here to finagle some quote out of me, walk out now before I have you escorted to the curb by a couple of big, burly men. I told you when you bailed on me that there'd be no special treatment." I couldn't help the smile that escaped. "What the fuck is that grin for?" he asked.

"Denton, I was just thinking two things. One, I miss working for you. That no-bullshit style of yours is in short supply out in the rest of the world. I don't think I fully appreciated it while I worked for you."

"And the other?" He crossed his arms over his chest, unimpressed with my compliment. Probably thought I was sucking up, hoping to be reinstated.

"The other is, I'm not sure I've ever seen you smile."

A huff-like laugh escaped from his throat. Although not quite a smile, it was in the vicinity enough for it to count. "You caught me off guard there."

"You were expecting groveling? Not today, Denton. I'm not here to get on my knees and ask for a quote, or a job. I'm bringing you a case." I pulled out Quincy's file and laid it in front of him. "I met a man recently who's been the victim of deed theft. You know the story: hard times, lack of cash, no access to counsel. Along comes someone who claims he has the magic bullet that will make all the problems go away. Before you know it, papers are signed, and the victim doesn't even realize he's signed away ownership of his home. Although the ongoing mortgage and an even angrier loan department are new surprises."

He flipped through the documents as I summarized for him. "Okay, looks like he's got something. But you could have passed this case on to a dozen different ASAs who would have been happy to do the legwork for him. Why are you pounding on my door?"

"Look at the address. Englewood. Three blocks from one of the shooting locations. I think there's a connection between these cases." I leaned back in my chair and paused, crossing my arms over my chest. "There are others in his neighborhood who've been victims of this same company, LRM Property Holdings. Are you aware of any of this activity?"

He tossed his glasses onto his desk and pinched the bridge of his nose as if a headache had just landed. I could see that I'd hit my mark. "I used to think your persistence was an attribute. Now I see it's just a pain in the ass. You're letting ambition fuel your imagination. Where is your evidentiary fact? Conflating this real estate scam with the shooting is beyond comprehension. I appreciate your chutzpah, but come on, Andrea, don't lose all legal standards of evidence in the process of getting your story."

"Well, let me broaden the landscape. Setting aside LRM for the moment, there's a company strategically buying up property in Englewood near the shooting locations. It didn't exist six months ago. It has offshore financial dealings in the Caymans. And the attorney involved in these transactions is also working with a certain alderman to obtain more-favorable zoning. An alderman who has connections with a large real estate developer who also happens to be a well-known name inside the highest level of city government."

I let everything fly, my words tumbling out rapid fire as if I were afraid that a pause would be an opportunity for Tierney to shut me down.

"Because I know you so well, Denton, that vein that's been bulging in your right temple tells me that LRM Holdings is a name you've heard before." He didn't acknowledge my comment, just looked at me as stonily as he would a defendant. "I'll leave you Quincy Harris's file with the understanding that his situation will be properly handled, as always. I'll pass on the additional victims as I have them." I paused, hoping for a response, but got none. I continued.

"It's clear that, at the moment, the rest of this conversation isn't something you're prepared to discuss. But you should know that I have every intention of continuing to pursue a connection between this real estate play and the highway sniper, despite your refusal to entertain that theory. If you want to talk about anything I've had to say today, you know how to get ahold of me."

I got up from my chair and turned to leave. Tierney kept his silence, but I could feel the shift in his energy as the cogs rotated and clicked into place.

“One last thing,” I said as I reached the door. “The attorney that set up LRM Holdings is the same guy who set up the company now gobbling up property in Englewood. His name is Porter Gladwyn.”

34

I'd been on Lake Shore Drive for all of four minutes when brake lights pulled me to a dead stop and out of my thoughts. After seeing Tierney, I had run home to get my car and was now on my way to Mezey Development. I intended to walk in and see if I could sweet-talk anyone into bragging about upcoming development plans. An unformed, ridiculous plan, but hell, why not?

If Nash was to be believed, the sniper was a hired gun. But why? What was the bigger plan? Real estate development was the only answer that made sense. The shootings could be a device for price manipulation

Can't exactly get top dollar for your home when bullets are flying past the windows. But it was hard to comprehend men so greedy they were willing to kill for a project. The magnitude of what must be at stake floored me.

The owners of those unsold properties might give me some answers. That is, if Brynn wasn't striking out as badly as I was.

I sure as hell wasn't learning anything new about the impact of summer road construction on traffic patterns. I'd moved about twenty feet in the last five minutes. Maybe Michigan

Avenue would be traveling at a better pace. Time to get off The Drive.

I flipped my turn signal and nosed over toward the beat-up white Cadillac on my right, hoping a wave at the driver would open enough space for me to squeeze in. Success. As I inched over, my phone rang through the Bluetooth system. With my eyes on the car in front of me doing a last-ditch maneuver into the exit lane, I tapped the button on the steering wheel and took the call.

"Hi, it's Erik. I know you're mad at me, but we need to talk."

Shit! Why hadn't I looked at the screen? Leave it to Erik to find me when my guard was down.

"Our attorneys can handle everything from here," I said. "Under the circumstances, it's best if we don't speak without a referee."

"Ouch! Having thoughts of inflicting bodily harm?"

"Only for the past four months."

Silence. Good.

"I only need a few minutes," he said, his voice losing its cocky edge. "I promise to be civil. I have a paycheck for you and a few documents. A couple minutes is all I need."

Items easily mailed. He must want something. I contemplated brushing off the request, but going in would give me an opportunity to pick up any notes Brynn had ready. The more data I had for Michael tonight, the better. I glanced at the clock. Tight, but I could still make it to Mezey before they closed if I didn't let Erik derail me.

"Fine. I can spare five minutes, but if this isn't all business, I'm gone." I tapped off the call before I could change my mind.

Traffic eased up once I was traveling west on Randolph. Unfortunately, my mood did not. If Erik was expecting a kiss-and-make-up moment, he was going to be disappointed. Each block closer I got to the office, the angrier I was at myself for even agreeing to meet.

I took a right on LaSalle and headed north, keeping my eyes peeled for a parking spot as I crossed Ontario. As usual, there was nothing. I circled, but wasn't feeling patient. The quicker I got in, the quicker I could get out, so I pulled into the alley behind the office, parked in an empty spot reserved for a neighboring business, put on my flashers, and prayed I wouldn't be here long enough for the owner of the slot to have me towed.

Brynn's face broke into a confused smile as I sauntered up to her cubicle.

"Please tell me you're back," she whispered.

"Nope." I shook my head. "Just picking up some paperwork from Erik. If you've made any progress on those calls, don't let me leave without a copy of your notes. I might have lined up some help."

Brynn gave me a quick nod and a lopsided smile as she threw herself back into the task.

Might as well get this out of the way. I nodded at a few of the surprised staffers and continued back to Erik's office.

As I stepped into the threshold of the open door, I caught sight of Borkowski leaning over Erik's desk. He was angled away from me and hadn't yet noticed my arrival. Why was he in here alone? His hand was on the desk phone. I watched as he seemed to be scrolling through Erik's phone log. Interesting.

My cell pinged with an incoming text, and Borkowski turned toward the sound.

"Oh?" he said, unable to come up with anything more eloquent.

Nice try on the diversion, but I wasn't buying it. *What were you looking for? Calls from potential purchasers?* I should probably chastise him for snooping, but in reality, I wondered if he'd found anything good.

"Where's Erik?" I asked instead. Whatever small bond we'd formed earlier in the day would hold for now.

"He, ah, went over to Starbucks. Said something about needing a double espresso."

"Seriously? We had a meeting. Tell him he missed his opportunity." I turned toward the door as Erik appeared, coffee in hand.

"I left that piece on your desk," Borkowski said quickly before scurrying out, his tone all business now that the window had closed on his surveillance expedition. He nodded his head at the phone as he left, a silent message to me. Keep quiet? Or I found something?

"Thanks for coming in," Erik said. "Things didn't end well the other day. I know, understatement of the year. You're probably not anxious to see me, but I'm glad you came."

"Do you have the documents?" I asked, trying to keep the conversation focused and emotions submerged. As much as I wanted to tell him what an ass he'd been, it wouldn't accomplish anything. Old story.

He unlocked a drawer in his desk and pulled out a file, but wasn't anxious to hand it over.

"What is it? Obviously you have something else you wanted to say. Please spit it out before my car gets towed." I shifted my weight to the other foot and hiked my purse up onto my shoulder, ready to bolt if this conversation diverted into our personal life. When he said nothing, I held out a hand. "Those documents...?"

He opened the file and gave me an envelope. "I had your payroll check cut early. Figured there was no reason to make you wait until next week."

I nodded thank you, appreciating his rare moment of thoughtfulness.

"You also have a severance check coming. Boss's discretion

can come in handy," he said, watching me for a reaction. "Six months was the best I could do." He handed me the file.

"Erik, I don't know what to say. Thank you. I didn't expect this." I flipped open the file, and instead of a check, legalese jumped out at me. Of course. I skimmed the document.

"I see there are strings attached." I closed the folder and felt my hands shake with rage as I glared at him. The brief moment of gratitude I'd felt had been squashed like a skunk on the expressway.

"It's a standard noncompete. Common in these situations. I'm sure you understand."

Common? No, but it would keep me on the sidelines and the highway shooting story locked on a flash drive, long past anyone giving a damn. Take the check and I'd be signing away any thoughts of a journalism career. I tossed the file back on his desk.

"Thanks, but I prefer a life without handcuffs."

I gave him one last look and walked out. Had Erik really expected me to take the money and go quietly? From his expression, it seemed he hadn't considered anything else. Sorry, good little girl went home long ago.

Brynn was ready with the copies when I got back to her desk. I thanked her quickly, promised to call in the morning, then bounded out of the office before my anger could consume me. Hopefully, I wouldn't be topping off my evening by having to cab over to the impound lot.

The warmth of the sun on my back and Brynn's notes in my bag were starting to ease my irritation as I turned the corner into the alley and moved past the dumpster.

Relief. The car was still exactly where I'd left it, but another vehicle had me pinned in. Probably the owner of the slot I was borrowing. Hmm, beat-up white Cadillac. Wasn't that the car that had followed me off the Randolph exit?

I stopped, pondering the situation, when suddenly someone grabbed my left wrist from behind and pulled my arm back and up into my shoulder blades. I gasped, and my bag tumbled to the ground. Before I knew what was happening, a forearm was thrust into my upper back, and I was slammed into the brick wall. Blinding pain shot down the side of my face as I made contact. My forehead and cheek were ground further into the rough surface as my assailant pushed the weight of his body into mine.

"Take my wallet," I managed to squeak out.

He yanked my arm higher until I cried out. My head foggy from the blow, my face pressed against the wall, I shot my eyes down the alley, hoping someone could see me. Could come to my aide.

"Don't say a word, bitch," he growled into my ear. The stink of cigarettes wafted up my nose.

My mind boomeranged, but in half speed, trying to understand what was happening, what he wanted, how I was going to get out of this. I blinked rapidly, trying to clear my head, trying to be analytical about the situation, forcing myself to notice what I could about the attacker I couldn't see. He was taller than me by maybe four or five inches. I could feel the weight of him, the dense, compact muscles of his chest and legs as he pressed against me.

His elbow now dug harder into my back, forcing soft flesh deeper into the rough brick. The surface was like razors tearing into my cheek, now warm and sticky with blood.

"You've been hangin' where you don't belong," he said, his breath warm against my face. "Askin' questions that ain't none of your business."

I forced myself to focus. Forced air into my lungs and out again. Forced the pain and the fear down deep inside so I could catch every nuance about this man and what he was saying. He released the arm across my upper back, but held tightly to the wrist pushed up between my shoulders. He pulled me back against him a few inches, my face now clear of the brick. His right arm came up along the side of my body, brushing the bare skin on my arm. I recoiled at his touch as he rested his palm against the wall. I could see the stubby fingers of his hand. The ragged nails. The elaborate tattoo that started at his wrist and sheathed his forearm. An eagle, a globe, an anchor, the words "Get Some." Military? I stared at the image, trying to memorize every detail, before he moved his hand to my waist and pushed his pelvis into my backside.

"You don't listen very well. You were told to stay out of Englewood. To stop talking to cops. I guess I'll have to find another way to get your attention," he said, his hand moving up my body, across my stomach, over my breast. I stifled a gasp but knew he could feel my panic as I tensed against his touch. His hand traveled to the low neckline of my blouse, fondling the silk until one finger reached skin. Then, in a single motion, he pulled aside shirt and bra, ripping off buttons and exposing me. Using the small bit of leverage that his movement had created, I brought one foot up against the wall, pushing and twisting, struggling to free myself as I screamed for help. In response, his hand became a vise on my breast until I shrieked in pain. Then with another yank of my arm, he shoved me back against the brick.

"Stay where you belong," he snarled into my ear, then released his grip and walked away.

As I listened to the sound of a car door slam and tires squeal down the alley, I clutched the wall, shaking, too terrified to move. I crumpled to my knees. My body trembling, I turned my back against the wall for support, closed my eyes, and pulled air deep into my chest, working the adrenaline out. Counting out the breaths in my head. In: one, two, three, four, five. Out: one, two, three, four, five. Slowly I regained control. The ripe smell of the dumpster that had shielded me from the street became tangible again. As did the rocks digging into my ass.

Releasing another breath, I pulled clothing over my scraped and bloody flesh and wobbled to my feet. My bag lay spilled just three feet in front of me. Kneeling, I picked up a packet of tissues and dabbed at the knot on my forehead, pulling back blood. Hurt like hell, but the bleeding seemed manageable. Now what? Go back upstairs and ice my head, which meant giving Erik another reason to hang on? File a police report on a man I could only identify by his forearm, which might also bring my assailant back? Or could I pull myself together enough to drive the ten minutes back to my apartment?

With unsteady hands, I gathered my keys and the contents of my bag and let myself into the car, quickly locking the door behind me. Leaning back against the headrest, I took a firm grip on the wheel to control the trembling, gathered what energy I had left, and allowed the tears to flow.

35

With fingers cramped from gripping the steering wheel so tightly I'd lost feeling, I let myself into my apartment. The tears had dried, the blood had dried. I remembered nothing of the drive home, focused instead on repeating over and over to myself the details of my attacker's tattoo, the sound of his voice, the choice of his words. Norman, my doorman, had rushed to help as I limped into the lobby for a second time, battered and bruised, offering to call an ambulance, the police, Cai. I declined, wanting only the security of my own home. My own bathtub. My own bed.

After securing the deadbolt, I bagged some ice, then shuffled off to fill the bathtub. Walter jumped up on the bathroom counter, welcoming me home, as I surveyed the damage. Abrasion on my cheek, a nice welt on my forehead, and an inch-long cut that had been the source of the bleeding.

I stripped, tossed the blouse in the trash, laid out the thickest towel I owned, and immersed myself in the hot water. Reclining as far as the slant of the tub would allow, I applied the ice pack and let the water be my release. Pushing away all thoughts of anything other than feeling the heat of the water and the soft expansion of my lungs, I let my body float until sleep found me.

Waking to bathwater gone cold, I toweled off, wrapped myself in a thick terrycloth robe, and downed some Advil before padding out to the kitchen to make a cup of tea. I curled up on the sofa with my Earl Grey in hand and Walter purring on my lap. I had just one thought on my mind: I was getting close.

The memory of my attacker's hands on my flesh flashed back. The thrust of his pelvis, his hand on my breast, his voice in my ear. My breath caught in my throat, and I gripped the arm of the sofa as panic seized control of my emotions. *Let it go. Slow it down. Focus. Fill your lungs and release.*

This is what he wanted. To put me into a cold sweat in the middle of the night, imagining how he would hurt me. To make me so afraid and weak that I would hide instead of fight. Instead he had given me a gift. He had shown me that someone wanted me off the story. And that meant I was pushing the right buttons.

At 7:30 p.m. the phone rang: Norman announcing Detective Hewitt's arrival. It had completely slipped my mind. After asking that he be sent up, I flipped open the door latch, then hurried into the bedroom to throw on jeans and a cotton shirt. As I heard Michael call out a hello, I took one last fruitless look in the mirror, dabbed on some concealer, and headed back toward the living room. There wasn't enough makeup in all of Sephora to camouflage my run-in with a brick wall.

Michael stood at the terrace doors, observing the view of the Hancock Building and giving me a moment to admire how the cut of his navy linen blazer showed off his strong shoulders and trim waist. He turned as I approached and gave me a smile that I felt in the pit of my stomach.

"Sorry I'm a little late."

As I got closer, his smile morphed into concern. His eyes

drilled into me as he lifted the hair off my forehead to get a look at the damage.

"I guess the ten minutes I just spent putting on war paint didn't hide the evidence."

"Makeup isn't going to cover up a goose egg that size. What happened?"

"Why don't we talk about it over a glass of wine?"

I didn't give him a chance to respond and moved toward the kitchen "Hope you're okay with rosé. My wine list is short right now. But I have a lovely Whispering Angel." I tipped my head toward the kitchen mess as I opened a bottle and poured. Handing him a glass, I sloshed a little over the side.

Michael rescued both glasses from my hands, lifted an eyebrow, and nodded toward the living room. I dutifully traipsed over to the safety of upholstered furniture.

We sat silently, getting the first sip of wine under our belts, while Michael grilled me with his eyes.

"Stop stalling. You were all in one piece yesterday. What happened?" He leaned over, took my chin in his hand, and gently turned my head to get a better look.

"This was a warning shot," I said, matching the intensity of his gaze. Any need to couch my words to Michael had evaporated in that alley. Like it or not, he was going to hear straight out what I believed to be true.

"A warning?" he asked. "That phone call you got was a warning. This is assault. Talk to me."

"I stopped at Link-Media for a few minutes early this evening. When I returned to my car, which was parked in the back alley, a man attacked me from behind. This"—I motioned to my face—"is where I made contact with the brick wall he shoved me into."

"You parked in the alley?" he said, as if this were some stupid blunder on my part.

"He wasn't there to mug me, Michael." I could hear the irritation in my voice. "I know it was stupid." I sighed and changed my tone. Michael was right. "He followed me. I first noticed his car on Lake Shore Drive. He followed me off the exit at Randolph. He may have followed me all the way from my garage. I don't know."

Michael said nothing, his jaw tightening as he digested my words. His fingers wrapped the bowl of the wineglass so firmly I thought it might shatter.

"He followed me to deliver a message. He shoved me into a wall and told me to stay out of Englewood. To stop asking questions about things that were none of my business." I paused. "To stop talking to cops."

I could see the comprehension dawn on his face. Gone was the relaxed laugh, the smile teasing at the edge of his mouth, the playful banter. In its place were impenetrable determination and anger.

As I waited for the interrogation I knew was coming, my phone rang in my bag at my feet.

"Sorry, I should have turned that off." I leaned down and switched off the ringer. As I pulled myself back up, Michael reached over and touched the edge of the wrap neckline of my top, holding back the cotton jersey that had gaped when I moved, exposing my scraped chest.

"Did he do this too?" he asked, his voice tight, as if struggling to control his tone.

"Yes."

"Did he touch you?"

"He pulled aside my clothing." As I said the words, I could again feel the brick against my flesh, his body pinned against mine, the terror as his hand clamped down. My breath caught in my throat, and I wrapped my hands over my knees to control the trembling as the emotions rocked me again.

Michael watched. His eyes now hard and black as they washed over my abraded skin.

"Is there more?"

Our gazes locked, and I nodded. "Bruising from his hand."

"What does he look like?" His voice was frigid, frightening me with his tone and the anger behind it.

"I never saw his face," I said. "He's Caucasian, muscular. Someone who works out a lot. I'd guess about five ten or five eleven. Tattoo on his right forearm. Elaborate. Colorful. Possibly military. It had a globe, an eagle, an anchor, and the words 'Get Some.'"

"'Get Some.' You're sure?" I nodded. Michael knocked back the balance of his wine, jumped to his feet, and bolted toward the door. "Lock up behind me. I'll be back in an hour, maybe two."

"Wait. Where are you going?" I rushed after him, confusion racing through me. "The shooting. We have to talk about what happened. I thought you..."

"I have to see Janek." He raised a hand to my cheek, caressing my skin. "I'm going to fix this."

"Michael," I said, my voice barely a whisper. "How did he know I had talked to the cops?"

36

I paced the length of my living room like a caged panther, weaving around plastic-sheeted furniture and boxes of tile as if they were rocks in my path. Did Michael seriously think running off without a word of explanation was going to work for me? Did he expect me to sit here like some quivering mess of femininity waiting for him to fix everything?

My description of the attacker's tattoo had rung a bell, and I could only imagine that Michael was tracking him down as I sat here alone in my protective tower. Running off to defend my honor in some macho moment of male bravado wasn't going to accomplish anything. Hell, I wanted the guy brought in, too—to find out who had hired him. Whoever had attacked me was simply the help. Guys in this league didn't get their own hands dirty. The prosecutor in me deserved to be part of the interrogation. And the lump on my forehead was my admission ticket.

I punched in a call to Michael, getting nothing on the other end beyond a recording. Damn it. Sorry, Michael, damsel in distress wasn't part of my repertoire. *Think.* What was the endgame? Big. Secret. Profit worth killing for. Ideas shot like pinballs in my mind, but nothing seemed to fit the bill. It was the scale of it all that was the key. The financial upside had to be astronomical.

Wine wasn't going to keep my head clear. I opened a bottle of water and stood staring at the notes still laid out on the dining table. Okay, so assuming that I was right about Langston, Ramirez, and Mankoff, they needed others to pull this off. Other financial players, connections to grease the wheels. If it took a village to raise a child, then it took a major city to pull this off. A city? A vague memory tugged at the back of my mind. Platt? What had Borkowski said about Platt? Nothing happens in this city he doesn't know about.

I grabbed my bag and headed downstairs to hail a cab.

Lights were still on in the Link-Media office when I arrived. I inserted my key and crossed my fingers. Click.

Borkowski, the lone employee still in the office at this hour, turned at the sound, a blank look on his face as he gaped at me over his glasses. I nodded, walked over to the side of his desk, and pulled up a chair.

"If you're hoping I have more dirt on your ex, you've wasted a trip." His expression didn't change, but his tone lacked the edge I'd come to expect as his eyes gravitated to my face. Given our earlier conversation, was I hearing sympathy or self-preservation?

"You seem unusually accident-prone." He nodded at my head. "Might want to consider adjusting some of your lifestyle choices—and getting a new insurance policy while you're at it."

"What's your connection to Nelson Ramirez?" I blurted out, needing to see his face as he responded. It wasn't the most sophisticated of tactics, but I was out of time and patience.

"What? You barge in here to ask me that?" His brow crinkled in confusion.

"I know you have a personal relationship with Ramirez. That you've, shall we say, done him favors in the past. I know the two of you had dinner recently, along with Anthony Langston and Matt Dubicki. So what exactly is the nature of your relationship with Ramirez?"

He scowled and turned his head away from me.

"The answer isn't on that wall, Art. Talk to me."

He huffed but turned back.

"Me and Ramirez go way back. High school days, before we ever had an inkling of how our lives would play out. We're still neighbors." He sighed. "About ten years ago, he helped my kid out of a jam. A big one."

"What kind of jam?"

Borkowski pinched the bridge of his nose and scrunched his eyes tight before continuing. "I guess I don't have anything more to protect. My son had a drug problem. One night I laid into him about it for the umpteenth time and he bolted. Got in his car and left, loaded up on Oxy. He ran a stop sign four blocks from home. Car coming through the intersection swerves to miss him, hits a tree instead. Driver was killed instantly. David didn't even know it happened, just kept going." Borkowski's voice cracked at the memory.

"Ramirez saw it all from his living room. Hell, the driver died on his front lawn. A seventy-year-old woman coming home from seeing her grandkids. He knows the car, knows it was David. Comes to my house in the middle of the night and tells me everything. Says he'll protect David. That he'll keep it quiet. Lie if he's asked about what he saw. Whatever it takes to keep my boy safe. Kid was only seventeen. And Ramirez has done that for all these years. So, yes, I've done him the occasional favor. Right or wrong, I owed him."

"What about your son?" It was all I could manage to say. I had been so prepared to believe Borkowski's motivations were financial that nothing else had crossed my mind.

"David never knew. He was in and out of rehab so many

times I couldn't find a way to tell him. That he wouldn't be able to handle it. I was afraid that it would be the one last thing that sent him over the edge. Didn't matter. Didn't change the outcome. He graduated to heroin not long after. Overdosed three years ago." The pain of countless sleepless nights was etched anew on his face. His body slumped forward, arms resting on his desk as he looked at me.

"I'm so sorry. I can't imagine how difficult that was for you."

He nodded. "Is that what you came for?"

"In part," I said. "You made a comment last week about Platt knowing everything that happens in Chicago. Did you mean that in a general sense of his job, or was there something behind the comment?"

Borkowski leaned back his chair, drumming the pencil in his hand against his leg. "What are you asking about? Why are you coming in here now with these questions?"

"I got the sense that you were alluding to some history or personal connection. That your comment was more than a statement about his role in city government. Was I mistaken?"

"Doesn't get much bigger than the mayor, does it, now that he's thrown his hat in the ring?"

I leaned forward and put my elbows on my knees. "You're not answering my question."

"Just trying to figure you out. You come down here after hours, letting yourself in to a business that no longer employs you, asking about my personal life and now an offhanded comment from days ago. What are you up to? Looking for a trash-talk story on the new mayoral candidate? Selling dirt to the tabloids?"

I felt my back rearing up for a fight, but the agony in Borkowski's disclosure stopped me.

"Were you just blowing smoke earlier when you complimented my honesty? Do you think I operate under reality TV rules?" I asked.

We sat quietly, scoping each other out, but both seemingly ready to test whatever our new relationship was morphing into.

He tilted his head and tossed the pencil on the desk. "No. I meant what I said. You're not a game player, which is rare in this industry and, quite frankly, not an asset. But oddly refreshing nonetheless."

I nodded a thank-you in honor of our silent truce.

"Platt has a complex history, to say the least," he said. "Twenty, maybe twenty-five years ago, long before he was on the political stage, he was a newly minted MBA with a healthy bank account burning a hole in his pocket, courtesy of his father's estate. He had a big old arrogant chip on his shoulder, even back then. So he hooks up with a buddy from business school, and they set out to rule the real estate world. Only, their first project kills a kid."

"What project? What was the business?" Paging back through what I knew of Platt's resume, nothing but civil service had ever been attached to his name.

"They built a three-flat, in Logan Square I think. They were playing with this concept of low-cost modular construction. Threw one together to test the waters before they expanded. Platt was the financial side of the duo, and being a numbers geek, it was only about the profit. Vendors were squeezed like turnips. He rode them hard, didn't care what they had to do to meet the budget or the schedule. Shortcuts. Substitutions. The end result was one of the back porches collapsed."

"What happened from there?"

"A twelve-year-old boy lost his life. Platt pulled in a cavalcade of lawyers. Used smoke and mirrors to shift the blame to faulty fasteners imported from China. Platt and his partner spent a boatload of money on legal fees and settlements to make it all disappear. Paid off everybody to hush it up, complete with heavy-duty nondisclosure clauses. It's as if it never happened. I only know about it because my brother-in-law was on the construction crew."

"And what about their company?"

"That's when Platt decided that using his family connections to entertain a career in government made sense. Distanced himself from the whole mess."

"What about his partner?"

"He took a different path. Followed the Chinatown business model. Shut down one company, six months later popped open another with a different name and a slight twist. They both walked away unscathed and eventually even wealthier. Couldn't have worked out better for them if they had planned it."

"What do you mean? How could a business disaster of that scale get washed away?"

"Haven't you ever wondered why certain companies seem to get all the city contracts? Why all the dough goes to the same people over and over again? Is it logical that no one can ever wins a bid that's cheaper or faster than the usual suspects?" He raised his eyebrows, waiting for me to make the connection.

"So you're saying it's cronyism. Platt has steered business to his former partner or helped him undercut the bid, and they've both profited from it."

"Ding, ding, ding. Give the lovely lady her prize. Now you're seeing how this works. You keep my secret, I'll keep yours, and in the process we both get what we want."

"Who was his partner?" I asked, dread filling my mind.

"It's a name I'm sure you'll recognize—Ty Mankoff, owner of Mezey Development."

"Platt's involved too," I said, my mind numb.

"What are you talking about?"

"The shootings. The highway sniper. Of course, there has to

be someone higher up." Borkowski was looking at me as if I'd lost my mind while I rambled.

"Kid, you're not making sense. How is Platt involved? What are you talking about?"

I told him everything. What I knew, what I suspected, the threats I'd received. When I finished, he took off his glasses and tossed them on his desk.

"This is going to tear the city apart. Let me help. Let me work Ramirez."

I nodded. "Let me run home and get the files so I can bring you up to speed. I shouldn't be more than twenty minutes."

"What is the development play?" he asked as I got to my feet. I shook my head.

"Platt, Langston, Mankoff, Ramirez, Gladwyn, Dubicki. They're all involved. Wait. Gladwyn." Something about his background tugged at the back of my mind. There it was. Gaming. Of course!

"They're trying to build a casino."

37

A casino. Yes, that had to be it. The first within the city limits. With Platt on board and likely the next mayor, they had the keys to the kingdom. And a casino plan potentially so profitable it negated rational thought. As mayor, Platt could grease the wheels with Springfield for a gaming license. The community fight might be tough, but with the state's precarious financial position, it was only a matter of time before city limits no longer mattered.

I kicked off my heels, then went over to open the terrace doors, needing a little fresh air and a moment to focus my thoughts. I sat on the chaise for a moment, jotting a quick text to Michael that I'd be at the office. As I hit Send, Walter jumped on the dining table, sending my neatly organized piles of notes flying. I tossed my phone on the chaise and rushed to mitigate the damage.

As I began moving documents I wanted to share with Borkowski into my tote bag, a sharp rap on the door pulled me out of my thoughts. Michael must not have gotten my text. As I hurried toward the door, it swung open. Erik poked his head around, immobilizing me where I stood.

"Hi," he said. "It was unlocked."

"That doesn't entitle you to walk in unannounced. What are you doing here?" My feet were moving instinctually, wanting to halt his progress, but he was already two steps inside the apartment. There couldn't be worse timing for another of Erik's pleading moments.

He smiled sheepishly as I reached his side, his eyes darting around the room.

"Not tonight, Erik. I can't do this now..."

Owen Platt stepped around the door, and I froze as he shut it behind him. My eyes swung from Platt back to Erik, and unease knotted my stomach.

"We were over at Spiaggia for dinner. Since you're just down the street, I thought we'd stop and say hello," Erik said, his voice wavering.

I searched his face, but he wouldn't meet my eyes. Bullshit. What was the agenda? And whose? He leaned over and gave me a peck on the cheek, holding his position longer than he needed to, as if lingering over the scent of my hair.

"You've met Owen, haven't you?" he said, pulling away.

"Yes, of course." I studied Pratt's face as we shook hands. As usual, his practiced smile was a mask for the ice behind his eyes. His grip was tight, too tight. Tight in the manner of a man who wanted no uncertainty of his power. Questions formed in my mind and fell right out, unasked. What do you say to a man when you know he's hired a killer?

"How about some wine?" Erik said, moving toward the kitchen, not waiting for me to offer. I stood open-mouthed, irritated at his familiarity, but willing to postpone my objection until I had a better idea of their mission.

I turned back to Platt, waiting for the tell, wondering what they had planned. Trying not to signal my wariness.

"I understand you have a stunning terrace. Why don't we go outside? The temperature is lovely," Platt suggested.

Alone with Platt was the last place I wanted to be, but I'd left my phone outside. "Of course." I motioned toward the door, but my eyes were on the remaining papers splayed over my dining table. Would Erik notice?

As all visitors did, Platt walked to the edge and lifted his head to look up at the X-braced exterior of the Hancock Building to the white band of lights rimming the one hundred-story structure, then down the eleven stories to the street below.

Platt made trivial small talk about my remodeling as we waited for Erik. The charm that had unnerved me in the past with its slickness now seemed to have sinister undertones. How far would he go to achieve his goal? To conceal his involvement? I glanced over at the chaise. My cell phone was in sight, but unfortunately not in hand.

Erik returned, glasses in hand, seeming to have ignored the mess on my table. And my banged-up head, I realized. Neither man had shown an ounce of curiosity.

They didn't need to ask. They both already knew.

No, not Erik, too. My heart shattered.

The two men filled the air with inane banter as we sipped our wine under the summer stars and felt the light breeze of the evening. With a hollow heart and every nerve on edge, I watched Platt, saying nothing, waiting for the drama to begin. I glanced back at the phone.

"Andrea, I hear you're considering a move back into legal practice," Platt said. "I'd be happy to introduce you to some of my contacts. You have the tenacity for corporate law, and the pay is definitely better in the private sector." His lips turned up in an attempt at a smile, but his eyes were sharp and calculating, as if he were daring me to challenge him.

I smiled at the two men. "You haven't done too poorly on the government payroll, Owen." I watched the flicker in his eyes that told me I'd hit my mark. "I'm sorry, but your source is mistaken. Thank you for the offer, but I'm going to give freelance work a shot."

"Are you sure that's smart, Andrea?" Erik said. "You could have a pretty secure future. Owen's willing to make the right introductions. It would be the best thing to do. Freelance work is unpredictable, and you have some hefty expenses in this apartment," he said, glancing back inside.

"What's going on?" I looked from Erik to Platt. "Why are you here? Why are you so interested in how and where I work?" The back of my neck bristled. I was tired of the dance already.

"Be practical, Andrea," Erik said.

I glared at him. Who the hell did he think he was? I was angry at his supposition, angry that he'd involved himself in Platt's insane scheme. How could he have been willing to take that risk? To go that far?

"Erik, why don't you go inside and give me and Andrea a few minutes to talk?" Platt said.

Erik nodded and, with a pained look at me, did as he was told. My stomach clamped down as I gauged Platt's intent.

"Let me grab my phone. I'm expecting a call." I said.

Platt hooked my arm as I turned to follow Erik, pulling me back.

"You can hear it ring. Let's chat."

"What is it, Owen? What game are you two playing?"

He chuckled to himself, enjoying my irritation.

"I think what Erik is trying to say is that I can get you reestablished."

He stepped closer to me, backing me against the parapet, until his face was six inches from mine. I could feel a cold sweat trickle down my back as I looked into the face of a man who knew no bounds. Would that include silencing me? I shouldn't have come out here with him.

"Let's look at this logically," he said. "You've left one career. Been fired from another before it even took off. You're about to be divorced, and the sad truth is women rarely fully recover financially. It's been a tough six months. I can help turn this situation around." He was whispering, but his voice was as sharp as a blade.

"In exchange for what? My silence on a certain real estate deal?" I stared him down, but couldn't suppress the adrenaline flooding my system. I pictured the path between me and my phone. Fifteen, maybe twenty feet. Would Erik stop me if I made a run for it?

"I knew I'd like you." His laugh was low and dead as he leaned in. "I like smart women, challenging women."

I stepped to the side, trying to make a move toward my phone. In one sudden movement, he grabbed my wrist and spun me around, pressing me hard against the stone. I gasped at the suddenness and the menace in his voice.

"Now, be that smart woman or we're going to have to find another solution to this problem." His breath was hot against my neck, his body steeled against mine, his fingers dug into the flesh of my wrist. My mind raced. How far would he take his threat? I listened for signs that Erik was close at hand and squirmed against Platt's grip. He just squeezed tighter and laughed.

"After all, you're distraught. Alone. No job. A husband who has betrayed you. People will be shocked at first, but who wouldn't understand that you might not want to go on? That the pain of all this trauma could be too much."

His arms came around me as he hissed these horrible things in my ear, and I knew he wanted me silenced, permanently.

I pushed against him as his arms tightened around me and

he began to lift. Wedging my knee under the cap, I braced my arms against the granite while Platt pushed me forward until I could see the sidewalk eleven stories down. I watched as the flower pot beside me was knocked over the edge and obliterated below me. And knew I would be next.

Wriggling in his grip, I spun my shoulder, aimed high, and slammed an elbow into his neck. Hearing him grunt, I kicked against the barrier, pushing, fighting for leverage. My bare feet slipped against the stone, and Platt regained his grasp on me, lifting me toward the edge.

"No!" I screamed for Erik and lunged toward the concrete planter on my right. Thrashing, kicking, clawing. I strained to get a hand on something solid as Platt lifted my legs.

My fingers clutched at dirt and plants, probing for the rim, for something solid to hold on to, as my feet hung over the edge of the building. With nothing but willpower to stop what was happening I screamed again, struggling with every ounce I had in me. As we fought, I heard Erik pleading with Platt to stop, felt Erik pulling at him, trying to force him to release me, but Platt would have none of it. As my body shifted, my hand brushed wood. A trowel. I grasped the handle and, with every ounce of strength, swung. As I felt the prongs hit flesh, a gunshot rang out, and I tumbled to the ground.

Lying in a heap of sweat and dirt and blood on the slate, with my mind fogged over, I sensed movement around me. I felt a body being pulled off of me. Felt myself tremble as the world around began to go dark.

38

A cold blast of air whipped at my shoulders, and I burrowed deeper under the covers. Why were these pillows so flat? Slowly, the faint sound of Willie Nelson trickled through in the background. The alarm? What happened to my classical station? I labored to shake off the sleep that cemented my eyelids. My body felt like marble, but the chirp of voices and daylight were pushing into my consciousness. Voices. Who was here? Platt! I threw myself upright.

"It's okay, Andrea. You're safe."

A nurse laid her hand on my shoulder and inspected an IV line in my arm. Michael and Karl Janek watched, from the end of the bed, Cai and Lane from chairs next to the window. "How about some water?" Cai asked.

I nodded and felt the hammering in my chest slow. The men said nothing as I drank.

"Last night. Were you there?" I asked the men after settling back against the pillow. Images and fragments of conversation drifted into my consciousness. Dreams or memory? I couldn't distinguish. Cai laid her hand on mine, a tear rolling down her cheek. Lane stood at her side.

"Yes," Michael said, his face wracked with pain. "How do you feel?"

"I think I heard a gun last night. Did someone get shot?" I asked reluctantly, hoping that the terror I was feeling in my gut was misdirected, unreliable.

The men looked at each other before Janek spoke. "As we walked in, Platt had you in position to go over the edge. I fired, and as I did so, Mr. Martin changed his position. He took the hit. I'm sorry, but he didn't make it."

Erik was dead? I stared at Janek. I was immobilized, unable to breathe, feeling tears stream down my face. We looked at each other for what seemed like months, the torment visible in his eyes.

"Thank you for saving my life," I said, my voice barely a murmur. I watched as a small weight slipped off Janek's shoulders with my words. "And Platt?"

"Your skill with garden tools incapacitated him, but he'll recover," Michael said. "He's talking."

"He told you about the casino plan?" I shot my eyes from man to man, looking for confirmation.

Janek nodded. "You figured that out?"

"Not until last night. I had most of the players, but hadn't connected Platt until recently. Apparently he and Ty Mankoff go way back, had a deadly build they swept under the rug with payoffs decades ago." I looked at Michael, wanting to take his hand, words unspoken between us.

"Funny, Platt left that part out," Michael said to Janek. "If he thinks that ratting on his buddies is going to help him get a lighter sentence, that history isn't going to help his case. Tierney will be overjoyed." He turned back to me. "As you suspected, Platt gave up Anthony Langston, Porter Gladwyn, Nelson Ramirez from Rami Concrete, Ty Mankoff from Mezey Development..."

"Don't forget Dubicki. The highlight of my career was hauling him in," Janek added, a satisfied smile crinkling his eyes. "The State's Attorney's Office is suddenly understaffed. Watch out, Tierney may come recruiting."

"I think I'll keep the perch I've got," I said softly. "What about the shooter? Who was it?"

"The group couldn't buy up everything they wanted fast enough for the world not to notice, so they had to get creative," Michael said.

"The deed theft," I said.

"Yes, but even that wasn't enough," Janek added. "Dubicki decided to add a little pressure. He hired this gangbanger he knew from back in the day and gave him carte blanche to scare a few more homeowners into selling. Dubicki claims he didn't hire the guy to kill anyone, but if prices took a dive in the process, all the better. But the guy turned the tables on him. He figured there was something big going on, so he started using the Dan Ryan as target practice until they coughed up more money."

"We don't think killing anyone was ever part of their plan," Michael said. "This was just about money." He paused and a pained expression crossed his face. "Andrea, you should know that Erik was involved. At least financially. These seven men conspired to purchase the land with the intent to develop a casino. And to mask their involvement in the process."

"I knew that Erik was trying to raise cash, but I got it wrong. I thought the business was in trouble." My mind was numb. How could Erik be dead? How could he have been involved in all of this? I couldn't process any of it.

"The shooter is the guy that attacked you," Michael said. "He's in custody. Your description of the tattoo pointed us in his direction. We've had dealings in the past. Platt's claiming Dubicki acted on his own, but that will be up to Tierney to ferret out. Apparently this was a preemptive strike. Platt knew that a casino was just a matter of time."

"And figured he was in a position to influence how and where and who made money on it," I said.

"Exactly," Janek said. "Mankoff would put in the bid, if you can call it that, when the politics had worked themselves out. Between Platt and Langston, they figured they could get it rubber-stamped. Set up another shell corporation to hide the ownership, and then this circle of men would cash in. No one would know that every detail of the deal had been rigged from the start. All they had to do was use the gang activity for cover as they plotted and they'd all get richer."

"Art Borkowski can fill you in on Platt and Mankoff's history," I added. Michael nodded and glanced over at Janek.

Stepping to the side of the bed, Janek held out a hand. "I owe you an apology. My stubbornness got in the way. I let my personal history with the media prejudice my investigation."

I took his hand and smiled.

"I'll go track down Tierney," Janek said glancing at Michael. "You probably have some catching up to do."

"Can you handle another visitor?"

I looked toward the voice, seeing only a large arrangement of peonies hiding the woman who carried them. Jenelle Platt placed the flowers on a nearby table, then took my hand. We looked at each other, locked in indescribable pain and sorrow.

"When you're well," she said, "let's have dinner. We have a great deal to discuss. He wasn't always like this. Ambitious, yes, but corrupt and heartless..." Anguish racked her body.

I squeezed her hand. "Was it you? The poems?"

She squeezed back and smiled. "Like Owen always says, not bad for a poetry major."

Janelle said goodbye and Cai gave me a hug as she left, telling me she'd back in the morning. Lane held back.

"I'm so sorry," Lane said. "I've been selfish and a horrible sister. Erik had me completely fooled." She couldn't meet my eyes.

"He fooled a lot of us." I pulled her in for a hug, all the tension of our relationship forgotten.

Michael stepped over as she left, and sat next to me on the bed. He lifted his hand, caressed my cheek, then leaned in. Our lips met.

"Don't ever scare me like that again," he said.

39

Standing in the doorway at Link-Media, I found my stomach full of butterflies. Everything had changed since the last time I had walked through these doors—Erik's death, the arrest of the other six men involved in the conspiracy, Jenelle Platt's announcement of her own mayoral candidacy, a news story that had rocked the country. *My* story.

Three weeks after being released from the hospital, I was here to face the staff. To answer their questions about the future. Since our divorce had not yet been completed, ownership of Link-Media had passed to me, and it was time to start making decisions. I unlocked the doors, flipped on the lights, and walked back to Erik's office. Brynn had packed up his personal things, but I could still sense him. I could smell his cologne. Hear his laugh. See him sitting at his desk. I choked back a sob.

"Good morning."

I turned. Art Borkowski stood in the doorway.

"When I heard you at the door, I expected Erik," I said, feeling the wound open back up. I was so confused by the emotional ping-pong going on in my head. Love, hate, sorrow, sadness, and the strange comfort that his last action had been to try to save my life.

"I think that's going to be the way it is for a while," Borkowski said. "For all of us. We're all grieving."

"Did you know? Did you know about Erik's involvement?"

He shook his head. "I knew something was going on, but I hadn't figured out what." His face held a pain and a humanity that I hadn't seen before. "As I told you, I thought there was a sale in the works."

"And you thought I was in on it, at least at first."

He nodded. "I figured if Erik was selling the business, you were probably involved, or your divorce was the cause. Either way, you were influencing him. I shouldn't have been so quick to assume. I shouldn't have been so quick to dismiss your talent as a journalist. Your work on this story was outstanding."

"So what do we do now?" I asked, letting the question linger in the air.

"I guess that's up to you as the owner. Sell it, close it, run it into the ground. Your call. I'm here if you need me. Or if you'd prefer that I step down, I certainly understand. I'll go quietly."

"Well, it appears that I'll be needing a new managing director. Interested?"

He looked at me and smiled. "Definitely."

Brynn stepped into the office. "It's so good to see you," she said as we embraced, both wiping away tears.

"I think it's time you have a real job. What do you think? Are you ready for your first byline?" I said to Brynn.

"I was born ready." She winked.

Together the three of us left Erik's office and walked out to where the staff was gathering. The momentum was ours, and we needed to embrace that. Tomorrow would bring yet another crime, yet another challenge, yet another story, and yet another version of the truth.

DID YOU ENJOY THE BOOK?

Thank you so much for reading LIES IN HIGH PLACES. I'm truly honored that you've spent your time with me.

Reviews are the most powerful tool in an authors' arsenal for getting awareness of our books to other readers. If you've enjoyed the story, I would be very grateful if you could spend a couple minutes leaving an honest review on Goodreads or Amazon.

NEXT IN THE SERIES

GET INFORMATION ON THE NEXT ANDREA KELLNER STORY

Fatal Choices - An Andrea Kellner Prequel Short Story
Lies in High Places - Andrea Kellner Book 1
The Last Lie - Andrea Kellner Book 2
Lies of Men - Andrea Kellner Book 3 - March 2019

I love to hear from my readers. Did you have a favorite scene? Have an idea for who I should kill off next? Jot me a note. I occasionally send newsletters with details on the next release, special offers, and other bits of news about the series.

If you'd like to follow the series, sign up for the mailing list at danakillion.com

ABOUT THE AUTHOR

Dana Killion grew up in a small town in northern Wisconsin, reading Nancy Drew and dreaming of living surrounded by tall buildings. A career in the apparel industry satisfied her city living urge and Nancy Drew evolved into Cornwell, Fairstein, and Evanovich.

One day, frustrated that her favorite authors weren't writing fast enough, an insane thought crossed her mind. "Maybe I could write a novel?"

Silly, naïve, downright ludicrous. But she did it. She plotted and planned and got 80,000 words on the page. That manuscript lives permanently in the back of a closet. But the writing bug had bitten.

Lies in High Places is her debut novel. Dana lives in Chicago and Florida with her husband and her kitty, Isabel, happily avoiding temperatures below fifty.

DanaKillion.com

ACKNOWLEDGMENTS

Writing a novel involves months, sometimes years, of plotting, planning, and fretting over every word, and mine was no different. It also involves the support and dedication of good friends and loyal fans.

Many thanks to my writing pals Kari Bovee, Shelly Blanton-Stroud, Pam Campbell, and Liz McCullough. They suffered through my horrid first drafts and blinding insecurities. Terrific writers all, watch for their books.

To my boys, Alex and Zach, I hope you live dreams of your own. And finally, to my husband Theo, thank you for having the courage to become the man you were meant to be.

Published by Obscura Press

ISBN-13: 978-0-9991874-1-8

DanaKillion.com

Made in United States
Orlando, FL
31 January 2022